Dangerous When Wet: Soaked in Praise

"There's never a shortage of drama—or humor—as Brickhouse chronicles his early years running behind his mother's (high) heels, his wild days in Manhattan, and his struggle with addiction." —*THE WASHINGTON POST*

"Packed with multiple fine threads in a rich tapestry." —MARY KARR

"A chronicle of [Brickhouse's] often tumultuous but deeply loving relationship with his mother that's as multifaceted as Mama Jean herself." —*ENTERTAINMENT WEEKLY* (GRADE A–)

"Jamie Brickhouse plunges into his dark days of boozing in *Dangerous When Wet*." —*VANITY FAIR*

"Compelling and funny... *Dangerous When Wet* is as tightly constructed as a well-crafted novel and as funny as an evening with Carrie Fisher." —*INTERVIEW*

"A delicious and touching memoir...Jamie creates a literary cocktail all his own: witty, blisteringly honest, and wickedly intoxicating." —PAUL RUDNICK, PLAYWRIGHT AND *NEW YORKER* HUMORIST

"Must-read...Brickhouse's blunt account of addiction and recovery is laced with twisted humor, a testament to the long shadow his mama cast over his life." —*OUT*

"Brickhouse's memoir is as revealing as it is riotous...a dark journey studded with gems of hilarity." —JOSH KILMER-PURCELL, COSTAR OF *THE FABULOUS BEEKMAN BOYS*

D1121348

BURNHAM MEMORIAL LIBRARY
COLCHESTER, VT. 05446

Praise for *Dangerous When Wet*

"*Dangerous When Wet* never feels like an Augusten Burroughs knockoff because the central characters—Brickhouse's grande dame of a mother, Mama Jean, and Brickhouse himself—are such true originals . . . Brickhouse has written a chronicle of his often tumultuous but deeply loving relationship with his mother that's as multifaceted as Mama Jean herself. Like her, it's glamorously tragic and howlingly funny in equal measure."

—*Entertainment Weekly* (Grade A–)

"Jamie Brickhouse has written a blisteringly funny, wrenching account of wrestling way too close to—and later loose from—booze, sex, and drugs, and his adorable, infuriating mother. Believe me: The gator wranglers from his Texas backwater hometown have it way easier. It's packed with multiple fine threads in a rich tapestry. The first of many from Brickhouse. Bravo!"

—Mary Karr, author of *The Liars' Club,*
Cherry, Lit, and *The Art of Memoir*

"Mama Jean takes center stage in Brickhouse's colorful memoir . . . There's never a shortage of drama—or humor—as Brickhouse chronicles his early years running behind his mother's (high) heels, his wild days in Manhattan, and his struggle with addiction. But in the end, this raucous memoir is a testament to his mother."

—*The Washington Post*

"As a blackout drinker and a 'serial fornicator,' Jamie Brickhouse was guided by two interrogative mantras: 'Sure. Why not?' and, courtesy of singer Peggy Lee, 'Is that all there is?' But *Dangerous When Wet* is far more than a witty chronicle of gin-soaked debauchery. It is, more importantly, a poignant, hilarious, and sharply observed story of a gay man's exchange of self-destruction and self-loathing for a quest for wisdom and a mature understanding of love. Move over, Augusten Burroughs. You've got company."

—Wally Lamb, author of *She's Come Undone,*
I Know This Much Is True, and *We Are Water*

"Compelling and funny ... *Dangerous When Wet* [is] as tightly constructed as a well-crafted novel and as funny as an evening with Carrie Fisher."   —*Interview* magazine

"Jamie Brickhouse's Mama Jean must take her place in the hall of fame where infuriating and unforgettable American mothers wreak havoc, break hearts, but finally instill survival. Surely there is a pedestal available far from Harriet Nelson and Mrs. Brady, close to the rowdy regions where Mary Tyrone lifts a cocktail and Joan Crawford waves a hanger. I loved this book. It made me laugh more than anything in years. Jamie is an original, entertaining voice and a totally wonderful talent."
                    —George Hodgman, author of *Bettyville*

"Jamie Brickhouse plunges into his dark days of boozing in *Dangerous When Wet*."   —*Vanity Fair*

"Everyone's got a mother, but Jamie Brickhouse was lucky enough to have a Mama Jean, a boisterous, loving, and bouffant Texas tornado. In *Dangerous When Wet*, Jamie's delicious and touching memoir, we find out precisely how Jamie became the sort of guy to purchase, at auction, 'a six-and-a-half-foot long, chestnut-brown, ranch-mink scarf,' which had once belonged to Joan Crawford. Under Mama Jean's tutelage, Jamie also came to appreciate the joys, and dangers, of a champagne cocktail. In exploring family uproar, the Holly Golightly allure of Manhattan, and the free fall of alcoholism, Jamie creates a literary cocktail all his own: witty, blisteringly honest, and wickedly intoxicating."
                    —Paul Rudnick, playwright, author,
                    and *New Yorker* humorist

"Must-read: Not every son can capture such a complex relationship with as much verve ... Brickhouse's blunt account of addiction and recovery is laced with twisted humor, a testament to the long shadow his mama cast over his life. That same shadow will be following you around days after you finish this book." —*Out*

"*Dangerous When Wet* is anchored by a character destined to become iconic: Mama Jean. The outrageously bold and bawdy Mama Jean teaches more about life in a single one-liner than a shelf full of self-help books. Brickhouse's memoir is as revealing as it is riotous . . . a dark journey studded with gems of hilarity."

—Josh Kilmer-Purcell, costar of
The Fabulous Beekman Boys

"Laugh-out-loud read . . . It's about a rather outlandish gay man and his codependent relationship with his larger-than-life Texas mom. It's really funny, but also heartwarming too."

—John Searles, *Weekend Today Show*

"Jamie Brickhouse has seen the darkness, and emerged a happier, stronger person. His book is sensitive and thoughtful, tinged with hilarity and heartbreak, and as bubbly as a champagne flute of Asti Spumante. Drink it." —Henry Alford, *New York Times* columnist and author of *Would It Kill You to Stop Doing That?*

"There's no shortage out there of addiction memoirs . . . but few include a mother figure as towering as Mama Jean."

—*Texas Monthly*

"An overly mature and flamboyant redhead, Brickhouse lived under the protective wing of his mother, a larger-than-life character named Mama Jean, whose personality could easily carry a Broadway musical." —*Houston Chronicle*

"Packed with laugh-out-loud humor and biting, rich pathos—reads like a novel." —*The Huffington Post*

"Top 10 Nonfiction Book of 2015: *Dangerous When Wet* is as out-rageously frank and honest as a memoir gets. It is funny, poignant, and gut-wrenching—often at the same time." —*Book Chase*

"It's hard to do justice to Brickhouse's dance-, song-, and celebrity-filled prose; escapades; good-natured storytelling; and unflag-ging hope. A funny, sad, and fine first book." —*Booklist*

"Brickhouse is an energetic, witty narrator with a très gay eye for detail who keeps it fresh." —*POZ*

"*Dangerous When Wet* is a fabulous new memoir... [at times] terribly sad, [it] is equally hysterical [and] well written. *Dangerous When Wet* shows us that with humor, hard work, support, and hope, [addiction] can be conquered." —*Lambda Literary Review*

"Campy yet touching memoir about [Brickhouse's] struggles with the bottle, his sexuality, and his mother, Mama Jean."
—*The Gay & Lesbian Review*

"Jamie Brickhouse serves up a riotous, rollicking memoir that, ultimately, is as sweet as it is outrageous."
—Neil White, author of *In the Sanctuary of Outcasts*

"Unabashedly campy but always candid." —*Kirkus Reviews*

"Jamie Brickhouse's flame-red hair may have faded, but his no-holds-barred account of his fairy-tale life gone bad sets the pages of *Dangerous When Wet* on fire... we wind up cheering him on as he struggles to find himself, sobriety, and redemption."
—Eric Marcus, author of *Why Suicide?:*
Questions and Answers About Suicide,
Suicide Prevention, and Coping with the
Suicide of Someone You Know

Dangerous
When Wet

*A Memoir
of Booze, Sex, and
My Mother*

Jamie Brickhouse

ST. MARTIN'S GRIFFIN ≉ NEW YORK

For Mama Jean, who wouldn't have it any other way

DANGEROUS WHEN WET. Copyright © 2015 by Jamie Brickhouse. All rights reserved. Printed in the United States of America. For information, address St. Martin's Press, 175 Fifth Avenue, New York, N.Y. 10010.

www.stmartins.com

The Library of Congress has cataloged the hardcover edition as follows:

Brickhouse, Jamie.
    Dangerous when wet : a memoir / Jamie Brickhouse.
        p. cm.
    ISBN 978-1-250-04115-9 (hardcover)
    ISBN 978-1-4668-3730-0 (e-book)
    1. Brickhouse, Jamie.   2. Alcoholics—United States—Biography.
3. Alcoholics—Family relationships—United States.   I. Title.
    HV5293.B75A3 2015
    362.292092—dc23
    [B]

                                                    2015005978

ISBN 978-1-250-08036-3 (trade paperback)

Our books may be purchased in bulk for promotional, educational, or business use. Please contact your local bookseller or the Macmillan Corporate and Premium Sales Department at 1-800-221-7945, extension 5442, or by e-mail at MacmillanSpecialMarkets@macmillan.com.

First St. Martin's Griffin Edition: May 2016

10 9 8 7 6 5 4 3 2 1

Contents

Part III: Palm Springs Follies (2006)

Part IV: The Hair Is the Last to Go (2008–11)

Acknowledgments

Allow me to raise a glass (some habits die hard) to family, friends, and colleagues without whom I'd still be soaking wet and swimming in a sea of words in my head, not on the page.

Cheers to:

My common-law husband, Michael "Michahaze" Hayes, who lived through most of it and he's *still* here. I love you.

Dad, who collaborated with Mama Jean to make me the man I am today and not only gave me his love and blessing to publish this book but gave me the opening line of this book. My brother Jeffrey for being my third parent and for all he did for Mama Jean at the end. My brother Ronny for just being Ronny and for calling me Pank.

My literary agent, Lisa Gallagher, who believed in the book ever since that fateful lunch at Le Veau d'Or and found the perfect publisher for it at St. Martin's Press. My talented editor, Charlie Spicer, whose passion and enthusiasm combined with his keen and ruthless editorial hand made this the best book possible. The peerless team at St. Martin's Press: Sally Richardson, Jennifer Enderlin, Jeff Capshew, Brian Heller, Tracey Guest, Laura

Clark, James Sinclair, Meg Drislane, Steve Boldt, Elisa "Legal Lisa" Rivlin, and Brittani Hilles. Special toasts to Michael Storrings for the marvelous jacket design, Jessica Lawrence and Joanie Martinez for launching the book, and April Osborne for her editorial support. Also photographer and friend George Anttila for the courage to take my picture.

Robert Allen and Mary Beth Roche and their marvelous team at Macmillan Audio—Brant Janeway, Samantha Edelson, Chealsea Pita, and Laura Wilson—for publishing the audio edition and letting me narrate it.

My writing teacher, Phyllis Raphael, whose rare gem of a workshop was the incubator for the book. By merely saying to me early on, "You need to be pushed," she pushed me. She also gave me invaluable editorial guidance outside of the workshop. Workshop peers, talented writers, and friends Kevin Brannon, Maia McCann, Wesley Usher, and Bruce Ward.

The superb writers Henry Alford, Josh Kilmer-Purcell, Wally Lamb, Eric Marcus, Paul Rudnick, and Neil White for blessing the book with their sparkling words; Will Schwalbe for being an early cheerleader and champion; especially Mary Karr, who not only gold-dusted the book with her endorsement but told me early on to "keep writing." Those two words were as powerful as rocket fuel and helped me enormously to "bring up a book."

My "analysts," the late and deeply lamented David "Dave" Eliseo (Helen Lawson thanks you) and the ever-present Dr. Anthony Demma (Blanche thanks you).

Three cheers and special toasts to close friends: Jason Brantley for always laughing at my jokes when others didn't; David "Big Daddy" Collins for being my first "real" reader; Stella Connell, who is always ready for a "sip 'n see"; David Cobb Craig, aka "DCC," whose taste and editorial precision devastate me; Nicole Todack Cubbage, who is my first and bestest BFF; Michael "Bunny" Hill for the first triage; Kevin Johnson for being a mentor; intervention angels Jennifer Naparstek Klein, Smith Patrick, and Janine

Tiago; Allyson Hancock Kinzel, who predicted all of this when I didn't believe it; Hedda Lettuce and Steven Polito, both of whom—bald or be-wigged—can always make me laugh; Mama Jean's friends and mine Dottie Crane, Nancy Dryden, Joan Gilliam, and Sissy Park; Jo Ann Miller for never turning her back on me when others did and for introducing me to Phyllis; John Murphy for being the first to show me a new way of life; Yann Samuels for the second triage; Keith Seabolt for his boundless generosity; Bob Stack for being the first to show me *how* to live a new way of life; Michael "Mr. Parker" Stainback for loving me "wet or dry" and reminding me that in writing this book "everything's at stake"; Debbie Stier for paving the yellow brick road out of the corporate forest; Warner gals Diane Ekeblad, Ellen Herrick, Patricia Keim, Kelly Leonard, Hera Marashian, and Karen McDermott; Stephen Wilder for introducing me to Cherry Grove; and Karen Wolny for telling me that Liz recognized the potential in me.

Dear friends, many of whom were early readers, whose encouragement and rah-rahs kept a flame burning under my writing chair: Ben Bruton, Adam Chandler, Nick Fiore, Stephanie Glass Flatten, Gene Giles, Michael Halliday, David Littleton, Jamie Malcolm, Kristen McGuiness, Lou Miller, Charles O'Connell, Richard "Bella" Iorio, Sara Nelson, Pam Radford, Kelley Parker, Mark Shenk, Mark Solan, Nickey Bohl Scarborough, Elizabeth Conn Waddill, Maggie Weir, and Suzanne Halbert Wohleb.

A final toast to that invincible bunch: my fellow alcoholics in and out of recovery (especially the Marybills), HIV-positive folk, suicide-attempt survivors, and people affected by Lewy body dementia.

To all of you, I take "a cup o' kindness yet for auld lang syne."

Author's Note

My father, brothers, and I each had our own deep, complex, and loving relationship with my mother, Mama Jean. This book is the story of my relationship with her told through the lens of my love affair with alcohol, the other dominant relationship in my life. Hence, my father and brothers often have only cameos here, but in the cast of our family they each had as big a supporting role as I did to Mama Jean, the star of our lives. Some of the names and places have been changed.

Ready or Not, Here Comes Mama! (2006/1987)

Whoever said you can't get sober for someone else never met my mother, Mama Jean. When I came to in a Manhattan emergency room after an overdose to the news that she was on her way from Texas, I panicked. She was the last person I wanted to see on that dark September morning, but the person I needed the most.

"She doesn't need to know about this," I told my brother Jeffrey, who sat in a dark corner of the room. "Call her. Stop her before she gets on the plane."

"It's too late," he said in a monotone. "She's already in flight."

There was no stopping Mama Jean.

At thirty-eight I had been living in New York City for sixteen years, almost as long as the time I spent growing up in little ole, flat-as-a-flitter, hot-and-steamy, oil-refinery-oasis, cancer-capital Beaumont, Texas. Beaumont is a southeast Texas port town on the banks of the muddy-brown Neches River with the smaller towns of Port Arthur and Orange, not far off of I-10. The Golden Triangle, this triumvirate of towns is called. With the corrosive winds of the Gulf ("guf") of Mexico a mere thirty miles away, Rusty

Troika is a better name. Pardon my dust, but I fled that backwater to New York City, where I had carved out a successful career in book publishing with some fancy executive-vice-president titles, alongside my architect boyfriend, Michael Hayes, or Michahaze, as he was known in our circle. "I am going to get sophisticated if it kills me," I loved to say, throwing back a martini, Beefeater gin, dry, up, with a twist. I was quoting a line from one of the many old Joan Crawford movies that taught me how to be glamorous and sophisticated. And it nearly did kill me.

I didn't need Mama Jean in the middle of this mess. I could imagine how she'd greet me. "God . . . *damn* it!" Her *goddamn it* was said with a pregnant pause after *god* that left the object of her scorn bracing for the explosion of *DAMN it!* "I knew you'd end up like this. I just knew it." I was tired of being in the red with her. The cars. Trips to Europe. College. The apartment.

I moaned at the thought and ran my hands through my copper-red hair, which was fading along with my looks. With an expressive oval face, and nearly six feet of skin and bone, I had never been handsome, but musical-comedy cute—the sidekick, not the lead—all bow ties and polka dots. Had there been a mirror and I'd had the courage to look in it, that's not what I would have seen. Gin-soaked at thirty-eight, my puffy complexion was redder than my hair, which was dissolving to a dull auburn, and my lanky frame didn't want to carry the yeasty dough I had poured on the middle. The lights in my brown eyes were off.

"Where's Michael?" I searched the gloom of the windowless room, lit only by a slash of jittery fluorescent hall light, for my Michahaze. We had been together almost as long as I'd been in New York, and he had never left my side despite all of my peccadilloes. *Did he get me here?*

"He left about an hour ago."

"Oh." *How long have I been on the gurney? What time is it? What day is it? How long until Mama Jean arrives?* Then panic again. "Oh, God. You've got to tell Michael to hide my . . ." I knew she'd be staying in our bedroom, and I didn't want her rifling through my drawers, which contained something more revealing than porn.

"I know. It's already taken care of," Jeffrey answered.

Big relief. I couldn't hide my drinking from her anymore—*have I ever been able to?*—but she didn't need to know *all* my secrets.

Lying on an emergency-room gurney, my primary concern wasn't who or what got me there. Well, I knew *what* got me there: the overdose of sleeping pills I'd taken the day before in my own bed—a cliché straight out of *Valley of the Dolls*. The prescription on the pill bottle read "Take as needed." I followed directions. All of that I could figure out later. I was worried more about what Mama Jean—my greatest champion and harshest critic—would say. I was still in denial—Jesus, I was barely conscious—but I was about to face the two most important relationships of my life: booze and Mama Jean.

I could never predict what was going to come out of her mouth. Had I been able to read her mind, I would have known, because whatever thought went through her mind was the next thing she said. Mama Jean could have had a great career in silent pictures. Anyone peering through a window into her house would instantly have known what she was feeling by watching her histrionic gestures, which were as broad and iconic as those of her favorite soap-opera stars. With her raven mane, which was always done to a tease, and her Rubenesque figure, her looks were reminiscent of Elizabeth Taylor's. She had the split personality of Auntie Mame and Mama Rose. She was every inch the star: self-made, image obsessed, demanding, with the patience of a firecracker, makeup camera-ready, and almost always in close-up. Like the quintessential Leo she was, her roar could be loud and fierce.

I thought of one of her iconic close-up moments with nineteen-year-old me. It was the summer of 1987, after my freshman year in college. She and I were at a turning point. For me, that first year away at college had been a liberating breather from her all-consuming love, a love that had always cloaked me like a cashmere blanket in August. For her, that year was a year of mourning: mourning over my deserting the nest, mourning over the loss of her idealized notion of me as her perfect child, and mourning over my newly declared homosexuality.

After that first year of splashing joyously in the waters of boys, booze, and drugs with impunity, it was a culture shock being back under her roof. To her, anyone who liked more than two drinks was a lush. Drugs were criminal. And sex? I can see her reflection in the makeup mirror dispensing her two warnings with a flick of her mascara wand: "A moment's pleasure isn't worth a lifetime of regret" and "A stiff dick knows no conscience."

I did manage to circumvent her warnings that summer and find a bit of glamour and excitement in the form of a ballet dancer I met at the Copa. Not the Copacabana. This Copa was Beaumont's "premier" gay bar, with delusions of New York glamour, located on a desolate corner downtown, which had been gasping for air since the mall smothered it in the seventies.

The dancer taught at Dolly Pepperdine's School of Dance, or Miss Dolly's, as everyone called it. He'd take me there late at night to show me moves at the barre Miss Dolly never dreamed of teaching. In the mirror, I could see we were being watched. The girls I had grown up with, in their little-girl pigtails and pink leotards, gazed at us from photos on the wall. Some even seemed to giggle.

The first couple of times I went out with the dancer, I lied and told Mama Jean I was going out with this or that high school friend. Before the third date—assignation, really—I thought, *This is ridiculous. I'm in college. She knows I'm gay. I'm nineteen. I'm an adult. Honestly, what's the big deal?*

I marched into the den where Mama Jean was supine on the peach velvet sofa in her maroon-and-pink, velour, zip-up caftan and gold slippers. This early evening she was watching *As the World Turns,* her "story." It had been taped earlier in the day on the VCR (programmed by me) while she was at work.

I genuflected at the corner of the mirrored coffee table by her head. "Uh, Mom," I said, my adult bravado starting to waver.

"Um-hm," she muttered, all but ignoring me as she stared at the TV and sipped a Diet Coke from a plastic, jewel-toned cup, part of a set originally meant for the pool. She hated to be disturbed while she caught up on her stories.

"You know, I'm not going out with Nicole like I told you earlier."

She was never a fan of Nicole, my best friend since high school. She thought Nicole was pushy and demanded too much of my time. Plus, she didn't wear enough makeup. I thought ditching Nicole as my evening date pointed us in a positive direction.

"Well, who are you going out with?" Her eyes were still fixed on the TV.

The familiar queasy knot in my stomach—LBD, as in lower-bowel distress—hit, as it always did, whenever I had something to tell her that I knew she wouldn't like. "Um, Carlos."

Her head spun at a forty-five-degree angle to face me. "*Who* is Carlos?"

"Carlos Novarro. Carlos Fitzpatrick de Novarro." That was the dancer's name.

She put down the Diet Coke and paused her story. Lisa, the reigning diva from *As the World Turns,* was frozen mid-gasp. I had Mama Jean's full attention. "Who the *hell* is Carlos duh Fitz-whatever?!" She stared me down with a this-better-be-good look.

"He's a ballet dancer."

"Is he *gay*?" she asked in the same way she would ask if he was a Democrat.

"Well, yes. That's kinda the point."

"Uh-huh . . ."

I decided to shift gears. "He teaches ballet at Miss Dolly's." I threw that out to legitimize him, give him a tutu of respectability.

Silence. She stared at the ceiling with her arms folded over her chest, her face locked in a frown.

I decided to try to impress her with his credentials. My experience with her was that all could be forgiven if you'd made something of yourself in the big city. After all, her childhood friend Henny had become an actor in New York and she always thrilled to see him in those insurance commercials. "Come quick! Henny's on TV! God, I remember how we used to put on shows in the backyard." Henny had recently died from complications caused by AIDS. The virus was still a mysterious and uncontrollable forest fire, big cities being the charred open wilderness.

"Well, you know, he used to dance with the New York City Ballet." I almost smirked.

"New York?!" The interrobang is a punctuation mark that combines a question mark with an exclamation point when a question is asked in excitement or disbelief. It was invented for her.

"Yes. New York City."

"Have you heard of AIDS?!"

"Have you heard of safe sex?"

"There are only *two* kinds of sex: *oral* and *anal!*" *She's forgetting vaginal, but that's her problem.*

I was speechless. She lay there, rigid as a corpse. After what seemed like an airless five minutes, I got up and left her to the daytime drama of *As the World Turns.*

When I returned from my date later that night, I slipped into the kitchen through the back door as quietly as a ballet dancer *en pointe*. The kitchen was dark, save for a swath of light spilling through the archway from the den. I turned my back from the light to lock the door. Through the door's window, I could see Mama Jean's black Cadillac sitting in the garage like a panther. When I faced the light, it darkened with Mama Jean's tall shadow, her bubble of hair a circle sitting atop the triangle of her floor-length, satiny nightgown. But once her gold-slippered feet set down stakes—one here, one there, about twenty-four inches apart—her shadow went vertical and she was live and in person. She placed her left hand on her left hip and her right hand on her right hip.

I couldn't see the angry glare in her eyes or her gritted teeth in the dark, but I could feel them. It was as if she had caught me bent over Miss Dolly's barre.

We were both silent for a moment before she fired like a machine gun her verbal salvo of interrobangs. Each shot was punctuated with the thrust of her perfectly sculpted, red fingernail.

"Where the *hell* have you been?!

"Do you know what time it is?!

"I've been worried *sick*!

"How *dare* you keep me up like this when I have to get up for work in the morning!

"Work that's paying for that precious school of yours!

"Work that pays for the car you drive!

"The car that you use to run the streets all night—with *no* regard for me!

"And you're *drunk*!"

She took a much-needed breath before firing her last shot: "Where the *hell* did you get that shirt?!"

Finally I spoke. "*You* gave me this shirt!" I was wearing a blue-and-green shirt she'd bought me because "it looks so pretty with your crowning glory," my copper-red hair.

She walked off in a huff. I stood frozen in place, afraid to take a breath.

Just when I thought it was safe, she reemerged. She assumed her previous hands-on-hips combat position for a final staredown.

The penetrating glare from her ominous shadow held me frozen for what seemed like an eternity before she spoke. Then out of the darkness her words came, no longer in the hysterical rapid-fire of her previous assault, but slowly, with the growl of a wounded lioness. Like a character in one of her soaps.

"You don't know what love is."

That's hitting below the dance belt. I opened my mouth but stopped short of responding, *A stiff dick knows no conscience, right?* Instead, I shut up while she made her final exit.

I stared at the empty shadow she left behind as I stood in my fog of booze, sex, and youth . . . wondering. I thought that her definition of love meant I had to do what she wanted, be her perfect Jamie Doll. I was wrong. It would take me another twenty years and getting sober from a silo of booze before I would understand what love was—Mama Jean's kind, anyway.

Part I

Golden Triangle (1968-87)

When you're good to Mama, Mama's good to you.

—John Kander and Fred Ebb, *Chicago*

The world wanders into many strange by-paths of affection.
The love of a mother for her children is dominant,
leonine, selfish, and unselfish.

—Theodore Dreiser

ONE

Break Out the Booze and Have a Ball

I had no business being a child. The playground and its mewling habitués were not for me. What I saw at my parents' parties and in movies and TV shows is all I wanted. To be at a cocktail party with a drink in one hand, a cigarette in the other, and my head thrown back in laughter was my idea of heaven. Everything outside of that was filler.

Before I could read, I loved looking at the photo albums of my parents' wedding day, April 24, 1965. I wondered why Mama Jean was in a cocktail dress and not a long, white gown and veil. But more than that, I was pissed off that my half brothers, Ronny and Jeffrey (nine and eight years older than me), got to go to the wedding *and* the reception, but not me. I couldn't stand the thought of missing a party.

My tour of the wedding always began with the black-and-white, eight-by-ten, glossy photo of Mama Jean's marriage announcement. She is in a pose you rarely see anymore: she gazes over her shoulder, which is in the middle of the frame, perpendicular to the viewer. I could almost tell that the triple-pleated shawl lapel of her chiffon dress was a blurry green, the color of a Spanish olive submerged in a martini. Her hair was one solid bouffant flip, a Cat Five—as in it could withstand a Category 5 hurricane, which was often a threat in semitropical Beaumont. The newspaper ran this photo as if she were a movie star, which she was to me.

Next I dove into the photo albums, starting with the wedding mass at St. Anne's Catholic Church on Calder Avenue, the church where I was baptized and already knew well its altar of pink and green marble statues flanking a disturbingly handsome Jesus on a cross. The photos were snapshots in black and white, three-and-a-half-inch squares with white borders. Most of the shots were taken from the rear of the church looking toward the altar so that you saw the anonymous backs of the wedding guests staring at the backs of my parents as they knelt before the priest. A permanent hush preserved these somber photos. I couldn't imagine that any of the guests spoke, or if they did, it was in whispers.

Opening the wedding-reception album was like unlocking a soundproof door on a party in full swing. I could almost hear the clamor of laughter, music, and clinking champagne saucers. These photos were in color—cotton-candy, *lickable* color. The women wore dresses of lemon chiffon, strawberry ice cream, birthday-cake blue icing, all trimmed with white gloves and crowned with matching pillbox hats. Mama Jean's miniature pillbox hat and veil were barely noticeable. Her hair was her crown. *Why don't the ladies still wear outfits like that?* Already I was nostalgic for a past I hadn't lived; felt as if then was better than now.

There was Dad—James Earl Sr., Bubba to his family but *never* in front of Mama Jean, J. Earl to colleagues, but usually just Earl—without a trace of gray in his close-cropped, dark hair, laughing as he fed a piece of bunny-white wedding cake to Mama Jean. He looked like Dick Van Dyke and had the comedic, easygoing personality to match. My brothers, Ronny and Jeffrey, six and four, were on either side of Mamou, Mama Jean's mother. She was the only redhead in the bunch and the person from whom I would inherit my red hair. *So where was I?*

It was explained to me a few times before I got it, accepted it really. Mama Jean, who grew up in Beaumont down the street from St. Anne's on Calder, got out of town for a while. After college at Louisiana State University, where she was a Chi Omega, she moved to Louisiana and worked as an elementary-school teacher. She met a man, Len, and he knew how to fly. He was in the Air Force. They got married in Beaumont at St. Anne's and were celebrated at the country club on the banks of the Neches River. Earl was at the wedding.

They left Beaumont for a honeymoon in Acapulco. After the honeymoon they went wherever the Air Force asked them to go—Louisiana, Alabama, Kansas—creating a Ronny in 1959 and a Jeffrey in 1960. Once, in August of 1963, when the Air Force asked Len to make a quick trip across Kansas with three other officers, he didn't come back. The plane went down in a wheat field. Everyone survived. Except for Len. Mama Jean, a brand-new widow at twenty-nine, put her boys in her new, black Ford Fairlane with shiny chrome bumpers and returned to Beaumont with a letter of condolence from President Kennedy. Earl was at the funeral, and he remembered thinking how pretty she looked in her black lace veil.

Three months later and just six days after President Kennedy's assassination, Mama Jean's father, Big Daddy, died in his sleep. "It always strikes terror to my heart whenever I hear *1963*," Mama Jean said ever after.

Earl had grown up in Beaumont too, but he never wanted to leave, save for his college years at the University of Texas in Austin. He had never married. Earl had been school friends with Mama Jean's older brother. That's why he got to go to her first wedding and to Len's funeral. When Mamou, who had always been fond of Earl (everyone loved Earl), ran into him at Luby's Cafeteria at the Gaylynn Shopping Center, a couple of blocks from St. Anne's, she told him to call Mama Jean.

He did. He took her dancing at the beaux arts costume ball in the Rose Room at the Hotel Beaumont. She was a señorita to his caballero. "I needed to have fun and I hadn't danced in a long time. Your father's a marvelous dancer." They were crowned the king and queen of the parquet after they jitterbugged the night away. She liked the way he moved. He liked the way she moved. Everybody liked the way they moved that night. With his ribald jokes— "A guy watches a wobbly floozy on a barstool and asks her, 'How many does it take to make you . . . dizzy?' She answers, 'Two. And the name's Daisy' "—he made her laugh for the first time in a long time. "And I needed to laugh," Mama Jean always said.

Once during their six-month courtship they were necking like teenagers in his red Mustang when she abruptly pulled away. She yanked her hand from the side of his rump and stared at him: "Did you just fart on my hand?"

He had, but he was going to let it go, so to speak. That's when he learned that Mama Jean never let anything go.

"Yes," he admitted.

"I can't *believe* you would fart on your date's hand."

"Well, you shouldn't have had your hand down there."

At that they broke up laughing. They always quipped that it was then that they knew it was true love.

On those early dates they both had a window into the future of what life would be like together. Dad remembers her getting out of the car and bumping into the headlight as she rounded the corner. She reprimanded the car with a "God . . . *damn* it!" and slapped the hood with her hand. "I'd never seen anyone get mad at an inanimate object before," Dad would recall. After a night of drinks and dancing, and more drinks, Mama Jean found herself in the driver's seat with an overserved Dad feeling no pain in the backseat. "I should have known then," Mama Jean always said.

At thirty-four, Dad was ready for a family. At thirty-one, Mama Jean had a family, and a new, little house bought and paid for with government money. A white, aluminum-sided, one-story "ranchburger" built in the fifties, this rectangular shoe box was topped by a pitched roof and fronted by a three-columned porch, door in the middle, two sets of windows on either side—a one-story mini–White House. It had three bedrooms, one and a half baths, living/dining room in front, open kitchen/den in back, attached one-car garage. The only thing missing in her new house was a father. Jeffrey had already asked her if she could get a daddy for Ronny and him at the 7-Eleven.

By 1965, Mama Jean was back at the altar of St. Anne's, but not in white. "You only get to wear white at the first wedding. After that it's tacky." As she wore that green dress, I was not even thought of, not even a twinkle in her eye. *How can there be a time in her life when I wasn't thought of?*

After that day it took three years for me to arrive. Their first stab at growing the family ended in miscarriage. When I finally made it out of the womb, in 1968, the stakes were high. I was placed in a crib positioned before one of the front windows of the mini–White House, as if on display. My brother Jeffrey said years later with good humor and a twinge of resentment, "It was like the second coming of Christ."

Mama Jean and Dad were hoping for a redheaded, brown-eyed baby girl. "Oh, I wanted a little girl so bad. So I could dress her up like a little doll," Mama Jean said. They were going to name me Julie. "Well, we came close, but there was something hanging between the legs," Mama Jean joked. Tally Whacker Baby was her first nickname for me.

Dad and Mama Jean danced throughout their marriage. I loved to watch them dance, because even if it was just the two of them and me watching, it felt like a party. They danced whenever their song, "More," came on the radio. A song meant to be danced to, meant to fall in love to, it had lyrics about the greatest love the world has ever known and being in a beloved's life every "waking, sleeping, laughing, weeping" moment. For them, those lyrics might have been a bit heavy-handed, but Andy Williams, Bobby

Darin, Doris Day, and Frank Sinatra sang that song to them wherever they went while they were dating. *Why don't couples have
their own song anymore?*

They fought just as well as they danced, maybe even better, and
they did plenty of that in front of me too. I always wished that they
would dance as much as they fought, so we could keep the party
going.

One of my earliest memories seems more like outtakes from a
dream, the before and after pieces having dissolved after waking.
There is no sound, only images that flicker like a home movie on
Super 8 millimeter film. I am standing in my crib before the
double-sash window and staring at a frantic Mama Jean, who is
on the other side, outside in the dark in her nightgown and robe.
Ronny and Jeffrey stand by her side, wide-eyed, their fingers
in their mouths. She is scaring me, the way she yells and impa-
tiently stabs her index finger at the middle of the window. I can't
figure out what she wants me to do. When I can't figure it out, she
shakes her head *no, no, NO!* I want to cry, but I don't want to make
her any more upset than she already is. *Why is she mad at me?*
Somehow I figure out that she wants me to unlock the window,
and my little toothpick fingers release the cold metal locks.
Mama Jean throws open the window and pulls me out of the
crib and into her arms. She runs with me to her blue Chrysler—
or was it her new, white Mercury Marquis? The next thing I
know, I am looking out the car window as she speeds out of the
driveway. The front door of the house is open; the light inside
casts a dim glow in the middle of the dark house like a night-light.
Dad comes running barefoot across the lawn, yelling and pointing as if he is trying to catch us. The memory ends there.

If their song was "More," mine was "Is That All There Is?" I must
have been around five when I saw Peggy Lee on some variety show
singing that haunting, fatalistic song. She was wearing about two

hundred yards of white, diaphanous chiffon. Her platinum-blond hair was upswept into a cascade of sausage curls, and she had a black dot on her right cheek.

"What's that?" I asked Dad.

He stopped drying the dish in his hand and stood in the middle of the room next to me. "That's a beauty mark. My God! Jean, come quick! You've gotta look at Peggy Lee. She's fat as a pig!"

A beauty mark? Just like that dot on Miss Kitty's face from *Gunsmoke,* a show I had zero interest in, save for Miss Kitty. *If only they would tell me when her scenes were on, I'd watch.* She was the only character from that show I remember besides Little Joe. Or was that *Bonanza*? Anyway, when Dad said to look at Peggy Lee, I looked. How could I not? She was mesmerizing, and "Is That All There Is?" hooked me from the first verse. Even though it is a very grown-up song, it wasn't *that* odd that it spoke to my five-year-old mind. It was a story song, after all. To the tuba vamp of a gentle oompah band, she told me that when she was a little girl, her father gathered her up in his arms and they watched their house burn as the whole world went up in flames. Her little-girl, pragmatic answer to the situation? With a shrug she asked:

"Is that all there is to a fire? . . . If that's all there is . . . let's break out the booze and have a ball."

Wow. That's my kind of little girl. I couldn't wait for the day that I could break out the booze and have a ball.

Around that time I took my first drink. It's a memory I didn't remember until after I stopped drinking. It wasn't a full drink, but a sip of one. It was Dad's. The memory is a Polaroid snapshot the color of autumn—orange, brown, and yellow—framed in knotty-pine paneling with my copper-red hair lighting the center. Dad was sitting on a sofa laughing; a Kent 100's cigarette dangled from under his mustache, which matched my hair, but curiously not his own. Mama Jean loathed that mustache almost as much as she hated his drinking. His drink was on the corner of the coffee table. The tumbler was swimming-pool blue, globular, with circular crater depressions throughout, like a glass moon. I liked those depressions because they made the glass fun to hold. Inside was amber liquid with frothy bubbles swimming among the "rocks" on top. That's what they called ice when it was cooling the brown stuff. *On the rocks.* I liked that phrase.

I don't know if Dad offered me a drink, or if I asked for a sip. Maybe I just took it. I know that I stood at the corner of the coffee table with my little hands pressed into the craters of that magic highball and took a sip of a drink that I knew was only for adults. I hesitated and let it stay in my mouth a few seconds longer than any other liquid I'd ever drunk. I winced and swallowed. It was as if I'd stepped inside from the oppressive heat of a Beaumont summer to the arctic blast of central AC: startling, mind-altering, and so refreshing. I don't remember any warm or fuzzy feeling or a feeling of *ahhh*. But I do remember the taste. It tasted like being an adult.

TWO

Press On

"Earl! Come quick! I think Jamie has a hard-on!" Dad came, as he always did when Mama Jean called, and stood next to her as she peered at me in my crib. He stared for a few seconds and a smile crept over his face.

He turned to her. "I believe he does. And it looks like he knows what to do with it."

She faced him with a mixed look of horror and fascination, and then they both cracked up. Maybe that's when I earned the nickname Tally Whacker Baby. I was two.

I have no recollection of this moment, but Mama Jean and Dad loved to repeatedly tell this as one of my early-childhood milestones. It's a shame that my baby keepsake book didn't have a place to record *Baby's first erection.*

I *did* know what to do with that thing, and I was fearless about using it. "Pressing," Mama Jean and Dad called it, because I did it lying on my stomach, my hands pressed into my gonads. I didn't realize it was something that simply wasn't done in public, like on the den floor in front of the TV, alongside the rest of the family. "Jamie, stop pressing" was a constant refrain. They never told me it was naughty or "self-pollution"—the official definition of *mas-turbation* from Mama Jean's 1952 edition of the Merriam-Webster dictionary—but to keep it to myself, so to speak. I sometimes forgot.

Once when I was pressing, I closed my eyes, and when I opened them, I was facing Mama Jean's Christmas-red toenails. They were spying from the trenches of the white shag carpeting of her bedroom. *Busted.* I looked up at her face, the window on top of the lookout tower of her body. "But it feels good" was my weak—and *completely* true—excuse.

As fearless as my pressing was, water was a different story.

From before I can remember, the mere suggestion of aquatic submergence was enough to make me "scream bloody murder," as Mama Jean would say. Dad could merely hold my toddler body between his outstretched hands over a motel swimming pool and I'd scream, "No! No! *NO!*" as I balled up like a doodlebug.

The brown surf of the Gulf of Mexico beaches nearby terrified me even more. I was convinced that if I went near that mass of spilled dark beer with its head of white foam, I'd be sucked in, never to be seen again. The shore was littered with stinging jellyfish that looked like inflated sandwich baggies—the shore was littered with those too—so who knew what lay beneath that dirty brown water? Whenever we drove to Houston, eighty miles away, and crossed the Old and Lost Rivers on that barren stretch of I-10, I'd stare at the vast body of water and spook myself into imagining I was bobbing in the middle of it in a black night, trying to reach shore. I had recurring drowning nightmares where I was either running from water or robotically walking toward it. Either way, it eventually grabbed me and swallowed me whole. The water was always dark, never transparent.

Even the bathtub faucet was a source of *terror agua* when Mama Jean washed my hair. In my early youth, she and I were on the same hair-washing plan: once a week and washed by someone else, hers by the black ladies at Town & Country Beauty Salon, mine by her.

Mama Jean had to hold a bone-dry, royal-blue washrag—folded to precisely the right width—over my tightly shut eyes so that no water could seep in. She'd plunge my head under the faucet for the shortest amount of time. Every plunge was a tiny bit of hell.

By three or four, I was able to get into a pool, but I'd only go as far as the steps. The built-in mesh underwear of my hula-boy swimsuit fascinated me to no end, but I was still miserable. I'd mask my misery—and utter boredom—with a façade of casual disinterest. I'd lounge with my elbows resting on the pool's edge and gently pump my legs in the water as if to say, *I'm fine right here, but you kids go on and have fun.* My lounge act was always shattered when the other kids got too close. "Don't splash me! Don't splash me!" I'd get out with the bogus excuse of having to pee. *I could have used a cocktail in those moments—something stronger than a Shirley Temple, please.*

My fear of water was temporarily replaced by a fear of something else: Mrs. Hammond. She taught me to swim when I was in kindergarten. She looked just like the Wicked Witch of the West's Kansas version, Miss Gulch. Actually, in her yellow, one-piece bathing suit and white bathing cap, she looked like a bald Miss Gulch. She taught swimming in her long, rectangular pool behind her old, white-stucco, two-story house in the old part of Beaumont. The streets there were lined with brick, stucco, and clapboard houses like the ones on *Leave It to Beaver* or *Father Knows Best,* as opposed to *The Brady Bunch*–like houses in our neighborhood. You entered through a side gate, bypassing the house, which was too bad, because I wanted to see inside.

As Mama Jean and I approached the gate, the other kids skittered past, hopping with glee, as if they were headed to a birthday party instead of certain death. Except for one girl. Her right arm was stretched to the limit as she no longer held, but pulled, her mother's hand. She squatted in resistance like a puppy on a leash for the first time. She was wearing a one-piece swimsuit with gold, orange, and red oversize daisies. *Cute suit.* I knew exactly how she felt. I knew such behavior would never fly with Mama Jean, so I continued the march of death with a brave face.

"Mary Alice, quit being such a pill and come on!" her mother said. She jerked her up and in the direction of the pool as she tossed her cigarette in the gutter.

I filed away the phrase *quit being such a pill* for future overuse.

Behind the gate was worse than I imagined. It wasn't the setup. That was great: a pool surrounded by a redbrick patio with black, wrought-iron furniture, thick, yellow vinyl cushions, and a yellow table umbrella with a white fringe. Tall pine trees and an octopus of a live oak shaded the backyard. *Nice. If only I didn't have to get into that pool.*

The situation around the setup was the problem. Mrs. Hammond, a skeleton draped in a skin of wrinkled frowns, was all business. Not once did she ask me where I got my pretty red hair or even comment on how cute my Hawaiian swimsuit was. She sternly instructed the parents that they were to go no farther than the gate. The kids were hers from that point until exactly eleven o'clock, and not a minute later. Or sooner. Parents were strictly forbidden to observe the lessons. If they showed up early, they had to wait on *that* side. She pointed to the street side of the gate. I wanted to find Mary Alice and make a run for it.

Mrs. Hammond's method of teaching was trial by water. We clung to a metal rail that ran along the shallow end of the pool, where she had lined us up like bobbing ducklings. After a quick demonstration of, say, the dog paddle, she snagged a victim at random to "sink or swim" for the class. If the hapless example sank and cried, the child was sent back to the shallow end to watch someone else do it right. My turn came during one of the first classes.

I was her assistant for the backstroke, which was lucky, because my face didn't have to go under the water. However, it was hell on my ears. She pulled my white knuckles from the metal rail and laid me flat on the water. Before I could sink, she grabbed the tops of my ears and dragged me in a zigzag around the pool. I squelched an ouch and somehow stayed afloat. She congratulated me before sending me back to the shallow end. I wasn't beaming the way I would have been after modeling a new outfit for Mama Jean. I was just relieved that the moment was over and my ears were out of her hands.

Near the end of one class I happened to look over at the fence. Mrs. Hammond had her back to it as she tortured Mary Alice with the backstroke. I saw Dad's smiling face peeking over. I almost screamed. He didn't know the rules. I shooed my hands at him and whispered, "Go away. Go away. You can't watch. She doesn't let the parents watch." He giggled and dropped his head just as she turned around with a suspicious squint of her eyes. I ducked my head under the water. Never had submersion been so easy.

During one lesson, while she was focused on teaching the budding Olympians the butterfly stroke, I got out of the pool and walked to the back door of her house.

"Jamie! Where do you think you're going?" Mrs. Hammond demanded from the pool, her hands clutching the ears of another floating victim.

I stopped and turned around. "To tee-tee?" I asked rather than stated. I did have to pee, but I really wanted to get inside that big, old house, which I could see was filled with beautiful objects not meant to be touched by children. Through the scrim of the gray mesh screen door, I saw a silent room full of furniture made with dark wood that gleamed with a roseate sheen, porcelain figurines, chairs with wings on them. Before I could open the screen door, I felt the chlorinated raindrops of the Wicked Witch of the Wet on my head. She grabbed me by the shoulders and made a sharp left with my body.

"No-one-in-the-house!" she said in a one-word bark. "If you need to tee-tee, tee-tee over here."

By the time she said "over here," she had grabbed my left hand and was dragging me to a corner of the house by the wax-leaf japonica hedge. She stood over me waiting. I looked up at her for a sign that here was "over here." She scowled and gestured to the spot on the ground. I focused on the carpet of rust-colored pine needles and waited for her to leave.

Drip. Drop. Drip. Drop.

She was still there.

"Well, go on!" she said.

Why won't she leave? I lifted up the elastic waistband of my trunks and slid both hands down. I fumbled for my tally whacker, but it was tangled in that built-in mesh underwear. We were in the shade, but I was so hot from shame, my face must have been as red as my hair. I continued to fumble. *Why won't it come out?* I saw her long, bony feet, the color of oyster shells, on either side of me, her body right behind me.

"Here. Let me do it."

Before I could ask, *Do what?*—knowing what *what* was—her left hand had grabbed the left leg of my trunks, mesh underwear and all. Her right hand took advantage of the point of entry and jerked out my tally whacker. She pressed it with wrinkled thumb on top and wrinkled index finger on bottom and aimed it toward the pine needles. My hands were still down the front of my trunks.

"Well, go on."

I didn't think I could go on, but I did. I shut my eyes so hard they hurt and turned my head away as if avoiding the sight of a doctor's needle. Instead of tears from my eyes, pee from my tally whacker flowed.

I don't remember the rest of the summer. It was my first blackout. Somehow I learned to swim, but how I don't know. My guess is that fear was the key. I can't recall any moments of aquatic triumph, say, diving for the first time and emerging from the water to the sound of Mrs. Hammond cheering, "Oh, Jamie, you did it! And all by yourself! Now, if we could just get you to pee with the same finesse." No, after our pee session in the bushes, my memory went dark until the last day, *graduation*—a word that meant "it's over." That's when the parents were invited poolside to see their precious angels reborn as water babies. I dove. I swam laps. I did the backstroke. All by myself.

"You're a regular Esther Williams," Mama Jean and Dad said with pride. I didn't know who she was, didn't know she was a swimming champion who dove to aquatic stardom in the forties and fifties in movies such as *Neptune's Daughter, Million Dollar Mermaid,* and *Dangerous When Wet.* How could I? I was five. But I got it that Esther Williams and water equaled real good.

The following summer my fear of Mrs. Hammond trumped Esther Williams. When it was time for aquatic fun in somebody's backyard pool, I wouldn't go farther than the steps. I was more afraid of the water than before because the fear was backed up with knowledge. And I had forgotten all the moves that Mrs. Hammond had taught me. Well, almost all of them.

THREE

Let Me Let You Go

O h, I wish I could shrink you back to age five. *That* was the
perfect age!" Mama Jean first said this to me just before I
started elementary school, and she never stopped saying it. It was
our first heart-to-heart. She told me this to prepare me—and, I
now suspect, herself—for first grade.

"Now, Jamie, all of your teachers may not love you or even like
you as much as I do," Mama Jean told me as she sat on her king-
size bed with me perched on her lap. The preamble was something
about entering a world of new people, strangers who might not be
as big a fan of mine as she was. She was talking about teachers in
particular. I was so addicted to Mama Jean's unconditional ado-
ration that I sought the same attention from other women, often
over the company of children. She had placed me on a pedestal and
I loved being there.

"Well, why not?" was my guileless response.

This made her hug me and laugh.

In the "perfect age" era of my childhood, before I started elementary school and before she went to work, I was her constant

companion. Those halcyon days were filled with sewing, shopping, movies, and hairdoing.

Before she was dressed, still in her nightgown and slippers, she would unfold yards of fabric on the long, black dining table next to her sewing nook in the back den. I'd gaze up at her from the floor as she cut, threaded, and then drove her Singer with her gold slipper on the pedal while singing and humming to the music of Burt Bacharach—"The Look of Love," "I Say a Little Prayer," "Walk on By"—that wafted through the gold threads of the hi-fi's speaker.

She copied the latest fashions for herself, such as a kelly-green knockoff of the Halston caftan dress made famous by Elizabeth Taylor and Liza Minnelli. The wide, dramatic drape of the dress from her neck to the bat-wing sleeves and down to the floor—the silhouette of a stingray—gave her the look of a goddess who could make anything happen. My favorite outfit that she made for me was a navy-blue, one-piece sailor suit worn with white tights to pose in for my Jane Butler portrait. We're not talking Olan Mills, that low-rent chain of portrait-photography studios. Jane Butler was the sought-after Beaumont society photographer. We weren't rich, but Mama Jean's "precious baby" deserved the star treatment. I was posed on the grounds of an old mansion—under a magnolia tree, gazing into a koi pond or popping out of a blooming azalea bush like a giant blossom.

When the sewing was done and before we left for our shopping adventures, she'd get ready. She never left the house without putting on her face.

"Where's my precious baby?" she'd call from her bathroom. I'd jump up from the floor in my room and run to her. She towered before her bathroom-sink mirror in her white bra and panties, an array of makeup laid out on the vanity of powder-blue ceramic tile. Staring intensely into the mirror—her work face on (lips curled over teeth)—she'd continue rubbing her face with a round sponge that made her skin tanner with each circular motion.

She'd cut her eyes in my direction and ask my reflection, "Where have you been, Lord Randall, my son? You weren't pressing, were you?"

"Playing." I'd smile bashfully. I didn't question why she called me Lord Randall, which is what she always called me whenever I had been out of her orbit for a time. I never questioned Mama Jean.

I'd watch in awe as she applied the liquid base, drew on her eyebrows, lined her eyes, and squeezed her eyelashes with a weird metal clamp. My favorite part was the lipstick application. She'd open her mouth wide, stretch her lips, paint them a vibrant red, pucker, and *POP!*

With abrupt, backward flicks of her wrist, she'd "run a rake"—a Pepto-Bismol-pink-handled comb that had about six needle-thin prongs widely spaced—through her hair to tease it out and cover any holes. Then she'd pull a pair of white panties over her fixed hair until they covered her fixed face, turning her into the headless horseman's wife or a figure in a Magritte painting.

"Why do you put underwear on your head?" I asked.

"So my dress doesn't mess up my hair," she answered, as if I had asked, *Why does our house have a roof?* and she'd said, *So we don't get wet.*

Then came the finale. She'd pull her dress over her decapitated head, wiggling her body with her arms straight up in a hallelujah gesture to let it fall into place. With both hands, she'd slowly peel away her big-girl panties. When they were at the back of her head, out of the danger zone, she'd fling them off to reveal her unscathed do and the masterpiece of her perfectly fixed face. Showtime!

In her white Mercury Marquis, a cake on wheels, we'd glide across town hermetically sealed in our own world with the AC on full blast and the radio set to KQXY, "The Beautiful Q," a station of instrumental versions of faded pop tunes. We'd shop for patterns at Ye Olde Sewing Shoppe, lunch at the counter of Sommer's Rexall Drugs, and drive through the automatic car wash on Calder on the exact lot where her childhood house had been. The house, an arts-and-crafts bungalow on stilts, hadn't been torn down. It had been moved across town. Every time we passed it and I pointed it out—never getting over that an entire house had been moved—she'd say, "God, I *hate* that house! And it keeps following me."

If it was Tuesday, we'd spend a good two hours at Town & Country Beauty Salon, because that was the day of her once-a-week hair appointment. (She'd have a comb-out in between weekly appointments during busy social weeks.) The beauty parlor—no one called it a salon—was a magic world, intoxicating to all of my senses: floral-scented shampoo, gaseous nail polish and hair dye, chattering women in a carousel of chairs on pedestals that went up and down in front of oval mirrors, all held together by a haze of hair spray. The ladies looked like characters out of a Dr. Seuss storybook. They were armless under black nylon smocks, and their hairdo-in-the-works hair was better than any cartoonist could conjure: antennae of silver foil, Vienna sausages of pink and blue plastic curlers, fireworks of hair teased all the way up to God. Their voices rose and fell along with the chairs that the beauty operators controlled with a giant foot pump. Certain words—the ones I listened hardest to—were spoken sotto voce (*cancer, divorce, silver plate*).

Visits to her friends where she could show me off and I could pretend to be an adult were my favorite parts of those days. Her friends all had children of their own, but I never heard about them when they were around me. They couldn't possibly favor their kids over me, the way they raved about my pretty red hair and sweet disposition.

"Oh, Jean, he's just *precious!*"

She'd gaze down at me in pride as she answered, "I know it. And he's so good. He never leaves my side. They broke the mold when they made him."

But I didn't just sit there like a China doll on Mama Jean's lap. I knew how to talk to her friends. I asked them about their hair, complimented their outfits, noticed the cars they drove. I was genuinely interested in what they had to say. It was much more intriguing than what was going on outside with the neighborhood boys.

Genevieve was an older friend of Mama Jean's we sometimes visited in the afternoon. She had a fixed, strawberry-blond do and freckly complexion. She'd greet us with a placid smile, a crystal glass attached to her hand. She lived in a big, two-story, brick house painted white, with live oaks in front and a swimming pool in back. The living room seemed bigger than our entire mini–White House. "I'd love to have a house like that someday," Mama Jean would say. I just wanted a two-story house. (All of her friends seemed to live in bigger houses than we did.) I dutifully sat on Mama Jean's lap or at her feet, but I ached to explore the entire house. All of the windows had wood shutters with louvers that Genevieve seemed to constantly adjust to either fill a room with light or keep it dark. I remember the living room as being mostly in shadow.

Then we stopped visiting. We hadn't seen her in a while, and when we drove past her house one day, I asked Mama Jean why. She didn't answer me until we got home. I asked her again. She stared straight ahead with her hands still on the wheel. "She killed herself. With a gun." She shook her head as if she were trying to shake errant pollen from her hair and dabbed her eyes. "I just can't imagine doing that to yourself. Nothing's ever that bad." She turned to me before opening her door. "She was an alcoholic. A *bad* alcoholic." That was the first time I heard that word. I was still the perfect age. I was five.

Mama Jean had been wrong during that come-to-Jesus talk before first grade about how everyone might not love me. My teacher, Mrs. Chambers, was smitten with me, and the feeling was mutual. She had a big personality like Mama Jean and even looked a little bit like her—dark bubble of hair, bright makeup. While Mama Jean favored jungle-red lipstick, Mrs. Chambers sealed her lips with frosted pink. Thrice daily she'd fumigate herself with perfume from an amethyst glass atomizer that sat on her desk.

Mrs. Chambers wasn't like the other teachers. She drove a navy-blue Mercedes. None of the others could afford to drive such a car. I knew from overhearing Mama Jean and Dad talking that Mrs. Chambers didn't need to work because she was married to a lawyer and they lived in a mansion out in the woods of Evadale. Before that they had lived in a big house on Thomas Road, what Dad called "the Flamingo Road of Beaumont" (where all the rich people lived). I lucked out by landing in Mrs. Chambers's class because I got the kind of attention to which I'd grown accustomed. She and I also had the same birthday, which sealed our bond.

In her class I found my ideal companion and first boyfriend: Eric Munson. We became fast friends during PE. As the other boys ferociously played dodgeball, we sat with our legs dangling atop the monkey bars discussing our favorite episodes of *Bewitched*. Dodgeball is a barbaric game in which opposing teams line up across from each other, red rover–style, but each player is armed with a large, red rubber ball. When Coach blows his whistle, the boys throw their balls at each other with intent to kill. *Kids are cruel enough. Why encourage them?*

Eric had eyes the color of the aquamarine ring Mrs. Chambers sometimes wore and blond hair like I'd never seen before, almost white it was so light. They called a kid with that shade of blond a towhead, which I thought was an ugly name for something so pretty. He even had wisps of it on his arms like a grown man. He was tall for his six years.

He seemed to be equally enamored of my looks. During coloring time, he'd send me love notes on manila paper like "Roses are red, violets are blue, your hair is red, and I'm sweet on you."

In the evenings we had long phone conversations, me talking on the wall-mounted dial phone in the kitchen. We took our cues from our mothers and the soaps we watched to mimic how ladies talk on the phone. I cradled the receiver between my ear and shoulder, hands free, so I could mock-file my nails or lethargically twirl the long cord like a jump rope. I always ended the conversation with "Well, let me let you go." That's how Mama Jean ended her phone conversations, but it was really she who wanted to be let go. It was the Southern way of dropping someone.

Soon we were hanging out after school and playing *Bewitched*. We didn't fight over who would play the starring, Elizabeth Montgomery role of Samantha, the witch. I took that role because Eric was so homosexually advanced he wanted to play Endora, Samantha's wicked, flaming redhead of a mother played by Agnes Moorehead. Eric perfectly imitated Endora's drag-queen mannerisms as he cast spells with a tornado of sweeping arms, arched eyebrows, and sucked-in cheeks. In our *Bewitched,* Samantha ditched her mortal husband, Darrin, after serving him a double martini and gallivanted across Europe with Endora.

This was a perfect game for Eric because he wanted magic, not reality. The house he lived in was also a 1950s ranchburger, not too different from our mini–White House. However, it wasn't as spiffy and clean as ours. The near-dead grandmother in the guest bedroom was supposed to be watching us because his mother, a nurse, was at work. He wouldn't say where his father was, but he assured me that his family had another house, a mansion with an entire room of glass furniture and a three-car garage filled with a Jaguar, a Rolls-Royce, and a Mercedes, just like the one Mrs. Chambers drove.

I remained close with both Eric and Mrs. Chambers after first grade. Eric and I had different second-grade teachers, but we still played after school some days. On other days I would stay behind as Mrs. Chambers's little helper, to stack her freshly graded papers or clean the chalkboard. On those afternoons it was just the two of us working in the empty classroom to the low roar of the window air conditioner and the aroma of manila paper, crayons, and her perfume.

As I helped her, Mrs. Chambers would let me in on the classroom gossip: "Travis Boudreaux can't concentrate. He's what they call hyperactive.... Kathleen Winslow is very creative, my star pupil, just like you were...." I even got to spend our birthday weekend with Mrs. Chambers and her family at her redbrick mansion in Evadale. Set back in the woods down a long, winding road, it was almost as big as the post office downtown and kind of looked like it, with its front porch of six soaring white columns. "I think she was going for Tara, but she wound up with a federal building," Mama Jean told Dad.

On one hot after-school afternoon, Mrs. Chambers called me over to her desk for a heart-to-heart. I sat down and met her gaze with a smile in anticipation of the latest gossip she was going to tell me. *Another parent-teacher conference with Travis's mother? The school is cutting back on manila paper? Show-and-tell is becoming more show than tell these days? Or is she going to invite me for another weekend at her federal mansion in the woods?*

"I want to have a little talk with you, Jamie." I loved little talks with big people. I held her gaze with eager anticipation. "Do you know the word *sissy*?" Her eyes narrowed and her head was cocked. I stared back at her. "Do you know what a sissy is?"

My eyes zeroed in on a close-up of her frosted-pink lips as she said *sissy*. Never wanting to show ignorance, even at that early age, I said, "I think so." I don't know if I did, or if I intuitively did. I felt that I was in trouble. I looked away from her lips and out the window at some boys laughing and playing tag around a lonesome live oak in the blinding afternoon sun. I turned back to her pink lips.

"Well, Eric might be a sissy. You know, people might think you're one too if you hang around him. Maybe it would be a good idea if you took a break from him for a while." Then she winked and ruffled my red hair to lighten the mood. "Just something to think about."

I don't know how much I thought about it, but I know that when

Eric came around after school I started making excuses for why I couldn't play. I was going to a birthday party. My parents weren't home and I couldn't have anyone over. I didn't feel well.

The last time I saw him before he finally stopped coming around, I was standing under the transom of the mini–White House's front door while he stood on the porch. As I made up yet another tale of why I couldn't come out and play, he didn't protest. He said limply, "Okay." His aqua-blue eyes were damp. We both knew that my excuse was a fairy tale. I finally broke the awkward silence with the only thing I could think of to say, "Well . . . let me let you go." He got on his bike and pedaled away.

Later that night I watched a rerun of *Bewitched*. When Endora popped onto the screen, cast a spell, and then disappeared with a whirl of her arms, it made me sad.

I was in junior high when I realized that Mrs. Chambers had been right: Eric was a sissy. I was one too. I rode my bike over to his ranchburger to see if we could pick up where we'd left off. I knocked on his door. A man I'd never seen before answered. Eric's father?

"Is Eric home?" Blank stare. "Eric Munson?"

"He doesn't live here anymore."

"Where did he go?"

"The Munsons moved to Kansas years ago."

FOUR

Driver's Seat

"Read the sticker price on that one," Mama Jean said, staring at a fleet of brand-new 1979 Cadillacs and pointing at the black one. We were cruising the lot of the Cadillac dealership in her silver Ford LTD under cover of night so no unctuous salesmen would hound her. Like cat burglars casing a mansion, we were shadowed in a film-noir chiaroscuro of moonbeams and parking-lot lights.

I obeyed her command; my eleven-year-old legs hopped out of her car to read the eight-by-ten printout stuck on the backseat window (the one behind the driver's seat). The Cadillac—as a Cadillac ought to be—was loaded. I read off the car's amenities: leather seats, illuminated makeup mirrors on the visors, power steering, power windows, power doors. Power.

I read the price and turned to her goggle-eyed. The Ford's electric window, a glass curtain black with night, disappeared into the car door to reveal her covetous face. "How much?"

"Fourteen thousand and eight hundred dollars."

"Well, I don't need leather seats. After you switch to velour, knock off some other amenities, and haggle with them, I could probably get it for eleven or twelve. But I'd need to sell at least two of those houses in Thomas Park before I'm behind that wheel." Thomas Park was the wealthy development at the end of Thomas, aka Flamingo, Road.

"But it says fourteen thousand."

"You never pay sticker price."

And she almost never did.

Mama Jean fell into real estate when she pushed Dad in 1976 to abandon our mini–White House and move to a bigger, better, brand-new house in a new development on the west end of town. It had four bedrooms, not three; two and a half baths, not one and a half; a detached, two-car garage in the back, not an attached one-car garage in the front; a fireplace; and a white terrazzo-tiled foyer. The best part: no aluminum siding.

Against Dad's protestations she started working when I was in first grade. As much as she liked playing the Southern hostess with her Haviland fine china and sterling silver (buttercup pattern), she was bored once I went to school. As she said in later years, "I'd rather be dipped in shit than go to another sip 'n' see!" (A sip 'n' see was a fine Southern tradition of paying a visit to the mother of the bride's house to "sip" tea and "see" the wedding gifts displayed on the dining-room table.)

She told Dad her plans over the phone when he called her from a business trip. "I'm going back to work."

"Why?"

"Because you don't make enough money."

"You most certainly will not!"

"I most certainly will. Besides, it's too late. I've already taken a job." That was her motto: act now, don't apologize later.

Dad was director of the Chamber of Commerce's Convention and Visitors Bureau. It was a high/low job: high profile/low pay. He got to meet all the visiting dignitaries who came to town—Miss Americas, Dr. Joyce Brothers, Pat Boone, even First Lady Betty Ford, who looked like Genevieve, and, according to Dad, had hands as sweaty and warm as fish left out in the sun. There's a photo of Mama Jean proffering me to Pat Boone as he blesses me with his hands as if he were the pope and I were the baby Jesus.

Mama Jean's and Dad's different ways of driving summed up their different approaches to life. He seemed more like a passenger than a driver, as if the car were on autopilot. He turned the key and tapped the gas pedal. The rest was up to the car. Mama Jean, however, had an aggressive, focused way of driving. While her foot assaulted the gas pedal, propelling her car in and out of lanes in search of the fastest route possible to "make good time," Dad seemed to float into traffic as if the car were a sailboat with a good wind behind it and magically glide to his destination. Someone was always in front of Mama Jean, slowing her down, getting in her way. When stuck behind a meandering driver who wasn't going left or right—or wasn't even going—she would moan, "Jesus. He didn't know whether to shit or go blind, so he closed one eye and farted." Dad was that kind of driver.

That first job she took was at the Southeast Texas Arts Council. It wasn't going to get her a Cadillac, but it did get her a fox stole and helped enough with Dad's salary that we were able to make the move to the new house. The Realtor recruited Mama Jean into the publicity department of American Real Estate. While she collected a modest salary, she watched the mostly female Realtors around her closing deals on their exclusive listings, cashing hefty commission checks, and hanging MILLION-DOLLAR PRODUCER gold plaques above their desks. Within a year she got her real estate license. Soon after, Beaumont's front yards were decorated with JEAN BRICKHOUSE EXCLUSIVE for-sale signs.

Dad had long gotten over the idea of Mama Jean's working and became her biggest supporter. He was already her biggest fan. The family photo albums are crammed with Dad's adoring shots of Mama Jean in an array of locations—next to an azalea bush in full bloom on Easter morning, on a hotel balcony in Acapulco, in front of a flocked Christmas tree—but always in the same glamour pose: hands on hips, right elbow point in front, left elbow point behind, right leg extended down to the right high-heeled shoe on point, and radiant smile in a head-on collision with the camera. My favorites are the candids he took of her looking into mirrors and applying her makeup. The one I love predates me. She wears a white dress accessorized by white ball earrings that drop from under her bouffant flip. She leans into a motel-room mirror with her lips stretched as she applies bright red lipstick. In the background is my father, his face blocked by the flash of the camera.

As her Realtor working hours became erratic—showing houses at night, sitting in empty "open houses" on the weekends—Dad took over in the kitchen, which meant we went from tuna casseroles with Lay's potato chips on top to veal scaloppine with mushroom rice. She was a back-of-the-box cook. He threw out the box. This role reversal was big news in town. The *Beaumont Enterprise* Sunday Lifestyle insert ran a cover story on Dad and Mama Jean's modern marriage: "She's a busy real estate agent who doesn't have time to cook for her family anymore. He's a gourmet chef who now puts food on the Brickhouse table every night." The story ran with a photo of Mama Jean sitting at the head of the table in the formal dining room. The glass table is set with her cobalt-blue and burnt-orange Imari china. Candles are lit and Dad is serving her his famous spinach-stuffed chicken breast with pine nuts. Never mind that he only made that for dinner parties and they only ate at that table for holidays and parties.

I was also a big fan of her career success. I called her Executive Woman, and she loved that. I relished the fact that *my* mommy wasn't a housewife like all the other mommies; that she brought home the bacon rather than fried it. I got to show her off at my school's career day. She was the star parent since she was one of the only mothers with a *real* job. A beekeeper mom got a lot of attention for the obvious reasons, but Mama Jean looked the best. She wore a seersucker shirtwaist dress and white leather sandals with cork-wedge platform heels.

I caught Courtney Butler pointing to her shoes and giggling with the girl next to her.

My face fell. "What?"

"Your mother's shoes don't have any backs. Why is she wearing slippers?"

"They're not slippers," I said indignantly. "They're *mules*."

Eventually, the town got to see Mama Jean as the big-screen star I knew her to be. When we heard the honk of a horn in the driveway one day, Dad turned off the stove, I put down my homework, and we ran to answer it. As the reflection of trees and blue sky disappeared on the driver's-seat window of a brand-new, navy-blue Bonneville, the Cadillac of Pontiacs, a beaming Mama Jean was revealed.

We knew this scene well—Mama Jean showing up in the driveway with a new car—but the first time it happened, Dad wasn't enthusiastic. In that foggy dream of one of my first memories, I was pulled from my crib through the window and fled in the middle of the night with Mama Jean and my brothers. I never knew if we were in her blue Chrysler or her new, white Mercury Marquis. My brothers filled in the missing blanks of the story. I now know it was her Mercury Marquis. Her *just-bought* Mercury Marquis. She had traded in her Chrysler that day without Dad's consent.

Dad wasn't happy and got drunk that day. On my family's way back from showing the car to Mamou, the fighting began while Mama Jean drove. Dad kept putting his foot on the brake. He was trying to take control of the car, take control of her. She pulled over and they both got out of the car. Ronny, Jeffrey, and little me sat on the backseat and watched them put on a show in a stranger's front yard. We all made it home, but the fight continued into the night until Mama Jean pulled me through the window from my crib and fled to Mamou's.

That was back in her nonworking days—a long time ago—before Dad officially handed over the reins, even though Mama Jean already had control of them.

Now Mama Jean honked the horn again. "Well, come on! Get in. Let's go for a drive! And I have something to show y'all."

Dad sat in front and I luxuriated in the cushy velour of the backseat and the intoxicating new-car smell.

"Don't y'all love it?!"

"Yes, honey. It's beautiful."

"It's not a Cadillac, but almost as good. I'm going to get that Cadillac if it harelips me. But wait till I show y'all what's on Calder."

As we approached Calder, right before I-10, we saw the American Real Estate billboard. Her face was plastered three stories high, announcing JEAN BRICKHOUSE: AMERICAN REAL ESTATE'S MILLION-DOLLAR PRODUCER!

FIVE

The Pink Pantsuit

U gh! My face looks like a melted candle," Mama Jean said, staring into her bureau mirror with her right hand in a strangulation clasp to hold back the loosening skin around her forty-six-year-old neck. I stood by her side, looking at me looking at her looking at herself in the mirror. She let go of her neck and tugged on the lapels of the pink pantsuit she was wearing with just a bra under the blazer and bare feet. This was the umpteenth time she had tried it on since she'd bought it two or three years earlier.

"And this suit doesn't fit right. It's too tight."

"I don't think so. It looks good," I lied.

"You're biased, darlin'. No. It was a mistake. I never should have bought it."

She was right. And pink wasn't her color.

Trying on clothes was a ritual she performed with me. She'd usually accessorize with two different earrings and two different shoes and walk into my bedroom with left hand pointing up to the earrings and right hand pointing down to the shoes and ask, "Which one goes better with this outfit?"

"Those and those," I'd say, pointing to my choices.

"Wouldn't you know it? Your father says these and these," she'd say, pointing to the opposite choices. She usually went with his picks.

The pink pantsuit was an impulse, off-the-rack splurge. It was inspired by the one Barbra Streisand wore in *A Star Is Born* and was at least two years and as many flared legs out-of-date. The modeling sessions of that suit were never joyous. This one happened at dusk just as darkness crept into her unlit bedroom. The suit was stored in the closet of the bedroom next to her and Dad's. It was my old bedroom, which had become the junk room when my brother Jeffrey moved to Houston at nineteen and I took over his room. The closet housed Mama Jean's overflow of clothes that she didn't wear regularly (such as ball gowns), that she had either slimmed or ballooned out of, or that she was waiting to make right, such as the pink pantsuit.

Deflated that the suit still didn't fit, she lay diagonally across her king-size bed, cast in shadow from the setting sun, and stared into space with her thumb in her mouth. I lay in sympathetic silence with her at the foot of the bed, absorbing her emotions, which filled the room like fog.

She sucked her thumb in moments of distressed contemplation. When she pushed Dad too far in a fight, throwing the money she was making in his face, and he was fortified with white wine, he'd swipe below the pantsuit blazer with "And quit sucking your thumb like a baby! That's pathetic!"

That was like stabbing a lion's paw. Her tears flowed and she'd flee the scene with "Shut up, Earl! You are so mean and hateful! *Hateful!*"

I often witnessed these fights because they rarely happened behind closed doors. They could explode without warning, anywhere, anytime. I hated to bring friends over for fear that Mama Jean and Dad would embarrass me with one of their fights. The explosions usually happened during our nightly family dinners at the kitchen table.

After one of those meltdowns, and after Mama Jean had fled the scene, I stood awash in my own tears, scraping the half-eaten food off my dinner plate into the kitchen sink. Dad rubbed my back as I said through hyperventilated sobs, "Why don't y'all get a divorce? I wish y'all would just get divorced!"

"We'll work it out, Jamie-poo," Dad said. "We always do." They separated not long after that.

Mama Jean pulled her thumb out of her mouth now and unbuttoned the pantsuit blazer. She broke the silence. "What do you think of that town house we saw?" She had taken me on house-hunting tours since the separation.

"I like it a lot!" I said overenthusiastically, trying to lift the gloom. I knew my role. It was to always be her happy little prince, always in a good mood. My sad or angry feelings were quickly negated with "Now, what does a little boy like you have to be sad about? Don't you know how much I love you?" *Yes, but can't I be loved and be sad too?* There was no room for anyone else's feelings. Mama Jean's emotions took up the whole house, like her clothes.

"I don't know. Maybe. If your father and I don't get back together . . ."

Maybe they weren't going to work it out this time. He was living at the Red Carpet Inn on I-10.

I liked the idea of divorce. I didn't look at it as Mama Jean and Dad not being married. I saw it as glamorous, something that all the trendy adults were doing. And it meant we might get to move into a two-story town house.

Mama Jean sat up in the nearly dark room and turned on her bedside lamp. "Well, we don't have to decide today."

I didn't know what I wanted that decision to be. I looked at her hair, now spotlighted, and pointed to it. "I see one."

She leaned her fixed hair in my direction. "Where? Come get it!"

I walked across the bed on my knees and came up behind her. She leaned her hair toward the light so that I could find the gray hair.

"Pull it! But pull it from the root."

. I did. "I see another one."

"God *damn* it! They come as fast as you pull them!"

I went to work on her head like a baboon picking lice out of another baboon's hair and pulled out four more. I balled them and handed them to her.

She looked down at them in her hand. "Those sons of bitches!"

She stood up and looked in the mirror and lightly picked her hairdo back into place with her fingers. As she did this, she spoke to my reflection, which was watching her.

"I don't know if your father and I ever should have gotten married." She removed the blazer and tossed it with a look of disgust onto the velvet love seat across from her bed. She looked back at my reflection. "But if we hadn't, then I wouldn't have you." I smiled up at her and she enveloped me in a hug. She looked away from my reflection in the mirror and down at my actual face. "And I couldn't live without you."

SIX

The Neon Lights Are Bright on Broadway

"Y"ou can have a champagne cocktail like me. But just *one*," Mama Jean said. The old-school, liveried waiter stood hovering over our table at the Russian Tea Room in New York City.

Dad, on the other side of the table from Mama Jean and me, looked at the waiter and ordered. "Uh, two champagne cocktails for them"—I was holding my breath that the waiter wouldn't give us any trouble since I was only fourteen—"and a vodka martini for me."

Mama Jean glared at Dad and shook her head. *"Earl."*

"All right, honey." The waiter waited. "Uh, two champagne cock-tails for them. I'll have a glass of chardonnay."

The waiter left. I exhaled.

At the thought of that champagne cocktail, I beamed as I had been beaming that entire week in early December of 1982. I was wearing a navy-blue, Shetland Polo sweater with black plaid wool trousers and Weejuns penny loafers, elated that I was finally in a climate cold enough to warrant such an outfit. I had finally made it to New York City and to "BROADWAY." We saw a show every night (*Cats, Woman of the Year* starring Raquel Welch,

Dreamgirls, Little Shop of Horrors). Our family may have been Catholic, but we worshiped theater.

"Now aren't you glad you came with us?" Mama Jean asked rhetorically. I had had the choice of going with the Monsignor Kelly High School drama club on the New York Easter-break trip or with Mama Jean and Dad in December. As I'd weighed my options, Mama Jean had said, "All right, but you're not going to be eating at Tavern on the Green and the Russian Tea Room with the drama club." I knew Tavern on the Green from the TV commercials where they secretly replaced their regularly served coffee with Folgers. I chose the December trip.

Mama Jean considered herself a New York insider since she had even lived in the city for a month two years earlier when she was in training to become a stockbroker. As a Realtor, she had sold a house to the new regional manager of a national stock brokerage firm. She impressed him and he talked her into leaving real estate "to make real money" as a stockbroker. She was one of two women stockbrokers in what was still a Southern good-ole-boys club. In the first year she made it clear that she was playing for keeps. When she overheard two brokers bragging about poaching clients from another broker, she poked her head in the door and said with a smile, "Hey, fellows. I heard what y'all just said. Listen to me. If y'all ever do that to me, I'll cut your balls off." By the second year those good ole boys watched in fear and respect as Mama Jean clawed out a chunk of the pie with her manicured, jungle-red nails and ate their lunch.

When Mama Jean was in New York for her training, Dad visited for a week. It must have been like a second honeymoon after they had gotten back together. They did what they liked to do best—after dancing—and saw a show every night and ate out at places like the '21' Club, where they had a lunch that cost the staggering sum of one hundred dollars. I knew that '21' was Joan Crawford's favorite restaurant from the A-earning book report I gave on *Mommie Dearest* in the sixth grade. I remember looking at the cover, which promised, "The #1 *New York Times* Bestseller, Soon to Be a Major Motion Picture!," and thinking, *When?! When?!* The tell-all book by her ungrateful adopted daughter should have made me hate Joan, but instead I became a lifelong fan and wanted to see every movie she ever made. I also couldn't wait to someday dine at '21' like Joan and Mama Jean and Dad.

All the Beaumont Country Club weddings I attended with them were dress rehearsals for this Russian Tea Room moment. I lived for those wedding receptions, when I could teeter on the edge of a gold vinyl banquet chair, dressed in my Sunday best, legs crossed, right hand curled around the stem of a champagne saucer, feeling like one of the adults. I was allowed a sip or two of champagne at weddings, as long as it was done under Mama Jean's watchful eye. The additional sips of champagne were done under her nose. Once a waitress called Mama Jean down when she saw her giving me a taste of her drink. "But he's *my* child!" she answered with a don't-tell-me-it's-not-okay-if-I-say-it's-okay look of indignation. I liked the taste of champagne and the instant pedigree of sophistication it gave me.

I had already had my first drunk a couple of months before this trip, when I felt my life opening up. I'd found the drama club, and in that club, my two new best friends, Nicole and Hunter. Not since Eric from Mrs. Chambers's class had I found friends that fit me so well. Nicole, two grades ahead, was in speech and debate and always spoke her mind. "James Earl, don't let me ever wear this dress again. It makes me look fat."

Nicole wasn't fat. She was tall and big-boned, with a round, smiling face and penetrating brown eyes. She always took charge, the kind of woman I understood. She made things happen, got us out of the house, much to Mama Jean's consternation.

"Mom, Nicole wants me to go to a movie tonight."

"You went out with her last weekend. That girl's pushy. Don't you want to stay home with me and watch *Dallas* and *Falcon Crest*?"

No. I want to go out with Nicole. "Well, I really want to see *Toot-sie*. It's supposed to be a great movie."

Mama Jean never said, "Go out and have fun." She always begrudgingly gave a yes with a layer of guilt: "All right for you, but you'll be sorry when I'm gone."

Hunter was a budding actor like me. We twirled the phone cords nightly, talking about how we were going to take over the drama club, ripping our classmates to shreds, and ending our calls with "Well, let me let you go." Hunter and I competed for Nicole's laughter with dueling impressions of our teachers and classmates. Hunter always won with his signature, showstopping impression of Faye Dunaway as Joan Crawford doing the "No wire hangers!" bit from *Mommie Dearest*.

My first drunk was with Hunter and Nicole. We drank like girls. Frangelico. Amaretto. Crème de menthe. And we got what we wanted: we got drunk. We found a dusty bottle of Frangelico liqueur at my house when Mama Jean and Dad were out one evening. Once the syrupy hazelnut lava had burned its way into us, we found ourselves lying on my bed, me in the middle between them, our heads at the foot, staring at the whirling ceiling fan. We laughed hysterically at the idea that the friar-shaped amber Frangelico bottle looked as if he could be the alcoholic brother of Mrs. Butterworth, the grandma-shaped pancake-syrup bottle. We thought everything we said was hilarious. I wasn't smashed, but perfectly buzzed, as if everything were underwater and I was floating weightlessly through it all. It was a perfect storm of joy. I had finally found friends who understood me. I was moving toward whom I wanted to be. I almost felt like an adult. The current that pooled it all together was booze.

As I surveyed the scene in the Russian Tea Room, I knew I had chosen the right way to see New York.

"Do you remember that scene in *Tootsie* where Dustin Hoffman meets his agent for lunch?" Mama Jean asked.

"Yes."

"Well, that was shot here." She flicked her diamond-braceleted wrist toward the red banquettes along the hunter-green wall. "Didn't I tell you this is a see-and-be-seen place?"

She was right. The trip from the entrance to our table in the back had been a celebrity minefield. At the front corner booth was the actress Ruth Gordon of *Harold and Maude* fame and her playwright husband, Garson Kanin. Two tables down was the comedienne Madeline Kahn, star of the Mel Brooks comedies *Young Frankenstein, High Anxiety,* and *Blazing Saddles.* At a table in the middle of the room sat a man with a bush of Crayola-yellow blond hair and a handlebar mustache. As we walked past, Mama Jean asked Dad in a stage whisper, "Look. It's that confetti-throwing fruit on all those game shows. What's his name?"

"It's Rip Taylor, honey," Dad answered, but I could have. Rip Taylor I knew. He was also on a Saturday-morning kids' TV show, *Sigmund and the Sea Monsters.* He had two trophies at his table: the lynx-fur jacket he was wearing and a comely, much younger black man. Even though Mr. Taylor wasn't ejaculating confetti, the flamboyant gestures of his fur-clad arms left fairy dust on the table.

With a nod of her head in his direction, Mama Jean said, "I want a lynx for my next fur. But full-length." She and I both wanted some of what Mr. Taylor had.

Where is that champagne cocktail? I needed it to keep my head from spinning.

It arrived with bubbles rushing for air from the sugar cube at the base of the tall flute, the champagne discolored to a rosy amber from the Angostura bitters.

Dad made a toast. "To Jamie-poo's first trip to New York. Maybe you'll be on that stage someday."

"I would love that."

"Yes, but that's a hard life," Mama Jean said before clinking her glass with Dad's and mine. I savored the first gulp of the drink, a mixture of dry bubbles sweetened by the sugar cube and given a zesty punch by the bitters. When it hit my nearly empty stomach, it made an instant impact. *Heaven.*

"God, I love a champagne cocktail," Mama Jean said.

"Too sweet for me," Dad said, sipping his dry chardonnay.

"Too bad we're not able to see Henny while we're here." Mama Jean was referring to her childhood friend who used to put on shows in the backyard with her. "When I lived up here during my training and Daddy visited, Henny showed us his apartment down in Greenwich Village."

"Well, it was two apartments," Dad said with raised eyebrows.

"He had combined two apartments, connected with a funny little crawl space. He took us through the crawl space, where he said his 'friend' had the other side." *Friend* was said in scare quotes. "We didn't get to meet his 'friend,' but I think they were more than friends. Like really, *really* good friends."

"Is his friend an actor too?" I asked.

"A dancer," Mama Jean said. "I guess they're happy, but I can't help but think that being . . . gay . . . is still a sad, lonely life for most people." I don't know what she based that on. Maybe the directors she brought in from New York to produce the annual *Luv Forum Follies* fund-raiser she started for the Junior Forum ladies club when she was president. She said they all drank, and one time she and Betty Jane Bundy had to drive one of the directors to the emergency room at one in the morning. When the nurse told Mama Jean he'd be fine once they removed the Coke bottle lodged up his ass, she said, "That son of a bitch!" Not in reaction to the Coke bottle but the one A.M. call, I presume. When I asked Betty Jane if this story was true, she replied, "Yes." Then she cleared her throat. "But it wasn't a Coke. It was Dr Pepper."

I looked away from Mama Jean across the room at Mr. Taylor and took two deep gulps of my drink. Just a week prior to this moment I had sat in the bathtub crying silently into the royal-blue washrag—the same one that Mama Jean pressed against my eyes when she still washed my hair—because I was gay. Not that I wanted to be straight. I was completely on board for the love of another man or men. *Bring 'em on!* But what would it do to her? I was always more invested in her feelings than my own. Everything I did in life carried the baggage of WWMJT?—What would Mama Jean think?

"Acting's a hard life too," she continued. "One in one hundred make it. And you wouldn't like struggling. You have expensive tastes."

"Well, to judge by this room, acting isn't a bad profession," I said.

"Yes, but you can't judge by this trip. I've only shown you the glamorous side of New York, not the seedy stuff."

I didn't mention the sights I'd seen in Times Square: a bronzed Adonis, three stories high, wearing nothing but Calvin Klein briefs (I hadn't been as excited about a billboard since Mama Jean's MILLION-DOLLAR PRODUCER one on Calder); and the marquis of the Gaiety, a series of light boxes of hunky men in various stages of undress, all of them winking, smirking, leering (its promise of "an all-male, all-nude gay revue" thrilled me as much as the Broadway shows we saw every night).

By the time the check came, I was feeling warm and doughy from the second champagne cocktail I'd snuck in while Mama Jean was in the ladies' room. New York was another universe compared to Beaumont, and the windowless Russian Tea Room was another planet within that universe with its flying saucers of cocktail-filled silver trays orbiting stars made of chattering celebrities. I wanted to stay there and keep drinking forever.

Mama Jean looked away from the check and over her frosted-gold reading glasses at me. "*Somebody* had an extra champagne cocktail." Then she glared at Dad.

"Oh, honey, it's vacation."

She sighed as she slid her credit card across the table to Dad. He slipped it into the leather case of the check and gave it to the waiter.

On our way out, we were bunched up in the bottleneck of the

vestibule, waiting in the coat-check line. I heard Dad's unmistakable stage whisper—"Jean, look who's in front of us"—and whipped my head around.

She looked. I looked faster. In front of us, waiting for her coat, was a fine-featured, statuesque blonde with a pixie cut fluttering over her heavily mascaraed, false eyelashes. She wore a tight-fitting, one-piece, black pantsuit and was talking and laughing with two men who matched her in height and good looks. Mama Jean made a silent, openmouthed *Oh!* of recognition that I could not share.

"Who is it? Who is it?" I whispered in desperation.

"Shh!" Mama Jean said.

I bugged my eyes loudly to ask the question again.

"It's Joey Heatherton," Dad whispered.

"Who's Joey Heatherton?"

"You don't know who Joey Heatherton is?!" they both hissed at me. They were always genuinely shocked when I didn't recognize a celeb. Like the time I asked them who the Muppet of a woman was talking to Johnny Carson. "You don't know who Carol Channing is?!" I was seven.

I looked at the lady in question again, as if another glance would unlock the mystery of who this obvious somebody was. It didn't. One of the men helped Miss Heatherton slip into her full-length mink. The false eyelashes seemed to weigh down her glazed eyes. She cooed and licked her lips as they expanded into an elastic smile. She locked arms with the men and walked onto West Fifty-seventh Street.

Mama Jean got her mink and locked arms with Dad and me, and we exited to embrace the exhilarating city outside: sharp cold, honking horns, clanging Salvation Army bells, nasal voices. Joey and her escorts were ten paces ahead of us.

Joey was flipping her artfully messy pixie cut to and fro between the two men as she cooed and cackled. One man goosed Joey at the waist. She squealed.

You can have Disneyland. Who needs that when there's New York? I thought.

I looked down the canyon of West Fifty-seventh Street and glanced up at the chorus line of towering buildings. Just as my gaze came back to earth, Joey screeched to a stop on the sidewalk. She tore open her mink, tossed her head back in a laugh, and threw her right leg over her head in the highest kick I'd ever seen.

The three of us stopped in our tourist tracks as strangers whirled past us. Mama Jean and Dad turned to me and said in unison, *"That's* Joey Heatherton!"

Joey closed her coat and kept walking, her ecstatic laughter leading the way.

I learned later that Joey had once been a movie star, had once been a TV star, had once been a Las Vegas headliner. Had once been. By that time she was better known for dancing provocatively in Serta mattress commercials in a hot-pink, bell-bottom, halter-top pantsuit. Four years after her high kick on West Fifty-seventh Street, headlines blazed, "Arrested for Drugs and Assault, Perennial Starlet Joey Heatherton Finally Crashes to Earth."

But the essence of what I knew about Joey Heatherton on that brisk December day, on West Fifty-seventh Street in New York City, was that I wanted to feel like her at that moment. And I never wanted to crash back to earth.

SEVEN

Lost in Acapulco

Somewhere in Kansas there's a photo of me. I've never seen it, but the details of that snapshot are almost as clear to me as every other detail of the day it was taken. I'm standing in the surf of a beach in Acapulco and flashing a virginal smile, my braces sparkling in the brazen Mexican sun like sequins on a Bob Mackie dress. Besides that smile, I'm wearing a pair of cornflower-blue, nylon, Ocean Pacific, short-short swimming trunks with three stripes in red, pink, and orange forming a *V* at the Velcro fly. Not a teaspoon of fat is on my fifteen-year-old frame, and my hair shines like a new penny. The ocean is behind me and I'm facing the Acapulco Princess resort, but I'm not looking at the Princess. I'm standing with my hands on my hips and inviting the photographer to stare back at me. Hard.

It was day two or three of a family vacation with Mama Jean, Dad, and my brother Jeffrey in 1983, the summer before my sophomore year. I was almost as excited to be there as I had been on that New York trip. Acapulco was loaded with the promise of glamour and excitement. I remember Mama Jean and Dad's stories about spending a week at a cliffside villa. And Jackie O spent her first honeymoon in Acapulco. Come to think of it, Mama Jean spent *her* first honeymoon in Acapulco. If I believed Mama Jean's talk about good girls not putting out before the gold band, I suppose she became a woman in Acapulco.

Ah, Acapulco. It had been a dream destination since I was five.

We didn't start out at the Acapulco Princess. We were booked downtown at the Holiday Inn Crowne Plaza. None of us were happy there, especially Mama Jean.

"Well, this looked a hell of a lot nicer in the brochure. And the place is full of Mexicans."

"Well, Jean, we *are* in Mexico," Dad said. "The Mexicans here aren't like the ones we have at home."

That night Mama Jean and Dad surprised us with a fancy dinner at the Acapulco Princess, which was twenty miles from downtown. Mama Jean primed me to be dazzled. "If you want to talk about swanky, you're talking about the Princess. I'm telling you, y'all won't want to leave."

We arrived at dusk, the palm-shaded road still dappled with sun. As we made the mile-long approach up the drive, I peered out the taxi window, eager for my first glimpse of the famed resort. I felt like Joan Fontaine as the innocent young bride in *Rebecca* as her jaded husband, Maxim de Winter, drives her through the forested path on her first approach to his legendary estate, Manderley: full of desire and anticipation but not knowing quite what to expect. The trees and tropical vegetation parted to reveal three ersatz Aztec temples of luxury. I gaped in wonder as we crossed the marble-and-stone, open-air lobby, which soared to the peak of the building with vine-covered balconies stair-stepped along the way.

"See. I told y'all y'all would like it," Mama Jean said.

We had a steak dinner and were serenaded by a mariachi band and had our photo taken with the band as we raised our salted margaritas. (I got to have a tropical drink or two when we were on vacation.) "You can have one margarita with dinner. *One*," Mama Jean said. After dinner Jeffrey and I explored a fraction of the 480-acre property. The resort sat on a private beach, and we saw two of the five pools, including a saltwater "lagoon" with a grotto accessed by swimming under a waterfall. Jeffrey dubbed it the Get 'Em Grotto because we saw a couple heavily panting and pawing each other at the entrance.

Mama Jean was right. We didn't want to leave, and thanks to her, we weren't going to. "Earl, I've got us two rooms here starting tomorrow."

"Are we going to be stuck paying for the rooms we've got?"

"I don't care. This is where I want to be. Besides, I'm paying for it."

I was with Mama Jean.

By two o'clock the next afternoon, Jeffrey and I were in room 1010, a white terrazzo-tiled affair with a balcony facing the beach. Mama Jean and Dad were in the same kind of room down the hall. By two-thirty Jeffrey and I were sunning by the lagoon with the Get 'Em Grotto, Mama Jean was shopping for silver, and Dad was reading the paper and having a glass of wine in the lobby bar.

This was Jeffrey's first family vacation since he'd announced to Mama Jean four years prior that, like her dear friend Henny, he was gay. Even though Jeffrey and Ronny were full-blood brothers and only seventeen months apart, Jeffrey and I were closest. Thin as the wing of a plane and tall as a skyscraper, he had sharp features inherited from his father and almost-black hair inherited from Mama Jean. We didn't look alike, but when we were younger, Mama Jean liked to dress us in matching outfits. Beige-and-red-plaid bell-bottoms with beige velour tops are the twin outfits that stick in my mind.

Jeffrey was my third parent, mentor, and best friend, and was forever inspiring me to fantasy and make-believe. After he told a six-year-old me about Ann-Margret's face-crushing fall on a Las Vegas stage, I reenacted the fall dressed in a blanket as my strapless gown. I fell off the bed I used for the stage and rushed myself to the bathroom for plastic surgery. Ronny, on the other hand, was a loner redneck who liked to race dirt bikes and go to Neil Diamond concerts. Mama Jean described him as marching to a different drummer. Maybe Ronny seemed to march to a different drummer because he *wasn't* gay.

Jeffrey's announcement was a double feature. Not only was he gay, but he was leaving the nest to move to Houston. And he was leaving with his boyfriend. I was eleven or twelve. I remember Mama Jean sitting in a burnt-orange wingback chair and crying. She explained to me that Jeffrey was gay and it was breaking her heart. When she asked, "Do you know what *gay* means?" I had a flashback to Mrs. Chambers asking me if I knew what a sissy was. "Yes." I didn't say anything else. I just listened with a poker face to mask my fear. Then she stopped talking. Her sobs were the only sounds in the room. I wanted to leave but was frozen in place on the floor at her feet. After she stopped crying and wiped the mascara running from her eyes like spilled ink, she looked down at me with a stare that could freeze lava and asked, "Do you have feelings like that? Because if you do, tell me now. I'll take you to see a psychiatrist."

I wanted to say, *If you have to ask . . . ,* but instead I answered with a clipped, high-pitched "Nope" and scurried to my room, where the original-Broadway-cast album of *Mame* was still playing. I'd known the answer to that question for a long time, ever since she'd asked me the first $64,000 question: if I had passed semen. I had.

I was already *interactively* reading the issues of *Penthouse Forum* that Jeffrey had left behind. They had bi and gay stories, so I knew what to do, knew what went on out there. I remember watching a report on television about what was then described as a gay cancer. Shots of shirtless men dancing at a disco were overlaid with a voice talking about how the promiscuous lifestyle of gay men might be spreading the new disease.

"Makes me sick," Mama Jean said in disgust. I thought to myself, *Don't stop the fun before I get there!*

By the time I hit that deck chair at the Get 'Em Grotto, I was ready. I hadn't confided in Jeffrey that I looked up to him in more ways than he imagined, and if he was bothered that Mama Jean hadn't extended an invitation to his boyfriend to join us, he didn't say. Instead we ordered a couple of piña coladas and simply basked in the sunshine of our Acapulco Princess good fortune. Jeffrey fell asleep on the deck chair. The piña colada that I quickly downed left me restless and ready for adventure. "Jeffrey, are you asleep?" He was. I left him there and meandered down the stone path that led to the other pools.

The first one was all water wings, inflatable sea horses, and shrieks of "Marco!" "Polo!" The kiddie pool. Ew. I kept moving. I found the adult pool. The scene there was a party, the pool an aquatic lounge.

I sat on the edge of the cement pond to soak in the scene. I wasn't afraid of the water anymore, just wisely cautious. The pool was enormous and curved in and out and ended—or began—with a swim-up bar under a thatched roof near a waterfall. The entire pool was shallow, since it was meant for lounging and libations. Every submerged stool at the bar was occupied by men and women holding a rainbow of umbrella-studded tropical drinks: yellow piña coladas, pink strawberry daiquiris, lime margaritas, blue curaçao Hawaiians. A woman in a macramé bikini and floppy hat was making out with a man wearing a gold chain. They both had savage tans. Spilling out from the bar into the chlorinated lake were pairs of men and women holding their drinks high above the water as their heads floated on the surface, besotted hippos. Shrieks of laughter rippled from one end of the pool to the other and back again. It wasn't that different from the kiddie pool, just another set of games.

Like a cat whose eyes go from lazy indifference to wide-eyed alert as it spots the only two birds in a forest of trees, my eyes zoomed in on the only two men in Speedo bikinis. They were frolicking in the middle of the pool. The one in the lime-green bikini was coquettishly posing for the one in the navy-blue bikini with red and white racing stripes on the side. Limey was tall and lanky like me, with curly brown hair and a light spray of freckles across his face and arms. Racing Stripes, the older one, was stocky, solid muscle, and almost short. A towhead, he had Windex-blue eyes just like my first-grade boyfriend, Eric. In a ricochet of penetrating glances, I caught Limey's eye, and he caught mine and tossed it to Racing Stripes, who threw the ball back in my court. *Tennis, anyone?*

I cocked my head to the side and smiled, with my arms in straight lines behind me, the silhouette pose of a sexy woman on a Mack truck's mud flaps. I wouldn't be surprised if I licked my lips. Limey posed for another shot, gazing over his left shoulder at the camera. Just as Racing Stripes cried, "Say cheese!," Limey pulled down the back of his bikini to expose a bare cheek like the little girl in those Coppertone sunscreen ads. When the camera clicked, he winked and shot his smile straight through me. If a bolt of lightning had struck that pool, I wouldn't have noticed. I was already electrified.

They got out of the pool and walked over to me. I pumped my legs in the water like Lolita and looked up as their near-naked bodies dripped on me. Racing Stripes took the lead and squatted on his haunches, offering his hand with a Pepsodent smile.

"Hi, I'm Vernon. This is Kelly." I shook Vernon's hand and Limey/Kelly squatted down to offer his hand.

"I'm Jamie. Nice to meet y'all."

"Want to take a walk?" Vernon asked, his head tilted in the direction of the beach.

"Why not?" I said, thinking, *I can't believe this is really happening.*

They told me that they lived in Kansas and were at the Princess for a company sales conference. "His job," Kelly clarified, indicating Vernon. *How old are they?* Kelly was probably Jeffrey's age, twenty to twenty-three. *Vernon?* I don't know. But they were hot. And they were men. That was all I needed to know.

"I'm here on vacation," I said, omitting *with my family.*

Making more small talk, we sauntered from the adult pool to the beach.

"Hey, why don't you stand in the ocean and I'll take your picture?" Vernon said.

"Okay" was my nonchalant reply, as in *Sure. I do this all the time. I'm used to it.* I walked out to the ocean and turned my back on the waves. "Here?"

"Just a little further back," Vernon said. "Yeah. That's it."

I struck my pose in the broiling sun, wishing I were in a wet bikini instead of my Ocean Pacific trunks—wishing I *had* a bikini. *Someday.*

Then I let the pose go as we waited for a parade of souvenir vendors to walk past.

They passed.

"Okay?" Vernon asked.

"Okay." I struck the pose again and flashed my thousand-watt smile of sparkling braces.

"Say cheese!" Kelly shouted.

"Cheese!" I shouted back.

"Jamie!" Dad yelled.

My smile melted as I turned my gaze from Limey and Racing Stripes to see Dad standing ten feet away from them with popped eyes and raised eyebrows. The adrenaline in my body was still pumping, but it sank from palpitations in my heart to a lump in my stomach. I robotically walked out of the ocean toward Dad, ignoring my new friends from Kansas. Out of the corner of my eye, I saw them drift away.

Dad held my gaze as I walked toward him. I couldn't read his furrowed brow as either a look of shock or worry. Probably both.

"Hi, Dad," I said as I reached him.

"What were you doing?"

"Just walking on the beach."

"Who were those guys?"

"I don't know. Just some guys. They asked if they could take my picture."

He stared at me, his face frozen in his brows-raised, eyes-popped look, but he didn't inquire further. "Well, you need to be more careful. Come on." He walked ahead of me and away from where Limey and Racing Stripes had been standing. I followed and we walked along the beach side by side for thirty minutes in silence. I didn't know what to say. I guess he didn't either.

At sunset that evening I found myself draining a frozen margarita back at the deck of the adult pool. Mama Jean was holding out her left wrist to model the collection of silver bangles she had bought that afternoon. Dad, Jeffrey, and I oohed and aahed on cue.

"I could shoot myself for not getting the necklace that goes with these. I'm just sick about it."

"Well, honey, you've already got plenty of silver," Dad said.

"But not like this. I'm going to have to go back to that store downtown before we leave."

"How about another margarita, Mom?" Jeffrey asked.

"Yeah. We'll get it," I said, taking the opportunity to sneak in one more.

"I don't know. Y'all might have to carry me upstairs if I have another," she said with her eyes crossed and her tongue sticking out the side of her mouth.

"Oh, have a second one, honey," Dad said with a head point toward the bar as he tilted his empty glass at Jeffrey and me. Jeffrey and I scurried off before she could change her mind.

We stood leaning on the circular bar as Jeffrey, to my right, ordered a round of drinks. Out of the corner of my left eye I saw a lightly freckled arm resting on the bar. Limey. I caught his eyes and smiled at him and glanced toward Jeffrey to halt him from speaking.

I turned away from Limey and said to Jeffrey, "Make sure mine is salted."

"Right." Jeffrey then called the bartender over to clarify the order.

Limey pushed a drink receipt toward me. I saw that he had scribbled "Room 910" on the back of it. He whispered in my ear, "Here's our room number. Call us. We'll be in our room for the next hour." His hot breath in my ear nearly melted me. I leaned harder on the bar as my left leg shot up behind me, bent at the knee. I turned to Jeffrey just as Limey was pulling away from my ear.

"Thanks!" I said to Jeffrey overenthusiastically. We gathered our drinks and joined Mama Jean and Dad poolside.

Midway through our drinks, I asked Jeffrey for our room key with the excuse that I needed to go to the bathroom. I took the key from Jeffrey and fought the urge to run to the elevator as I caressed the piece of paper with "910" scrawled on it. Jeffrey and I were in 1010, so they were directly below us. I saw this as a good omen. I rang them from 1010.

Vernon answered, "Hello." His voice went up in anticipation on the *lo.*

He said that he and Kelly were going to a big company dinner that night and then out to the bars downtown. *The bars!*

"Oh, I wish I could go," I said, twirling the phone cord, "but I have dinner plans."

"Maybe you could come to our room later? We should be back from the bars by midnight." Each time he said "the bars" I tingled. "Want to stop by then?"

"Sure. Sounds good," I said with bravado, wondering if I could make it happen.

"You're not hungry?" Mama Jean asked as I pushed my enchilada *verde* around my plate.

"Too many chips and guacamole by the pool." I was too excited to eat. I hadn't been this excited since the day before my first drama tournament in junior high.

"Uh, y'all don't look now"—Mama Jean leaned her head forward—"but look at the next table."

We all started to turn.

"I said don't look. But I want y'all to see this couple at the next table. Okay, look now. But quick."

We looked. A man was staring intently into his woman's eyes as he fed her a piece of lobster claw. When she reached the end of the lobster meat, she began fellating his finger and moaning.

We all turned back to each other with our eyes bugged.

"My God! Can you believe that?" Dad said.

"I told y'all."

"I'll bet they're the couple from the Get 'Em Grotto," Jeffrey said.

I looked at my watch. Ten o'clock. *It's my turn in two hours.*

"Jeffrey? Jeffrey?" I whispered. He didn't respond. In the blackout dark of 1010 I listened intently for the telltale signs of his deep sleep and heard the steady metronome of his breathing from the next bed. "Jeffrey, are you asleep?"

I pulled on a pair of white shorts that I had placed under the bed earlier with the room key already in the pocket, left on the extra-small T-shirt that fell just above my belly button, and slipped into my Top-Siders. I used the pinstripes of the outside hall light framing the door as guide and goal to tiptoe my way through the dark room. Once I was in the hall I actually skipped down the corridor. I took the stairs, rather than the elevator, to the ninth floor, below.

Scurrying down the back stairs seemed to add intrigue to the adventure.

Nine-ten. My heart was running a race as I knocked on the door. Limey cracked open the door and smiled hello. I could tell he wasn't wearing anything. That was damn thrilling, but I would have preferred that he greeted me in his lime-green Speedo.

"Come on in." He let me in and I saw that he had a towel loosely draped around his waist.

I walked down the small entrance hall past the bathroom, where Racing Stripes stood at the sink brushing his teeth, wearing only his white, bikini Calvin Kleins, like the briefs the bronzed Adonis wore on the Times Square billboard. He looked at me in the mirror and garbled, "Hello."

I sat on the corner of their bed until Limey came in dressed in a T-shirt and shorts, followed by Racing Stripes, still in his Calvin Kleins. We talked for a little bit about their company dinner. They'd had fun at the gay bars downtown and were leaving on an early flight the next morning. They lived together in Kansas and had been a couple for three years. Limey was seated next to me. Close. Our legs touching. Racing Stripes was sitting on the other bed across from us doing most of the talking. Limey was twenty-three. Racing Stripes was thirty-two. "I'm eighteen," I lied.

"Do you like Acapulco?" Limey asked.

I turned to his face, our noses almost touching. "Yes. Very much." I felt as if I were talking in slow motion, aware of my lips as every syllable left them. Then Limey gave me my first kiss. He tasted of bourbon. I already had a taste for bourbon. Ingested this way, it was as exhilarating as that first sip of whiskey when I was five. It tasted like it did then. It tasted like being an adult. To this day I'm a sucker for whiskey breath.

In the fog of that kiss Racing Stripes materialized. We tumbled into a blur of tongues and mouths and stiff dicks and oohs and aahs. I was in the middle, and I loved every second of it. My first time and I was spoiled. *Will I ever be satisfied with just one?* The sex was like a Harlequin romance: everything but penetration. *Sure as hell beats pressing.*

I don't remember dressing, just the image of them peeking at me from behind the door, Limey's head on top of Racing Stripes' until I disappeared up the stairs. I almost floated up those stairs, I was so giddy. *I am a woman now.*

I slipped my hands into my pockets and tensed my shoulders with delight. In my right pocket was the room key, and something else that wasn't there before. Paper. I stopped walking and pulled out a wad of peso notes, worth about fifty dollars. As I stared at the money, I thought, *They think I'm a whore. I'm no whore.* I walked back to their room. The door was shut. I piously slid the money under the door.

Back in my hotel room, I lay in my bed, playing back the video of the entire day, alternately flattered and insulted. Finally, at six A.M., I slipped out of the room again to see if I could catch them before they left. *To get the money back? For another round?* Their door was ajar. I pushed it open. The room was empty. The closet bare. The soiled bed unmade. They were gone. And so was the money.

I always imagine them back in Kansas boasting to their friends about the copper-headed Lolita they picked up at a pool in Acapulco and nearly lost on the beach, but who couldn't be bought— or at least wouldn't take a tip. And every time they tell that story, I imagine them pointing to a baby grand piano lousy with a collection of silver-framed photos. In the center is a picture of a metal-mouthed kid brazenly smiling in the Mexican sun as he stands in the surf of an Acapulco beach—forever virginal, forever fifteen.

EIGHT

Bottoms Up

How are we feeling this morning?" Mama Jean asked as she pushed open my bedroom door, her way of knocking.

My mouth feels like a desert highway at noon, my head like an overblown balloon, and I just might upchuck into my underwear drawer. Right. Now. What I actually said with a forced smile that hurt my face was "Fine."

I had been to the Monsignor Kelly High School spring dance the night before with my de facto girlfriend, Maggie, and was experiencing my first colossal hangover, the maraschino cherry to top off my junior year. This educational year had left me street-smart, but not exactly street*wise*.

"How was the dance? Did you and Maggie have a good time?"

Maggie and I had been going out for a few months. She was edgy and weird, in the drama club like me, and drank. *My kinda gal.* She went by Margaret until she met me. I called her Maggie, as in Maggie the Cat from *Cat on a Hot Tin Roof.* She should have called me Brick, as in Maggie the Cat's alcoholic husband who wouldn't put out. I wasn't actively looking for a girlfriend as a beard, and Maggie wasn't a beard. More like a goatee, since I don't think I was fooling anyone but maybe her, Mama Jean and Dad, and a couple of nuns. She'd receive the most tasteful corsages, orchids usually, and always wrist, not breast, so her dresses, like her virginity, would remain unscathed.

"Oh, lots of fun," I said, not looking at Mama Jean as I tried to remember just how much fun I'd had. But only three hazy snapshots remained from the school dance:

Repeatedly scooping a Dixie paper cup into an Igloo cooler filled with red punch at someone's parentless house. "Hey, what is this anyway? It's good!" I asked the crowd around the cooler. "Everclear! One hundred and ninety-proof! Illegal in most states!" answered some blond jock with bloodshot eyes.

Bouncing like Tigger from Winnie-the-Pooh *to the B-52's ode to a beach bacchanal, "Rock Lobster." The lyric "Boys in bikinis!" conjured Acapulco and made my loins tingle.*

Throwing up blood—blood? No, it was the punch—all over the white porcelain urinal of the school bathroom.

Then black.

How did I get home? I saw my clothes piled neatly on the chair next to my desk. *Schwoo.* At least I didn't get caught. *How did Maggie get home?*

My drinking prior to that school dance had certainly caused lapses in judgment, but never giant lapses. Booze had always been the ticket to fun, and I sought it whenever possible. For my weekend outings, I'd skim from the house liquor cabinet. On nights when Mama Jean and Dad were out, I'd play amateur bartender with Dad's cocktail-recipe book from the fifties, *Bottoms Up.* The sexy cover featured a busty, blond floozy wearing nothing but opera gloves, black high heels, and a lopsided smile. She was loosely draped over a saucer champagne glass like a pair of stockings, three sheets and several panties to the wind, her image repeating like wallpaper. I discovered recipes for cocktails that I had only seen in old movies: sidecars, sloe gin fizzes, pink ladies, Manhattans. *Bottoms Up* unlocked the key to the drinks I wanted, the Holy Grail being the martini.

Martinis were forbidden in our house. The mere suggestion of a martini launched Mama Jean into retelling "The Legend of the Dinner Roll Martinis." "Earl can't have martinis anymore. That time we were in Colorado and he had I don't know *how* many, and the next thing I knew, I looked across the table and he was like this"—she made her drunk face (lopsided head, eyes crossed, tongue hanging out)—"and he started throwing dinner rolls across the table. After that, I said, '*Uh-uh!* No more martinis.'"

Dad always rolled his eyes and sighed. "Honey, that was *one* time."

"Well, one time too many," she said, getting in the last word.

I was a toddler when that happened, but the oft-told legend left me thirsty for martinis my whole life. I couldn't imagine what was so lethal about them, or complicated. Whenever they popped up in old movies, there was debate about "shaken or stirred," "don't bruise the gin," "just a whisper of vermouth." Like most things that adults do that seem so complicated when you're a kid, the martini was surprisingly easy, but I had to improvise. With no cocktail shaker in the house, I used the Pyrex measuring cup. We had no proper martini glasses, so I poured the magic potion into one of my grandmother Mamou's gold-rimmed crystal champagne saucers. The recipe called for three ounces of gin and one ounce of vermouth. My first taste: *Ew.* I'd never had gin. I thought it tasted like a Christmas tree, and the vermouth part of it was just shy of gasoline. But I was determined not only to finish that drink, but to acquire a taste for martinis. *I am going to get sophisticated if it kills me.*

Those first martinis were extremely wet. Not just in terms of the liberal amount of vermouth I was naively using, but where I drank them. I sipped them nude in the swimming pool that Mama Jean put in when I was a freshman. I did know how to swim by the time the pool was installed, but it had taken a while. After the terrifying summer with the Wicked Witch of the Wet, I spent the next two summers back on the steps of the pool. When I was nine, we joined the country club. At the bar that overlooked the pool, I used to sit eating maraschino cherries and talking to Clarence the bartender. I was finally coaxed down from my barstool into another go at swimming lessons when I saw the instructor: a tall, tan, blond college student with a Mike Brady perm. He was kind and gentle and patient. He never helped me pee, although I'm not sure I would have minded. He even got me to jump off the high dive. That took several seconds—minutes?—of standing on the edge of the board, staring down at the water, and chanting to myself, "Do it. Just do it. Just. *Jump*," before I would close my eyes, scream, and jump.

Mama Jean and Dad had a rich social life, so I had plenty of nights to myself to hone my nude bartending skills. I'd set Mamou's champagne saucer on the edge of the pool, take a deep gulp, and float on my back to the sounds of the rediscovered Burt Bacharach songs of my early childhood—"Make It Easy on Yourself," "I Say a Little Prayer," "Walk on By." "The Look of Love" was my favorite song to float by. Sometimes I'd drift under the white stone lion, Mama Jean's zodiac avatar that stood watch at the deep end of the pool. I'd let Leo drench me with the steady stream of chlorinated saliva spewing from his mouth. I was breaking two of Mama Jean's rules: no martinis and no glass by the pool.

As fun as those solo, nude drinking nights were, I still craved drinking while dressed up. The Neches River Festival provided the ideal venue. It was *the* society event every spring. High school senior girls were presented as princesses in a weeklong round of festivities that culminated in the coronation of the NRF queen at the Julie Rogers Theatre downtown. The winning princess was always beautiful and almost always from an important family. The queen would reign that night at the ball and the following day in a parade downtown on the arm of the king, a middle-aged to simply aged, rich man. Like most Southern extravaganzas, it was a beauty pageant with money attached.

Senior boys usually escorted the princesses, while juniors were requested to pull up the slack for the duchesses, the out-of-town gals. As a junior, I was happy to be an escort and thrilled to don the requisite white jacket and captain's hat.

I was paired with a duchess from Port Arthur. Port Arthur was a depressed refinery town twenty miles from Beaumont. Apparently, the Duchess of Port Arthur was already royalty—refinery royalty—since her daddy was an executive at one of the plants. Clearly, she'd been treated like a princess her whole life and wasn't happy about her reduced status as duchess. She had a lemon-yellow bob of curling-iron ringlets and wasn't much bigger than Shirley Temple. At the coronation—princesses all wore virginal white, duchesses wore anything *but* white—she was outfitted in a bubble dress of chewing-gum-pink taffeta. The skirt puffed out from the waist to a bubble of pleats and then curled under at the knees, giving her squat figure the look of a giant taffeta beach ball.

She had taken an instant dislike to me from the moment we met at the coronation rehearsal. She wore a sickly smile that looked as if she had just smelled the flatulent fumes of her refineried Port Arthur backyard and barely said hello. *Perhaps her ultrasensitive nose sniffed me out for what I was.*

After the coronation, I couldn't turn the key fast enough in the ignition of my teal-green Pontiac Sunbird, which Mama Jean had given me earlier that year, so I could drive the Duchess of Port Arthur to the ball and dump her into the arms of her doting parents.

"Do you have any Excedrin?" the Duchess of Port Arthur whined, her head turned away from me.

"What?" I said as I pulled out of the parking lot.

"I have to have some Excedrin. I have a sick headache." *A sick headache? Who gets sick headaches except bitter old women? Bit-*

ter young *women, I guess.* I wasn't packing Excedrin, so we drove all over town looking for it. It was late, almost eleven P.M. Most places were closed. I found some Anacin at a 7-Eleven.

I held it up in the store window for her approval while she sat waiting in the car. She screwed up her soured face to weakly yell, "It *has* to be Excedrin. I *only* take Excedrin."

I slammed the Anacin on the counter and left. Two stores later I found Excedrin.

"Here you go." *Pills for the Pill,* I wanted to say. Then with mock enthusiasm: "It's extra-strength! Didn't want to take any chances!" I opened it and gave it to her with a McDonald's Coke I had wisely picked up during our search. The Duchess of Port Arthur took her medicine.

I reached under my seat and pulled out the bottle of Jack Daniel's I had stashed for the ball and had been sneaking swigs off of during the coronation. "Do you mind?" I held up the bottle. I didn't wait for her to answer. "This is *my* Excedrin." I smiled at her as I poured liberally into my Coke. "Extra-strength."

After the ball I raced downtown to the Copa, the gay bar, which wasn't far from where the coronation had taken place. As I walked toward the bar, still wearing my Neches River white jacket and captain's hat, I noticed a tall, lanky man, maybe twenty-three, with longish, dark Duran Duran hair. He stood under the streetlight on the corner and winked at me. Inside was a glow-in-the-dark, ersatz New York City skyline. I was the belle of the ball—the real Neches River queen—as I danced on the cheap parquet floor with a new partner for each song: Wham!'s "Careless Whisper," Duran Duran's "A View to a Kill," and Madonna's "Crazy for You," the first song Maggie and I danced to.

I made out a few times at the bar. Between sloppy kisses flavored with Jack and Coke, I glanced in the mirror behind the bar and caught glimpses of what others saw: captain's hat askew, bow tie dangling around the neck, lopsided smile—a drunken sailor in need of an escort. But I didn't find the escort just right for me.

On my way out of the bar I passed the Duran Duran man, who was still under the streetlight. He smiled and winked at me again as he puffed on a cigarette.

"Hey," I said.

"Hi there." He flicked his ash.

"What's up?"

"Nothing much. I'm staying not far from here."

"Really?" I asked with a lopsided smile.

"Yeah. Wanna go there?"

I was thrilled by this cinematic tableau: a sexy stranger, nonchalantly smoking on a desolate downtown sidewalk corner lit only by a streetlight. A surge of electric tingles radiated to the ends of my fingers and toes as I jumped at his proposal.

I zigzagged to my Sunbird and offered him the passenger seat, which was still cold from the Duchess of Port Arthur.

We got in the car and held each other's gaze.

"So why didn't you come inside and say hello to me?" I asked.

"Well, I was working."

"Working?"

"You know what I am, don't you?"

"Um, a fag like me?"

"Well, yeah. But I was selling, you know. Out there on the street."

"Really?"

"Yeah. I'm an 'escort.' But I'm off duty now."

Now I was really turned on. "I'm an escort too." I took off my hat and tossed it onto the backseat. "Also off duty."

I put the car in gear and closed one eye to focus on the dotted line of the road since I was seeing double. I carefully drove just under the speed limit of thirty miles per hour, aware that I was drunk. I was convinced that I drove better drunk because I was extra-cautious. I believed that when I drove drunk, I didn't do anything stupid or take any risks.

He lived—or was staying—in a garage apartment behind a dilapidated Victorian. We climbed the outside staircase to enter a room filled with ball gowns draped over every surface, lit only by a dim-watted floor lamp. Rising from the gowns and perched on an ottoman was a wisp of a man with long, blond, permed hair and traces of lipstick and mascara on his face. He was hunched under the lamp, painstakingly sewing silver sequins onto a ball gown that he held in his arms and across his lap like the dead Jesus resting on Mary, a drag pietà.

"Don't mind us," my escort said.

The man looked up and over his reading glasses, his needle and thread suspended in midair. "Oh, Mary, don't y'all mind *me*." He had the soprano twang of a piney woods mawmaw. "She's gonna be up for *hours*. I don't know *how* she's gonna git all these gowns done by the ball next Sunday." He—*she?*—made a sweeping gesture around the room. My gloom-adjusted eyes could see that the gowns rivaled any I had seen at the coronation in embroidery, bugle beads, and sequins. *More Cher than beauty queen.* I could also see that they were about ten sizes up from Cher.

"The ball?" I mouthed to my escort.

"The big Miss Gay Southeast Texas drag ball next Sunday."

"Oh, *Mary*," the seamstress said, his eyes fixed on me. "You gotta cuuum!" He gave my outfit a once-over. "Trust me, honey. It will blow out of those muddy, snake-infested Neches River waters *inny-thing* you saw toniiight."

I couldn't reply. I was paralyzed by a combination of fascination and horror that made me want to turn around and leave. Obviously, the Seamstress did drag. Drag made me nervous. He was one of those "high-flying fruits" Mama Jean talked about. Like the ones that worked at her current beauty parlor, Fame.

Shit. What if the Seamstress works at Fame?

"We're going to slip into the bedroom," my escort said.

"Slip away, Marys! Slip away!" the Seamstress said, wafting the needle and thread in her right hand before she returned to the intricacy of her sequins. "Y'all have fun. Lord knows, *somebody* should."

We pushed to the floor the backless, strapless, non-bubble gowns that were lying on the bed and took the Seamstress's sage advice.

A few weeks later mysterious blood was on my post-BM toilet paper. *Weird.* A week later blood was in the toilet. *This can't be good.* A blind man's search with my hand discovered mysterious little bumps down there, like fleshy moles. *Surely they'll go away.* They didn't. A self-examination with one of Mama Jean's makeup mirrors revealed little, white hamster pellets. *Oh my God. What are they?*

For I don't know how long, I would reexamine myself and see that they were growing. The alien hamster pellets were forming little bouquets. I'd sit on the toilet, my head in my hands, a diseased version of Rodin's *Thinker. I can't sit on this much longer.* I told no one. *Who am I going to tell?*

I remembered the free clinic in the black part of town. It took a few merry-go-rounds the block before I got up the nerve to go in. As the only white boy (the only *boy*) in the waiting room, I was, as Dad liked to say, "nervous as a whore in church."

"Oh, *honey!*" the fat nurse, a white version of Mammy, explained as she examined my exposed butt. "You've got cauliflower growing out of your ass! We can't handle this here, hon. You've got to see Dr. Faudi."

My sphincter tightened at the mention of Dr. Faudi's name since I went to school with his son. "Isn't there anyone else?"

"No, hon. He's the only proctologist in Beaumont."

I made an appointment, but I didn't get past Dr. Faudi's gatekeeper: a pageboy-blond nurse with red lips that bled into the Kabuki-white powder spread on her face. After I told her my problem, she stared at me as if I had cooties. *Well, I guess I did, but shouldn't she be used to this in her line of work?* With disdain and the same fart-smelling expression of the Duchess of Port Arthur, the Nurse of the Bleeding Lips told me that the doctor couldn't see me without insurance or my parents' consent. *Didn't she know how hard it was for me to be there?* Her judgmental glare seared my entire body with shame and I hated her for it.

I told Dad that I thought something was wrong, that I was having pain going to the bathroom. No need to get Mama Jean involved. Dad took me to his physician. When I exposed myself to the avuncular doctor, a Captain Kangaroo type, he said, "Oh. Oh. Uh, well, son, it appears that you have anal warts. And they're awfully . . . florid."

I couldn't resist. "Kind of like a cauliflower bouquet?"

"Well, *yes*. That's a good description. Now, son, I can't take care of this. You're going to have to see a proctologist. And the only proctologist in town is—"

"—Dr. Faudi," I said in unison with him, but under my breath.

Dr. Kangaroo didn't tell Dad that I had anal warts, just that I had to see Dr. Faudi. Dad, to my relief, didn't ask any questions, but he did have to bring Mama Jean in on it. He made the appointment and I returned with both Dad and Mama Jean to Dr. Faudi's office, where the Nurse of the Bleeding Lips sat waiting. This time she greeted me with a powder-cracking smile. I mirrored her fake grin as I walked past her to Dr. Faudi's examination room.

Dr. Faudi confirmed what I already knew. Yes, I had anal warts. Yes, they were a cauliflower bouquet. Yes, he was the only proctologist in town. Had I had anal sex with a man? Yes. Did my parents know I was gay? No. Did we have to tell them I had warts? Yes, because they had to be removed surgically, in the hospital.

He agreed to keep the cause of the cauliflower bouquet a secret. The warts he had to let out of the bag. He called Mama Jean and Dad into his office and explained that I had anal warts, a virus. Dad was silent with his eyebrows raised. Mama Jean listened intently to Dr. Faudi, but looked at me out of the corner of her eye. I avoided her glare.

"But *how* did he get them?" Mama Jean asked. Someone was always to blame in her book, and she needed to know whom.

"There are any number of ways one can contract this," Dr. Faudi said, his shoulders in a but-who-knows-how shrug.

"Like *what*?" Mama Jean asked.

"Oh, say in the locker room, from sharing a dirty gym towel."

"A *gym* towel?! But he hasn't taken PE in almost two years!"

Mama Jean was confused. Her eyes scanned the room from me, as red-faced as a pimiento, to Dad, with his eyebrows raised, to Dr. Faudi, whose shoulders were still shrugged. Thankfully, she didn't pursue it any further. On our way out, we all stepped over the imaginary gym towel left behind on the floor.

After the surgery Mama Jean bought me Always minipads to help with the post-surgery "flow." As she handed me the box, she said, "I thought I was done with this stuff after my hysterectomy."

The spring dance with Maggie was a few weeks after the surgery. By that time I had recovered and was ready to go out and celebrate, but it wasn't the dance that was memorable, since I remember almost nothing of it. What I can't forget was the dooms-day promise of that seventies song "(There's Got to be a) Morning After." As Mama Jean stood peering over my shoulder, eager to hear *all* about it, I stared into my underwear drawer with nothing but those three snapshots of memory from the night before.

"You got home awfully early last night," she said in a singsong voice.

"I didn't think it was *that* early. Did I wake you?"

"Wake me? Darling, I believe *I* woke *you*." Her head was cocked to the side as her tongue pushed out her right cheek. I didn't know what to say, so I took the Fifth. "You don't remember our little conversation?" she asked with a wide smile and blinking eyes.

LBD (lower bowel distress) hit. I couldn't tell if it was caused by my hangover or the trap I was falling into. "We spoke?"

Her smile widened as she pushed aside my clothes and sat in the chair next to my desk, an antique from Mamou's house. Hanging over it were the *Playbill*s of all the Broadway shows from the New York trip, which Dad had framed for me. Mama Jean clapped her hands as she hit the chair. "Oh, let me tell you *all* about it! It's a real good story."

Busted. And Mama Jean loved to bust.

"Your father and I got home at eleven from Yum Yum and Dan's party, and there was your car. I looked at Earl. 'What's Jamie doing home this early?' We opened the back door and there was your shirt. Oh! And then a sock in the den. Then a whole *trail* of your clothes, like Hansel and Gretel's crumbs, leading to your bed."

"Really?" I said incredulously, which was sincere.

"Yes, *really.* I whispered, 'Jamie? Jamie?' Then I tapped you on the shoulder. *'Jamie?'* You shot up in bed and said, 'What?' I said, 'Have you been drinking?' 'Huh?' you asked. I said, *'Jamie,* have you been drinking?' Well, at the *top* of your lungs you screamed, 'I'm *DRUUUNK*!'" She raised her eyebrows and laughed. I was about to join her, but she shut off her laugh midstream like a water faucet and fixed me with that lava-freezing stare of hers. "And you don't remember *any* of that?"

"I don't think I do."

She told me that she called Maggie, who told her that she had driven my car home.

I explained about the Everclear punch. That I hadn't known what was in it, which wasn't a complete lie. That I'd had the good sense at the dance to know I was drunk and needed to leave before I embarrassed myself. The "good sense" part was a lie. I skipped over the upchuck in the school bathroom. That I'd known better than to drive, so I'd asked Maggie to drive me home. I omitted that I didn't remember leaving the dance or the drive home or the disrobing from kitchen door to bed.

"I'm going to let you off easy this time and not punish you," Mama Jean said. Then with a finger point: "But you and I are headed for a falling-out if this happens again. I hope you've learned your lesson. Listen to me: You better watch the drinking.

It's in your blood. On your father's side. He, and Pawpaw before him, liked it *way* too much."

I stood there flush with shame, feeling as if I were five and had just been caught pressing. I nodded yes in silence for a few seconds to let her know that I had absorbed what she'd said and that I agreed. "Yes, I think I've learned my lesson."

"Good. You've got too much going for you to let that get in your way. With your grades and talent, you can do *anything*. You can be a writer." She was proud that I was editor of *The Spectator,* the school newspaper, and that I'd had a story published in the *Beaumont Enterprise,* "Christmas Is in the Closet." *No comment on the title.* "Or a diplomat!" *A diplomat?* "So *don't* let the drinking get in the way. It's not worth it."

I wanted to say, *Jesus. Relax. It was just* one *night.* Instead I nodded in agreement.

She got up and looked down at the pile of last night's clothes. Before she left, she pointed to a lone sock. "I think its mate is in the den."

I had learned my lesson that year. No more duchesses. No more whores. And no more Everclear.

NINE

Destiny

W here in the *hell* have you been?! I can *never* reach you."
Mama Jean's voice was long-distance, but, as always, her
words were loud and clear. "Where in the hell have you been?" had
long since replaced "Where have you been, Lord Randall, my
son?" from my childhood days.

"Well, I was in class, then at rehearsal . . . busy," I said, two hundred miles, and a world away, from her. I looked down at the gold-
and-onyx ring on my finger. She had given it to me four months
earlier for graduating seventh in my high school class with the
words "No mother could love a son more than I do."

It was the fall semester of my freshman year in college. I had
landed at Trinity University, an exclusive ivory tower of a liberal-
arts school five hours from Beaumont, in San Antonio. *U.S. News
& World Report* annually dubbed it "the Ivy League of the South-
west." Wisteria League was more like it. What *U.S. News & World
Report* didn't tell its readers was that Trinity was rumored to be
thirty percent gay. And I was happy to raise the percentage.

I'd enrolled in a playwriting class. Mama Jean and Dad had proverbial front-row seats. They were eager to see my work, so I mailed

them a dot-matrix printout of my first assignment, a five-minute opening scene for a comedy about a straight girl and her gay best boyfriend, who might actually be in love with her. I based it on my friendship with Nicole.

"We read your scene and just *loved* it," she said, speaking for herself and Dad. "We're so proud of you!"

"I'm glad y'all like it."

"I don't know how you do it. I couldn't write my way out of a paper sack. You sure don't get that from me. That's *all* your father."

"Maybe I can write 'em *and* star in 'em." I was still harboring dreams of being an actor, but I wasn't going to dare major in theater.

"No, you need to be a writer. *That's* what you should be doing! I'm telling you, your ticket is the writing. And remember what I've always said: *you* control your destiny."

I never believed her all the times she said that because I believed that *she* controlled my destiny.

"I can't wait to read how the rest of the play turns out." After a pause she continued with an uncharacteristic hesitancy in her voice. "You don't have tendencies like that? Do you?"

Tendencies? I am a full-blown sodomite. I hadn't planned on telling her then, but she asked. Actually, she had already asked—that time in junior high—but this time I pulled a Mama Jean and spoke the truth of my mind and my heart. "Yes. I do."

She shouted away from the phone, but her voice still pierced my eardrums. "Earl! *Earl!* Pick up the phone! *Now!* Jamie's on the line. He has something to tell us. *Earrr-rul!* Where in the *hell* are you?!"

She cried and told me she should have seen it coming. I thought she had seen it coming when I was five and danced along with the opening credits of *I Dream of Jeannie*—hands over head in a prayer gesture, hips swaying left to right, feet pointing in opposite directions—or when she dressed me up as Marco Polo for my fifth-grade history class, down to her pantyhose for tights, and I never wanted to take off the outfit.

Dad remembers this phone call differently. He says that he was already on the phone and he was the one who asked, "Are you writing about yourself? Do you have tendencies like that?" I think I remember Mama Jean asking the question because she was always the one to speak any truth that was as clear as the lipstick on her mouth.

But Dad might be right because he could see, while she was still in the dark. When it came to any flaw in me (and homosexuality was most definitely a flaw in her mind), she was blind and fiercely protective.

A few weeks after the call, I went home for a visit and Dad took me out to our first father–gay son lunch. "Your mother seems to be surprised, but I think I realized a while ago." Neither of us brought up that long walk in silence on the beach in Acapulco after Limey and Racing Stripes took my photo. Nor did we mention the case of the cauliflower bouquet and the dirty gym towel in Dr. Faudi's office.

"You know that we love you no matter what you are and we want you to be happy." Sip of chardonnay. He looked back at me with his eyes popped and brows raised, that look of his that said more than he could speak. "Just be careful."

"I will."

"And don't march in any of those parades."

During that first semester of college, I popped the cork of liberation to imbibe in love, lust, and libations. I dove fearlessly into the deep end of the buoyant water of boys, booze, and late nights free of Mama Jean's morning-after inquisitions. Within six months— no, it was six weeks, but college years are like dog years—I had lived so many lives, opened so many windows, run so many ways: from *Doctor Faustus,* to Byzantine Madonnas, to Ecstasy pills, to meeting and shedding two sets of new friends, to my first boyfriend.

After I dropped the H-bomb on the phone, I told Mama Jean

with the bravado and naïveté of first love that I had found a boy-friend: age-appropriate, fellow-freshman-classmate, myopic, in-tellectual Michael Parker. He was about five-ten with a smattering of freckles on his pale complexion. His baby-soft hair was return-ing to its natural light-brown shade as vestiges of a platinum-blond dye job faded. Somewhere along the way he became Mr. Parker for his Edwardian demeanor and acerbic tongue. He'd rest his chin on his hand and gaze wide-eyed from behind his glasses—or "spec-tacles" as he preferred to call them—ready to critique and dissect whatever you were telling him, which he never took at face value.

We met over Fuzzy Navels (peach schnapps and orange juice—*barf!*—but it got the job done) at somebody's dorm-room boy party. I wowed him with my impressions of Carol Channing and Faye Dunaway as Joan Crawford. He wowed me with his erudite con-versation, which he delivered in vocabulary-rich, complete sen-tences, as if he'd scripted his dialogue before going out.

"The way in which you re-create Miss Channing's persona is *astounding*." And: "My God, you as Faye as Joan is incredible, but have you seen Miss Crawford's Oscar-winning performance in *Mildred Pierce*?"

"Not yet," I said, ashamed.

"Well, you should. It's sublime."

"Have you seen *Breakfast at Tiffany's,* my favorite movie—and book—of all time?"

"Of course," he said without hesitation. I later discovered he hadn't.

After the Fuzzy Navels wowed us both, I drove him to a back alley in my Pontiac Sunbird, where we consummated our love in the backseat. I almost ruined the spontaneity with my "Not on the seat" cries of concern about staining the upholstery.

Mr. Parker wasn't a theater queen—he knew Latin, history, and spoke Spanish fluently—but he was an old-movie queen at a young age, like me. Our first real date was cult-movie night on campus. The feature was what I now know is a camp classic, *Lady in a Cage*.

It starred Olivia de Havilland in her scream-queen phase as a heaving-bosomed widow trapped in a house elevator while her live-in homosexual son is away for the weekend and thugs invade her gewgawed home. I told him that my mother had a figurine of an eighteenth-century lady just like Miss de Havilland's. A few scenes later one of the thugs shattered the figurine. We grabbed each other and Nellie-screamed in horror, our relationship cemented with that movie.

I jumped the gun in telling Mama Jean about Mr. Parker. We only lasted six weeks. Mr. Parker threw me over for Colton. Colton had three traits that obsessed Mr. Parker: he was pint-size, blond, and an ambigubod (as in undeclared sexuality, which made him an instant turn-on to Mr. Parker).

Mr. Parker and I agreed to be friends, and two weeks later I was getting ready for a party Mr. Parker and his roommate, Ed, were throwing. No reason to miss a party. My party outfit was all-black. I had cast off the preppy clothes that Mama Jean had bought me (for evening wear, anyway) and was trying to blend in with the "clad-in-blackers," as we dubbed the cool club kids with their two-toned hair and cassette tapes of the Smiths and the Cure and New Order. I wore a black turtleneck, black Girbaud jeans, and black Weejuns penny loafers (one last vestige of preppy). I crowned the outfit with a black beret from a thrift store. I thought it was a brilliant stroke of fifties beatnik chic.

I arrived late because I had to strike the set of a show I had been working crew on, and I bitterly resented it. The party was raging when I arrived. The bread box of a dorm room was packed with moussed and gel-spiked heads bobbing to the Smiths (rumored to be real, live homosexuals) plaintively singing "How Soon Is Now," about being human and needing to be loved like everyone else. Over the Smiths' forlorn wail, I announced my presence with a bray of "Oh my God! You're all drunker than I'll *ever* be!"

Uproarious laughter. Immediate attention on me.

"Oh my God! We thought you'd *never* get here," Mr. Parker said.

"Me either."

"You need a drink!"

"Yeah, I need a drink."

Someone handed me a paper Dixie cup filled with store-bought ice, cheap rum, and orange juice. I downed it in two gulps and thrust the empty cup into the air like the Statue of Liberty's torch. "I need another." More laughter.

"I love your outfit," someone said.

"Thanks. Very Audrey Hepburn in *Funny Face,* don't you think?"

"Huh?"

"Never mind. Think beatnik."

"Can I try on your beret?" someone slurred.

Before I could answer, the beret was lifted from my head. As I took giant gulps to catch up to the party's buzz, my beret bopped around the room like a beach ball to the Pet Shop Boys singing "West End Girls." The last place I saw it land was on Mr. Parker's head as he danced with a blasé Colton.

I was thrilled that my beret had become the hottest party favor since a fat joint. But I wanted it back. My outfit was incomplete and I was certain I had hat head. In between gulping drinks and gyrating to Mr. Parker's favorite band, New Order, I would swing my arm in the air as if it were a dance move, but really to fluff up my hair.

By the time the Bangles were singing "Walk Like an Egyptian," my dance steps were more Frankenstein monster than pharaoh deity. I ran my hand through my still-flat hair. *Where's my beret? I* want *my beret.* As soon as I thought it, I said it. Something I only did when I was drunk.

"Where's my beret?!"

"I don't have it."

"I think it's over there."

"No one's seen your silly beret."

"Where's my beret?" I was like a dog *without* his bone. "I *want* my beret!"

I surveyed the room, which was now a quarter full with the die-hards bopping to Bananarama's "Venus." No one had my beret. I searched the room with the singular focus of King Kong lumbering through New York City on a quest for Fay Wray, pulling up pillows and bedspreads and tossing them down when I didn't find what I wanted.

I laser-beamed my inquisition at Mr. Parker. "Where's my beret?"

"Jamie, darling. I haven't seen your beret."

I scowled. "*You* took it."

"Honestly, Jamie, I don't have your beret."

Straight out went my right arm like an unhinged gate. It swung fast and loose until the palm end of it crashed into Mr. Parker's right cheek, making a soundstage effect of a slap, only it was real.

Stunned silence except for Bananarama still chanting about Venus, *"Yeah, baby, she's got it!"*

I never saw that beret again.

I woke up the next morning feeling as if *I* had been slapped in the face. Not just because my hangover was award-winning, but because I couldn't fathom that I had actually hit someone. *I am a lover, not a fighter.* I liked to joke that when straight men get drunk, they fight, but when gay men get drunk, they fuck. *How did I cross that line?*

After that first year of ecstatic freedom I was back in Beaumont, where summer had covered the town like a wet towel after a scalding shower. Being back under Mama Jean's roof felt as oppressive as the humidity. The ground was lousy with Mama Jean land mines. Not long after she informed me that there were only two kinds of sex—oral and anal—and cryptically declared, "You don't know what love is," another Mama Jean explosion erupted.

"Don't you ever, *ever*, refer to yourself that way! That makes me sick!" Mama Jean's rage was pointed—with the help of her mascara wand—at the parody of *The Spectator*, our high school newspaper. I was making it for my friend Nicole because that's the kind of silly stuff we did to amuse each other to break up the boredom of a summer in Beaumont. "You should have more self-respect than that."

I stood silent, half-dressed for my summer job at the White House (not *that* White House, but Beaumont's fledgling answer to Neiman Marcus), and stared down at the mock *Spectator*. I had foolishly left it exposed on my desk, sitting below the framed *Playbill*s.

What had ignited her rage was the headline I'd written over my graduation photo: "Fashion Fag & Drama Queen Jamie Brickhouse Saves the White House." She couldn't handle the *fag* part. *Would she prefer I use her word*, fruit?

"And I'm not paying for you to go to that fancy school so you can be an actor. You can try that *after* you graduate!" Poof! She was gone. Her fuse burned down the hallway from my bedroom to her bathroom.

I pushed the parody *Spectator* into the trash and continued to get ready for work.

When I was in high school, she had bought me a trunkful of new clothes, each outfit carefully coordinated by her. A day later I said something that hurt her feelings—I don't remember what—and she retaliated by grabbing all of the clothes and storming off with them to her room. We made up and she gave back the clothes. But the message was clear: anything I did that she didn't like meant I didn't love her. And I'd sooner go naked than leave the house without her love and validation.

That summer I made a decision. I wouldn't major in theater. I'd major in something vaguely creative but more practical, communication, with a focus on journalism, and I'd audition for plays on the side. The booze and the sex I was in control of. They were all mine and she couldn't stop me from chasing them. Her idealized image of me—though already fractured—I would keep separate.

Booze. Sex. Her love. Unwittingly, I'd created a kind of golden triangle that left me standing in the middle of a highway. The only problem with standing on that yellow, broken line is that the traffic passing you by in both directions will eventually kill you.

Part II

Mr. Golightly (1990-2006)

*Promise me one thing: don't take me home until I'm
drunk—very drunk indeed.*

—Holly Golightly, from *Breakfast at Tiffany's*
by Truman Capote

*After the first glass, you see things as you wish they were.
After the second, you see things as they are not. Finally,
you see things as they really are, and that is the most
horrible thing in the world.*

—Oscar Wilde

TEN

Swingin', Baby, Swingin'!

I was standing at the antique art deco bar Mama Jean had reluctantly bought me after I moved to New York. In my left hand was a lit cigarette and a martini. In my right hand, a cocktail shaker. I was about to refill the martini glass of a party guest, a friend of a friend.

"How's the party going?" she asked.

"Swingin', baby, *swingin'!*" I laughed and refilled her martini glass.

She took a sip of her martini. "Mmm. You make a mean martini."

"Thanks. We're hanging a sign over the door like McDonald's: BILLIONS *OVER*-SERVED."

She cackled at that. "Remind me again. You're from *where*?"

"Beaumont, Texas. It's a small town in southeast Texas, near Houston. But my whole life I knew I was destined for New York. The summer I graduated college I took the Radcliffe Publishing Course, a postgraduate course in book and magazine publishing. I mean, I came here to get into publishing, but I really came here because I *had* to be in New York."

"New York must have been culture shock after Texas."

"No. The first eighteen years of my life was culture shock. *This* I understand."

I smiled as I surveyed the crush of people in the Upper West Side Manhattan apartment that I shared with my boyfriend of a year, Michael Hayes, or Michahaze, as he was known, because of the rapid-fire way he pronounced his first and last names when he cranked up his East Tennessee dialect. We lived in the kind of apartment I'd always seen myself in—brownstone walk-up, wood floors, exposed-brick walls—and threw the kinds of parties for which I was born. The apartment was a reverse clown car as a parade of people poured into the narrow room to the competing sounds of Deee-Lite's "Groove Is in the Heart" and the blasting door buzzer. "Could somebody just *lean* on the buzzer?" I shouted across the sea of bobbing, laughing, swilling, talk-yelling heads. At the far corner of the room two wasp-waisted boys and the Rasta Ecstasy dealer disappeared into the sliver of a bedroom Micha-haze and I shared. *I wonder when my X will kick in?*

I met Michahaze in 1990, six weeks after moving to New York to break into publishing. Whenever people asked us how we met, we told them in Central Park. It was September 23, the first day of fall. I was walking my roommate's dog. Michahaze was jogging. We went out a week later. "That's so romantic," girls would gush.

It's actually impolite to ask gay men where they met because the answer is rarely polite. It's almost never at a party or through friends. It's more likely cruising on the street, at the bathhouse, on the phone lines (in those days), or, at best, at a bar. Michahaze and I did meet in Central Park, but in the Ramble, the Brothers Grimm wooded area of winding paths famous for watchers of birds and seekers of snakes—the one-eyed kind.

It was twilight. I wasn't having any luck until a blond wearing a gold shirt, jeans, and a suede backpack materialized under the newly lit streetlight. The blond smiled. I smiled. He motioned me up the hill with his head. I followed.

The sex had a tenderness that I hadn't felt in situations like that, and he possessed a sweetness that I'd never experienced with anyone before. When it was over, rather than immediately separating and walking away with an awkward "Thanks, man" or "See you around," we hugged each other. Intensely. For a long time. Neither of us wanted to let go. When we finally did, we stared into each other's eyes in the semidark of the new night. We walked hand in hand out of the park. Under the streetlight he looked at my hair: "Oh, you're a redhead. Like me."

I looked at him. "You're not a redhead. You're blond." *I'm not picking out china patterns yet, but if this is going anywhere, there can only be one redhead in this relationship.*

"Strawberry blond," he conceded. With his close-cropped and side-parted hair, he was a boyish thirty-two to my twenty-two. He was as adorable as the dentist from *Rudolph the Red-Nosed Reindeer*. Then I saw his eyes. They were unlike any I'd ever seen before—a blue-green but with a halo of gold around the pupils. We went out a week later on a real date. I brought him a bouquet of purple irises, the Tennessee state flower, and he took me to dinner at Yippee Yi Yo, a Texas country-cooking joint. He told me that he'd been looking for me. Just months before we met, he was in Scotland and paid a visit to a legendary tree where people leave a garment and make a wish. "My wish was to meet the love of my life," he told me. "I tied a tube sock to a branch and made my wish." *To think that I can be had for the sacrifice of a tube sock. A jockstrap would be more romantic.*

I had been looking too. The only real boyfriend I'd had before Michahaze was Mr. Parker, but that was only for six weeks when I was a freshman in college. Since then I had had a cavalcade of men, but no boyfriends. Some people were serial monogamists. I was a serial fornicator. *Some people call that a slut.*

The guys I actually dated tended to have big personalities like mine, but turned out to be no-count flakes from Carlos Fitzpatrick de Novarro on. Michahaze was unlike anyone I'd ever gone out with before. While I was usually "on"—telling jokes, doing impressions, talking about old movies and the theater—he was reserved and soft-spoken, talking about politics and ways to improve life in the city. He was an architect, which impressed me. I had wanted to be one before I discovered the theater (and realized all the math involved in becoming an architect).

But Michahaze was an eager audience member, always ready for a good time. Early in our courtship we were two sheets to the wind one Sunday morning, conjoined with the sashes of our robes, Bloody Marys in hand and dancing. I shouted, "At last! I've found someone who likes to drink as much as me!"

Best of all, he called when he said he'd call. He showed up where he said he'd show up, usually meticulously dressed in a plaid blazer, bow tie, and silk pocket square. After nine months I moved in with him to the Upper West Side apartment on West Eighty-second Street.

Michahaze had his first audience with Mama Jean at the Royalton Hotel not long after we had moved in together. The Royalton was where he had taken me for drinks on one of our early dates. It was the chicest hotel at the time, with its Alice-gets-drunk-in-Wonderland-fantasy lobby. Mama Jean and Dad were perched on a chartreuse velvet sofa under horn-shaped sconces, she sipping a champagne cocktail, he drinking a glass of chardonnay.

Mama Jean never quite bought the Central Park story, at least the way I told it. "Now, let me get this straight," she said. "You were walking a dog, and Michael just stopped running, turned around, and said, 'I believe I'll have some of that'?"

"Pretty much," I said.

"I don't quite get how that works, but okay." Even with the sugarcoated facts, she managed to extract the essence of our meeting. I presented Michahaze in his ocher-and-maroon-plaid blazer and bow tie. Dad rose to greet us in his navy-blue blazer and red paisley tie. Mama Jean remained seated in her black linen dress and held out her hand for Michahaze to shake. He shook it, and as he did, I caught her glancing at me wearing one of Michahaze's bow ties and plaid jackets. She didn't recognize the outfit, hadn't bought it. The tie around my neck was almost as tight as my sphincter hovering above that velvet sofa.

"I'll have a Manhattan," I told the clad-in-black cocktail waitress.

"A Manhattan?" Mama Jean cocked her head. "Isn't that a little strong? I thought you liked champagne cocktails." She glanced at hers.

"Too sweet."

She rolled her eyes and sighed.

I sat there in silence as Michahaze told Mama Jean about his rising career as an architect, but mostly as she and he discussed my budding career in publishing. I was working in the publicity department of a major trade publishing house. They talked about me in the third person, as if I weren't there.

"Well, this is a good start, but he really needs to be writing. That's what he should be doing. He gets that from Earl."

Dad smiled. I nodded. Michael agreed. The moment wasn't unlike the parent-teacher conferences I was allowed to sit in on when Mama Jean and the teacher discussed my talents and how best to direct them.

Mama Jean also tooted her horn about how far she'd come with gay acceptance. "I can't tell you that I was happy when Jamie told me he was gay, but when I hear about parents turning their backs on their own children because of that, it makes me sick. Earl and I were visiting our friends Yum Yum and Dan. Dan started going on about the fags this and the fags that." She gritted her teeth and lowered her voice, as she must have with Dan. "I told him, 'You better watch it, Dan. I'm the mother of two gays.' He didn't *dare* say another word after that." *I'll bet he didn't.*

After my two Manhattans and Michael's Southern charm,

sprinkled with just the right amount of praise—for her outfit and for producing such a marvelous son—had worked their magic, I relaxed. I excused myself to the bathroom.

I looked at myself in the bathroom mirror and adjusted Michahaze's bow tie. *This is going well. I love him and I think she likes him.*

I pranced down the royal-blue-carpeted runway of the hotel lobby back to our table. My prance ground to a halt and the smile on my face went slack when I saw the cloud that had formed over our table. Mama Jean was dabbing tears from her eyes. She was talking to Michahaze, and Dad was looking away from them and scratching the back of his neck. When he saw me, Dad gave me his raised-eyebrows look and took a sip of his chardonnay.

"I hope y'all are careful."

"Of course, Jean."

Dad interjected. "Now, honey, don't get all worked up."

"Well, I can't help it, Earl. I *am* worked up!" She turned her back on him, shot a quick glance at me, and fixed Michahaze with a steely glare.

"What happened?" I asked, looking at everyone.

Mama Jean ignored me. "Because if anything ever happened to Jamie, they'd have to lock me up and throw away the key." Her face was in close-up, an impenetrable wall of moistened makeup and don't-fuck-with-me stare.

"Mother." (I always called her Mom, but this moment required Mother.) "Don't worry, we're safe."

"Okay, but promise me. *Promise.*"

"I promise." With one raise of the eyebrow I gave Michael the "Now you know what I mean about Mama Jean" look. I glanced at my watch. "Well, we better go if we're going to make our dinner reservation."

Mama Jean handed Dad her credit card, and he took care of the tab. As we left the lobby, she pulled me aside. "Well, I'm impressed." When Mama Jean said this about someone, she meant not only that she liked the person but that she respected him. "Michael is *really* fine." She meant *fine* as in "high quality." "You can see that he's so meticulous and conscientious about everything he does—I haven't seen you wear that jacket before—and he knows how to behave." Pause. "It's better that you're gay. I could never share you with another woman."

ELEVEN

A Frog in Cha-Cha Heels

I was two sips into my martini the first time I saw supersize drag queen Divine in a baby-doll nightie throw a monumental fit on Christmas morning. I was at the Works, a gay bar around the corner from our West Eighty-second Street apartment. The bartender had turned down the music so the entire bar could watch the TV screen as Divine, playing Dawn Davenport in John Waters's cult classic *Female Trouble,* tears open her present expecting the cha-cha heels she has her cholesterol-encrusted heart set on. Her face is as excited as, well, a child's on Christmas morning, as her father and slip of a mother look on. When she pulls out a pair of low-heeled, sensible shoes, her face falls and she explodes in anger. "What are *these*? These aren't cha-cha heels! I *told* you the kind I wanted!" She throws a tantrum to rival that of a drugged-out rock star in a hotel room, stomps on those *wrong* kind of shoes, and buries her whimpering mother under the toppled Christmas tree. "I hate Christmas!" Divine shouts, and flees the room, a blubber of sobs.

The entire bar was laughing. Except for me.

I felt exposed, as if John Waters had snuck his camera into the living room of Mama Jean's dream house during the Christmas morning that had just passed and from which I was still recovering. I thought of those old Polaroid commercials that showed the idealized reality of family holidays instead of the shit shows they actually were. I sucked down my martini as everyone around me seemed to laugh maniacally, their mocking faces taunting me like reflections in a fun-house mirror. It had been one hell of a Christmas, emphasis on *hell*.

Since I'd been living my New York dream come true, Mama Jean had been in her custom-built dream house for a few years. She and Dad had made it to Flamingo Road, a lifetime away from her loathed childhood house on Calder.

The front of the terra-cotta-colored stucco house with teal-green trim was Palladian in its symmetry: wide, triple-pane windows on the two ends of the house, slightly set back from the robust middle. Three tall windows were under the pediment of a high-pitched gable that sported a decorative oval window of leaded glass.

I remember the first time I saw it, when I returned from my junior year of college in London. I was slack-jawed from the moment I walked into the house—the foyer with its pink marble floor and padded fabric walls led into the twelve-foot-high living room, which flowed into a large, formal dining room, which opened onto a gallery of three sets of glass double doors, which opened to face a brick courtyard—to the moment I saw the new car she had waiting for me in the garage with a giant red bow that Dad had tied around it.

Unlike the formal living room of the previous house, with its Ethan Allen Chippendale knockoffs, which was never lived in but always sealed off and frozen in time like Miss Havisham's wedding-banquet hall, this living room was meant to be shown off. The room was filled with antiques—Impressionist paintings in gilt frames bought at auction, a silver serving tray that once belonged to the movie star Gene Tierney. Hanging above the custom-made sofa of pale pink damask was a tapestry depicting a woman riding a horse on a fox hunt.

Dad pointed to the tapestry. "It ought to have a title, like a great painting."

We cocked our heads and squinted our eyes, concentrating on the tapestry as we took up the title challenge.

"In Pursuit?" I said.

"Uhn-uh," Mama Jean grunted.

"The Fox and the Lady?" Dad said.

"No," Mama Jean and I said in unison.

Mama Jean sat up in her chair. "I've got it." She clapped her hands. *"Cunt on a Hunt."* The name stuck.

She loved that house and loved showing it off almost as much as she loved showing me off, especially at the annual Christmas parties she and Dad threw for *le tout* Beaumont. In front of the glass doors looking onto the back courtyard was the Christmas tree that I "helped" decorate. That meant that Dad and I did the work and Mama Jean directed: "No! Put Scarlett right in front— right there—in the middle where that bare spot is. Yes! That's almost perfect." (Dad had given her a Scarlett O'Hara ornament to make up for the coveted Scarlett doll she'd never received as a child.) The ten-foot artificial tree with twinkling white lights and pink and gold bows all over was crowned with a giant bow at the top from which matching streamers cascaded.

At one of those Christmas parties, right before the guests arrived, Dad took a photo of a thin Mama Jean holding her champagne flute of Asti Spumante, beaming with regal pride in front of the garland-festooned fireplace as three gift-bearing Wise Men made of gold Venetian glass marched in profile across the mantel.

Christmas was always her favorite time of the year, and she was forever trying to compensate for the disappointing Christmases of her childhood on Calder Avenue, with scrawny trees under which longed-for gifts such as the Scarlett O'Hara doll never appeared. Each Christmas had to be bigger and better than the last, and the Christmas tree, which was bigger and more elaborately decorated each year, could have no bare spot.

She loved giving as much as she liked getting. As kids, we always got what we wanted. Ronny got his dirt bikes. Jeffrey got his birdcages, fish tanks, mini-greenhouses, and everything that went in them. I got whatever toys I asked for, except for the Barbie makeup head, but then I intuitively knew never to ask for that. Dad had the burden of getting her what she wanted. One Christmas he gave her an expensive silk wrap dress of wide vertical stripes in bold primary colors. Mama Jean was a bold, color-loving gal.

She opened the box and unfurled the dress. She forced a smile as she held it up to her body. "Well, it's the right size."

"Honey, all those bright reds, blues, and yellows will look gorgeous with your dark hair," Dad said in pale imitation of the kind of remarks Mama Jean would say when giving us clothes.

"I guess so." She forced a smile. She was a terrible liar.

"You don't like it."

"I *do* like it. I do." Those were the days when she couldn't afford *exactly* what she did like.

I wanted so badly for her to like it. She wore it to a dinner party, and I oohed and aahed at the sight of her in it as she and Dad left the house. I told her that she looked just like Elizabeth Taylor. She'd heard this before and immediately posed: head turned in profile, lips in a sultry pout, glancing over her shoulder. "You think so?"

"Oh, yes."

When they returned home, she said that the hostess of the dinner party opened the door and said, "Well, hi, Jean! Come on in with that loud dress." I could see Dad's face fall. She never wore the dress again.

At the Flamingo Road Christmas parties, I was always expected to be on display as her living ornament. The annual holiday

routine quickly became Michahaze and me spending Thanksgiving with Mama Jean and Dad in Beaumont, and me back
solo for Christmas.

After my first year in New York, Mama Jean offered to fly Michahaze and me to Beaumont for Thanksgiving. (There was no
question that I would be home with her for Christmas.) *But Thanksgiving* and *Christmas, two visits barely a month apart?*

After a day of showing Michahaze the sites of Beaumont, she
let us in on her plan. "Now, since y'all are here, I would love it if
y'all could help decorate the house for Christmas."

"Christmas? We just finished Thanksgiving supper," I said.

"I know, but I've got y'all here *now,* and I love my house when
it's decorated for Christmas. I'd leave it that way all year if I could.
Besides, I bought your plane tickets. It's the least y'all could do."

The pattern was set. Michahaze and I would spend Thanksgiving in Beaumont decorating her house, and good gay son-in-law
that he was, he always brought a large, expensive ornament for
the tree. BOHs (balls of honor), Mama Jean called them. I would
return solo a scant month later for the party, Christmas, and to
de-decorate the house. *Lather. Rinse. Repeat.*

Michahaze spent the holiday with his family in Tennessee. We
didn't think we had rights to alternate Christmases together with
each other's family or simply have Christmas with just the two of
us in New York, rights that our straight, married friends enjoyed.
We were old-school queens in that way.

Every Christmas was the same party with the same decora-
tions, and the same food, and the same people. Mama Jean was always dressed to the nines; her favorite hostess gown was a
floor-length, lipstick-red St. John Knits dress with rhinestone buttons up the front, from Neiman Marcus. St. John Knits were
the haute couture of rich, white Republican ladies. She'd parade
me around as her living ornament and brag about me: "He's up
there in New York working on all kinds of big books, like *Scarlett,* the *Gone with the Wind* sequel, and Madonna's trashy book."

Don't get me wrong. I loved it. I basked in the praise but I felt like a fraud, because I was working *with* writers, as opposed to *being* a writer.

Then there was Christmas itself. I couldn't stand my losing battle in the gift-giving sweepstakes. Mama Jean always went out of her way to give everyone what they asked for and what she thought they needed. When it came to choosing gifts for her, no matter how hard you tried to guess her tastes, the gift was never right unless she had chosen it. I fantasized about someday striking it rich and returning all she had given me and more, presenting her with that one gift that would balance the bill. We all learned that it was best to get her what she wanted, no matter the cost. Besides, you'd never be able to give her more than she gave you.

She had become obsessed with a pattern of china called Tobacco Leaf. She had a twelve-piece setting and was eagerly grabbing accessories—planters, vases, cachepots, anything with that damn pattern of cobalt blue, pink, green, and gold. The catalog copy at Gump's in the Houston Galleria best described the pattern:

"Tobacco Leaf, one of the most prized of Chinese Export patterns, was developed circa 1780. The design shows the leaves of the flowering Nicotiana (Tobacco) plant upon which a small phoenix perches bearing a flowering twig in its beak. The joyous exuberance of the Tobacco Leaf pattern is undiminished by time."

The summer before that Christmas, Mama Jean and I were at Gump's in Houston.

"Come look. Quick!" she called. She was holding a Tobacco Leaf–patterned frog. "Isn't he precious?"

"Just adorable."

"If you were thinking of getting me something, *this* would be it."

She raised her eyebrows as she put it down. *Excellent. Christmas is taken care of,* I thought.

Months passed before I called Gump's to get the frog. By the time

I did, they were out of it, but they had a bunny rabbit in the Tobacco Leaf pattern that was just as cute. And for the same price: $120. *Kind of steep on my entry-level publishing salary, but if that's what the lady wants . . .*

On Christmas morning I was playing Santa, grabbing presents from under the tree and delivering them to everybody. Mama Jean sat on the sofa in the living room underneath *Cunt on a Hunt*. Dad had just gone to check on the turkey in the kitchen. I knelt at Mama Jean's slippered feet and presented the distinctive Gump's box with its black grosgrain ribbon.

Mama Jean's face was as excited as, well, a child's on Christmas morning. "Is this what I think it is?" She untied the black ribbon.

"Well, go ahead and open it."

She started to lift the lid on the box.

"I think you'll like it, but . . ."

"If it's what I think it is, I'll *love* it!"

"Well, it's not *exactly*—"

She spread apart the tissue paper inside. "Oh, and I have the *perfect* spot for this . . ." She pulled out the Tobacco Leaf . . . *"Rabbit?!* No!" She held the terrified rabbit at eye level and screamed at it. "This isn't what I wanted! I wanted the frog!"

"Well, they didn't have the frog. But don't you think the rabbit is just as cute . . . cuter?"

"No! Not when I wanted the frog! Why can't anyone ever get me what *I* want?"

I tried to explain, but it was like reasoning with a drunk. Or a lynch mob. Dad ran into the room to come to my defense. This was a rare moment because fights like this were usually between her and him or her and one of my brothers, but never with me. If he got involved in a fight with my brothers, it was to take her side.

"Oh, stop it, Jean! I can't believe you."

"Shut up, Earl! This is between Jamie and me." But she made it between him and her to make it no longer between her and me.

"No wonder your mother hated Christmas. She always said that there was no pleasing you."

"Don't you *dare* bring my mother into this!" By now the water-works were flowing (mine and hers).

"You always ruin Christmas!" she screamed at Dad, and ran sobbing from the room, abandoning me and the Tobacco Leaf rabbit. The next thing I heard was the screech of tires as her Cadillac shot out of the garage. I wanted to hurl the rabbit onto the pink-marble hearth and leave it shattered for her to see, but I couldn't. She might have done that, but I wasn't allowed to get angry like that. There was only one star in that house.

When I found myself in the Works, the gay bar around the corner from West Eighty-second Street, watching the Divine clip, it was too soon after that Christmas for me to laugh.

"Would you like another?" a shirtless bartender said to me.

"Excuse me?"

"Ready for another?" He pointed to my empty martini glass. *How did that happen?*

"Yes. Beefeater gin. Up. Make it a double."

"But it's a martini."

"Then don't even *think* about the vermouth."

I stared at the TV screen, which had been abandoned by Divine and replaced with a video of Madonna voguing. But I didn't see Madonna. I saw that Tobacco Leaf rabbit where it had taken its final resting place on the living-room shelf, next to a jade-and-ceramic tree. It sat in silence, forever mute about its provenance.

The joyous exuberance of the Tobacco Leaf pattern is undiminished by time.

TWELVE

Verboten in Zurich

It was nearly five A.M. when I came to in a Rodeway Inn motel room on the side of I-10 in Beaumont. The blond-tipped Walmart employee I had picked up at the Copa earlier that night lay snoring beside me.

"Shit!" I looked at my watch in disbelief for the third time. *How did this happen?* I asked myself, remembering how my much-needed night of freedom from Mama Jean's house was supposed to be fun and painless: easy out, easy in, no one gets caught. I resented having to spend another Christmas in Beaumont, where I didn't feel as if I could be an adult, which meant I couldn't drink the way I wanted to drink. At twenty-four, I still felt like a teenager in her house and had to lie that I was going out with friends instead of to the Copa for a few drinks and maybe a little . . .

Well, I had the few drinks and had by midnight found myself a hot little country boy who worked at Walmart. I sprang for the room. I had it all figured out. We'd be in that room and done by one. But I hadn't counted on one thing: passing out.

"Shit! Shit! *Shit!*" I roused Walmart. "Come on, babe. We gotta go."

"How about one more round?"

"No, ma'am! I've gotta go." I frantically pulled on my clothes.

Maybe Mama Jean will still be asleep. But if she's awake . . . This fiasco had to come just a day after she was still smarting from reading my journal, which detailed the exploits of a trip Michahaze and I had taken that October to Paris, the Loire Valley, and uptight Zurich. The pages were lit with Parisian bathhouses, booze, and a colossal fight in Zurich.

Michahaze and I became one of those couples you see fighting on the street and wonder why they can't do it elsewhere. I now know how those public fights happen. They're an explosion that's been building but comes with no warning. It doesn't often happen in private, because it takes external events to light the bomb. *Douse liberally with alcohol and enjoy!*

We were in Zurich, guests of Michahaze's rigid, Swiss ex-lover, Lars. It was near the end of what had been a lovely vacation—Paris for three days (just Michahaze's best friend from college, Big Daddy; Michahaze; and I); then on to the Loire Valley, where Lars had a farmhouse; finally to clean, controlled, *dull* Zurich. *Switzerland is the Canada of Europe, and my apologies to Canada.* I couldn't appreciate the surrounding gray Alps, the winding cobblestone streets, or the centuries-old, turreted buildings. All I could see through the steady mist of drizzle was a land and a people obsessed with the forbidden, aka *verboten*. Everywhere I turned absurd signs told me what I *couldn't* do in Switzerland. U-turns: *Verboten!* Sawing a park bench in half: *Verboten!* Nude skiing: *Verboten!*

I got into a discussion with Lars and his girlfriend about my favorite drug, Ecstasy. *Girlfriend? What is that about?* Lars's already straight back stiffened further, his thin lips pursed tighter, and his beady eyes got narrower as he said, "Vell, this Ecstasy is *verboten* in Switzerland."

"Well," I said as I took a swig from my glass of red wine, "it's *verboten* in America too, but we still do it!"

After nearly a week under Lars's controlled roof in the Loire Valley and then at his apartment in Zurich ("Today ve vill do this and that—but not that—and eat at precisely seven thirty-five p.m."), Michahaze, Big Daddy, and I finally had a night of freedom without Lars, who had another engagement.

Having drunk only wine the whole trip, we were on a quest for a stiff drink of vodka, and Lars was adamantly opposed to the idea. "You don't want to buy vodka in Switzerland. It is *very* expensive."

"We'll pay! We'll pay!" we cried. Reluctantly, he led us to a store where the best vodka we could find was Smirnoff. We bought a fifth and polished it off before going out. There was no ice in the apartment, so we drank warm vodka tonics. *I'll go to any lengths for a drink.*

After a dinner of wine and cheese fondue, we headed for the gayborhood, excited about a young night of options before us—maybe Michahaze and I would try a bathhouse. We had visited one in Paris and had a three-way, which wasn't our first. We had also had a three-way at our apartment on Gay Pride Day the previous summer. It happened after a day of drinking and after the Ecstasy kicked in, so kind of organically. (These situations occurred without us setting parameters and usually me pushing the boundaries.) In the Loire Valley, Michahaze and I had wonderful sex several nights in a row. We hadn't been so passionately regular for months. Despite the sex, I would find myself bored during after-dinner conversations, and the fantasies of leaving Michahaze—thoughts that had been gnawing at me for over a year—kept creeping in.

We went to a lovely *rendezvous* bar (Swiss term for a more social and formal boîte, as opposed to a *cruise* bar, a pickup joint). We bellied up to the bar and ordered a round of drinks. At the end of the bar stood a dream of a man in black trousers, a black turtleneck, and a hunter-green wool blazer. Tall and dark, he had the sexy stubble of a two- or three-day holiday from shaving. He was dreamy, the kind of man I would order. I remember once complaining to Michahaze that we didn't have many gay friends. His reply: "That's because you try to sleep with everyone we meet."

I quickly introduced myself, Michahaze, and Big Daddy, and we asked him about the scene, which cruise bars and baths we should hit. Felix was his name. He lived in Zurich. He had a lover, also Swiss, but the lover lived in New York. Felix gave us the rundown. It was too late for the baths, as they closed early. He knew lots of bars. Why not follow him to one?

At the next bar, while Michahaze and Big Daddy struck up a conversation with some people, I moved in on Felix. With the bluster of a third of a bottle of vodka and change, I told him he was beautiful. That I wanted him. The feeling was mutual, he said. I told him that I wanted us to be naked and told him explicitly what I wanted to do to him once we were naked.

With a lick of his smiling lips he said, "Perhaps we should go for a walk?"

"I don't think my lover would like that." I quickly rethought that. *We have gone to a bathhouse. We have had three-ways.* Fortified with liquor courage, I asked Michahaze if he minded.

He minded. "Just what are you saying?"

"Just kidding."

Too late. I had crossed a line. No going back. I explained that I hadn't thought he would mind since we had just had a three-way in Paris. Michahaze couldn't believe his ears. I couldn't believe my mouth. We stood in the seedy, smoky, crowded, small bar and melted down.

I'd been having doubts for the last year, I told him. "I think you're a wonderful person but I don't know if I love you anymore. I think I need to be on my own."

"Are you saying it's over?"

"Yes, I'm saying it's over."

The look of stunned hurt on his face, like a child who has just been hit, was harder for me to take than his next move. He took off his ring and shoved it in my hand. "You're *horrible!* Just *horrible!*" His hurt had burned into anger. "What would your mother think?"

"Don't bring her into this!" But she was always there, even when she was an ocean away. She constantly haunted my thoughts, especially when I was doing something of which she wouldn't approve. The mantra in my head wasn't WWMJD? (What would Mama Jean do?), but WWMJT? (What would Mama Jean think?). She became my conscience, a termagant sitting on my shoulder in her lynx-fur coat and shaking her finger. I kept air-biting her finger until she went away, the way our dog Brennan used to do when she scolded him.

I took off my ring and put it in my pocket along with his. While he repeated how horrible I was, I fondled the rings in my pocket and shook my head humbly in agreement. I heard the ping of something hitting the stone floor. I thought it was a coin. Before I could stoop to see what it was, the bartender was showing us out the door. Our behavior was *verboten* there.

We continued our fight on the cobblestoned street. I told Michahaze he needed to go home to get away from this. He refused. I begged him to let me get a cab. After a breathless silence, I said, "Well, I'm going back in the bar." Even though I was saturated with guilt, I still wanted Felix and was on autopilot. A stiff dick knows no conscience, as Mama Jean always said.

Practical Michahaze emerged. How would I get back home? What would I do for the rest of the trip? Despite all of the horrible things that I had said, he was still trying to salvage what was left of us and look after me, which made me feel even more guilty and still in love with him. We finally left together in silence and went back to the apartment. Michahaze crawled into bed and I crawled on the floor, still in my street clothes, to further humble myself.

"I wish I had a gun, Michael, because I'd kill myself. You're right. I am awful."

His face turned away from me in disgust. "Oh, stop it. Go to sleep."

I felt for the rings in my pocket. Only one was there. That ping on the stone floor I'd heard in the bar had been my ring. I returned to the bar the next day to look for it, but like the black beret from college, it was never to be seen again.

I wanted that ring back. I wanted Michahaze back. Michahaze, despite my drunken transgression, never left.

I had written down this tale in my journal, which also contained enchanting tales of recreational fun with drugs such as Ecstasy. Mama Jean helped herself to the journal on that Christmas visit. "I'm worried about you. *Seriously* worried about you," she said, glaring at me as my red diary sat in her lap. "Do you know what you're doing? The drinking is bad enough, but do you know what that drug, Ecstasy, does to your body? I've read about it." She crossed her arms in a giant *X* to let me know that she knew the slang term for it, but the gesture looked more like a giant *verboten* sign. "And going into those seedy places in Paris where you can catch God knows what. Remember, Jamie, a moment's pleasure isn't worth a lifetime of regret."

Do I call her Pandora for opening my red box? No. I didn't bother to register anger because I knew that the contents of the diary trumped my feelings. Besides, the journal was under her roof, so fair game. I told her that I was an adult and was having a little fun. That I was in control of it. Careful. Blah, blah, blah.

Now, back in Beaumont at Christmas, a day or so after that revelation, I was dragging in at five A.M. My hopes that she was still asleep were defeated when I walked in the back door and the lights were on. I walked down the hall to the open double doors of her bedroom and sheepishly looked in.

Dad, looking drained, was standing just inside her bedroom.

"Jamie, your mother has been up all night, worried sick," he said like a weatherman announcing a hurricane that's about to—

Hit!

"God . . . *damn* it!" Farther into the cavernous room of peachy pink sat Mama Jean in her floral nightgown on the edge of her king-size, floral bedspread that matched the floral fabric of the quilted headboard that matched the floral fabric of the window drapes that matched the floral wallpaper behind the bed. *It is a not-so-secret garden.* She was holding the phone in her hand. She slammed it down on the cradle and screamed, "Where the *hell* have you been?! I've been calling all over town, not knowing if you were dead or alive." *Dead seems like a better option for me right now.*

"I fell asleep at a friend's," I lied.

"A friend's?! Bullshit!" Her teeth were bared and her eyes were narrowed in a white-hot glare.

"I'm sorry. I'm sorry" was all I could say.

"You ought to be on a couch somewhere!" Her phrase for anyone whom she felt was in need of psychiatric help. I was speechless.

As I walked away, she fired one more shot. "And I feel sorry for Michael!"

THIRTEEN

The Short and Long of It

L es Hommes Bookstore was a mere two blocks away from the Works gay bar. I sometimes popped in there for a quickie after a night of carousing, if nothing panned out at the Works, which I had renamed the Last Chance Saloon. Les Hommes was not a Barnes & Noble or a cozy little hole-in-the-wall specializing in used and rare books. It was a gay porn shop with "buddy booths" in the back for impromptu assignations. I don't think any books were traded there, but the patrons were certainly used if not rare. *Les hommes* means "the men" in French, *merci beaucoup*.

It was on a side street, and even though booze wasn't served, it had a speakeasy feel. The gray metal door with its twelve-inch-square, blacked-out window faded into the streetscape. You wouldn't notice it unless you were looking for it. A buzzer was at chin level next to the door. I rang and was immediately buzzed in. I made the cut. I climbed up the dimly lit stairs, careful not to trip on the peeling linoleum. Even though it was a flight up, the place had a distinctly subterranean feel, like entering the underworld. At the top of the stairs I passed through another door (no buzzer required for this one).

The main floor was harshly overlit. Fluorescent lights exposed a wide assortment of children's fairy-tale videos: *Pinocchio, Bambi, Cinderella*. Mayor Rudy Giuliani had recently cleaned up sleaze in the city, and the ridiculous compromise that businesses such as Les Hommes had to make was the devotion of prime shelf real estate to family products. I didn't browse the selection, but walked directly to the bulletproof Plexiglas cashier window.

"One for the back," I said, and pushed my eight dollars through the money slot. The Indian man behind the window rang me up on the manual cash register, staring through me like a zombie. He could have been a tollbooth clerk on the New Jersey Turnpike. *Kah-clunk,* I heard as he depressed an unseen button to release the turnstile that allowed entry to the buddy booths. Above the turnstile a plastic sign read NO REFUNDS. NO REENTRY. NOT RESPONSIBLE . . . The FOR LOST OR STOLEN GOODS line had broken off. But NOT RESPONSIBLE just about summed it up for a place like this.

The buddy-booth section consisted of a long row of plywood cells along a grimy hallway of broken red and yellow tiles lit by slightly dimmer fluorescent lights. The booths were no more than three feet square and featured a small screen with flickering blue movies. The rows of doors opened in with metal slide locks near the top.

I had been here before, and it was never a sure thing. The clientele usually seemed old and desiccated to my twenty-seven-year-old eyes, but occasionally a hottie lurked behind one of the plywood doors of the place, reminding me of a porno version of *Let's Make a Deal.*

Tonight the pickings were slim. I walked the hallway like a jailhouse warden on patrol for final bed check. A crypt keeper in booth number one. Several well-oiled porn stars in booths two and three (on the screens, that is). Darkness Invisible in booth number four, which is to say that the door was cracked open, but the transient resident was hiding in the shadows. *Never a good sign.* A tall, skinny man with extreme blond highlights gave me a one-eyed leer on his own patrol down the hall. He appeared to be drunker than I was. I ignored his gaze as I walked silently past him. An unspoken rule of etiquette in venues such as this is that no words be uttered, lest anyone break the mythological sexual tension looming in the stale air. The man in the last booth was a bit of an oasis. He was about my age and height. Dark brown hair. Slim. Good haircut. His five-o'clock shadow added to his sex appeal in a George Michael kind of way.

I gave him the look of love and loitered outside his booth. He seemed to return my gaze, so I approached. He raised his hand in halt and said, "I'm taking a break." *Ouch*. When words are spoken, they are those, and they are the gentle way of saying "go pound sand."

Not only did it hurt, but it infuriated me too. *Taking a break from what? All of the pageant winners strutting their stuff on this dingy runway? I'm just as good-looking as he is. I'm certainly better-looking than the other choices at hand! And wasn't he giving me the eye?* Then I realized that he was eyeing the video screen above my head in the hall. *Oh, the humiliation of unrequited love.*

I retraced my steps and checked out the booths again in the bored way you repeatedly check the refrigerator between commercial breaks hoping that food you want to eat that wasn't there before will magically appear. After a couple of strolls, I went back to Darkness Invisible. I stood outside the cracked door, but couldn't even see a pair of blinking spook-house eyes. The door creaked open to reveal more of the booth but no occupant.

"Psst. Psst."

I looked for the source.

"Psst. Psst."

I looked down. Darkness . . . *Visible*. There he was. A little person. A *very* little person. About four foot eight. A dwarf. *Aren't there two kinds of dwarfs, proportionate and disproportionate?*

He beckoned me into the booth with a hand wave and a nod.

I thought I had tasted the full range of male flavors, but this was a first. As I stood there contemplating, he gave me another nod. *What to do?* It's an adventure, new frontier. *Oh, why not?*

I entered his booth. The porno screen cast a grayish-blue light, but kept the room in enough shadow to hide the filthy floor. He stood in a corner by the door. He seemed to be all head and torso resting on baby legs, a putto come to life. He was cute in his red plaid shirt and khaki pants, his brown hair short and combed to the side. He looked young, but do dwarfs ever look their age?

As soon as I latched the door, he pulled down his britches. Out popped a staggering prize of manhood. It would have been an eye-popper on a six-foot-two man, but on a four-foot-eight man, it was truly a third leg.

Definitely a disproportionate dwarf.

He invited me to sample his supply. I accepted by squatting on my haunches. That merely brought us to eye level, crowding the corner. He scooted away from me to the corner diagonally opposite. Remaining on my haunches, I let my upper body fall to meet him, bisecting the booth. I grabbed on to his hips as I dipped my head, my profile nearly grazing the nasty floor. I went to town on his blue-ribbon-award winner, my body performing a painful modern dance that would have made a Martha Graham dancer ache. *Never have I worked so hard for so little and so much at the same time.*

Mama Jean always intruded in times like these. *WWMJT?* The first time I had sex with a black man she was right there. As the man took me from behind and my head was bobbing up and down in a one-two motion, a miniature apparition of Mama Jean in her pink, full-length nightgown floated in front of me waving her index finger left and right: "Don't play *Guess Who's Coming to Dinner* with me!" *She didn't warn me about dwarfs.*

After I had gorged myself for a while, he tugged on my crotch. I panicked. Mine was nowhere near the size of his. In fact—oh, I'll say it—his dwarfed mine by comparison. *Will he be disappointed?*

Will he laugh? He kept tugging. Finally, I stood up and fed him with ease. After a while he broke the silence and suggested that we see if anyone wanted to join us. Maybe he was disappointed.

"Sure. Why not?" I said.

We turned and faced the door. Since he'd made the suggestion, I waited for him to take the lead and open the door. Nothing. Then I felt a tug on my trouser leg. I looked down. He was pointing up. I followed the arrow of his index finger to the door's latch in front of my eyes. *Oh.*

As I unlatched the door, a million little questions buzzed in my head. *How does he reach the buzzer on the street? How does he pay the gatekeeper at the cashier booth? Or does he slip below the gatekeeper's radar and get in free? Is he ever mistaken for an actual customer for the fairy-tale videos?*

We didn't get any takers, nor was there anyone we wanted to take, so we went back to each other. I reached down to pick him up at the hips. Before lifting, I asked, "Do you mind?"

"No. Whatever gets the job done." *You can't argue with success.*

So I lifted him like a proud daddy and made a human pacifier out of him. My flying putto was in heaven. I was in the clouds. When we finished, we left each other the way most such encounters ended: "Thanks, man." "Yeah. See you around."

What a fun little adventure, I thought. *And I owe it all to alcohol.*

FOURTEEN

Is That All There Is?

"Play it again! Play it again!" slurred Mr. Parker like a drunk at a bar begging for just one more drink. I did as I was told and pointed the remote control at the CD player and hit repeat. For the fourth time Peggy Lee's whispery voice haunted the living room of West Eighty-second Street with "Is That All There Is?"

Mr. Parker, who had remained my best friend since the "Where's my beret?!" college night, had just moved to New York from Los Angeles. He was staying with Michahaze and me for a couple of weeks until his boyfriend, Bunny, joined him to find their own place. We were having four A.M. nightcaps after another night of carousing.

Since he'd hit town, I was showing him every bar, boîte, and ballroom I frequented, high to low. We had taken Peggy's advice to break out the booze and have a ball. Every night. Michahaze had opted out of this night. "I've had enough," he said with the implication *Haven't you?* I hadn't. *Perhaps he doesn't like to drink as much as I.* Was it a school night? Probably, but at twenty-eight I had no problem making it to work after a late night. Or three.

In a louche, seen-it-all, resigned demeanor, Peggy sang verse after verse about a life of tragedy and letdowns, from the fire at her
childhood home, to being bored by the spectacle of the circus, to
the end of a first love, while being backed up by a tuba vamp. Each
disappointment was met with the question "Is that all there is to
a ___"—fill in the blank. A fire, a circus, love? Her answer? Keep
dancing and boozing. Have a ball.

"My God, that song is brilliant!" Mr. Parker said with his head
thrown back and his arms stretched out with his palms facing
up, as if in religious supplication.

"Shhh!" I whispered. "Michahaze is asleep." I pointed my head
toward our bedroom. It was nearly four A.M..

Mr. Parker held an index finger to his mouth in a grand *shhh* gesture. "Right. *Right,*" he said, sotto voce and bug-eyed. "But I have
to say that this song may be the greatest song *ever.* And Peggy may
be the greatest singer in all of Christendom. God, I'm a Peggy Person." He looked at me with besotted eyes and asked me rhetorically,
"Jamie, are *you* a Peggy Person?"

"You better believe it!" I slurred back, mirroring his goggle-eyed
glaze. "Peggy People are the luckiest people in the world."

"That's right, *baby!*"

I took a gulp of one of the bourbon on the rocks I had poured for
us. I thought of myself as a little boy and that first moment of being instantly mesmerized by her ghostly figure wrapped in a
massive cloud of white chiffon and singing that song on some
variety show. My appreciation of Peggy's oeuvre had since expanded beyond "Is That All There Is?" to her big-band swing days
to her cool "Fever" jazz days and beyond. Her breathy voice was
so sensual, a feline purr, as if she were your lover singing next
to you in bed; her phrasing so nuanced and subtle that the meaning of the songs as interpreted by her were perceived in flashes,
the way lightning can illuminate a dark room just long enough for
you to see what you need to find. With her minimalist phrasing

she could nail the essence of a song by her pauses, what she didn't say. Like the best painters and sculptors, she knew that the deepest meanings often reside in the void of negative space.

In "Is That All There Is?" her father takes her to a circus, which she describes with a wink in her tone as "the Greatest Show on Earth." Her voice rises at the end in a question, so that you can almost hear her ask, "Right?" But she doesn't say it, it's implied. Her assessment of the spectacle of clowns, and dancing bears, and pretty ladies in pink tights? "I had the feeling that something was missing. I don't know what."

"Most people think of this as the ultimate downer song." Mr. Parker launched into his critical analysis. "I don't. Conversely, I think it's a celebration of the spectacle of life in all its joy and tragedy."

"Well, she *does* say that she's not ready for that 'final disappointment.'"

"Oh! That 'final disappointment.' What a brilliant line. It's a total *alkie* song." He looked heavenward and opened his mouth like a choirboy as he sang, "She's fan-*taaas*-tic!"

"And what will she be doing when that final disappointment comes?"

We answered in unison, "She'll break out the booze and have a ball."

We took gulps of drinks and marinated in the meaning of the song as we let Peggy finish it uninterrupted. In the final verse she says that as fatalistic as her outlook may appear, she's not going to end it all, and when that "final disappointment" comes, she'll face it, the way she has faced the rest of life. She rephrases the song's question as a statement that she'll keep dancing and drinking "if that's all." Pause. "There." Pause "Is." Followed by a final vamp and bump bump of the tuba.

We sat in silence and drank, staring ahead.

Then Mr. Parker spoke. "You know, I have her phone number."

"What do you mean?"

"I mean to say that I have her phone number. Right here in my wallet."

"What are you talking about?"

"A friend of mine who knows I'm a *major* Peggy Person worked at one of the hospitals Miss Lee frequented. You *know* she was always in and out of hospitals."

"Oh, I know. I read her autobiography. She described more ailments and near-death experiences than . . . than Elizabeth Taylor."

Mr. Parker pulled out a folded-up, laminated piece of paper. He waved it at me. "I keep all the addresses of those near and dear to me so I can send letters and postcards from wherever I am. My friend slipped me Miss Lee's phone number and address. You know it is one of Bunny's and my dreams—dream number thirty-*two*, I believe—to open a bar called Is That All There Is? Anyway, I have her number."

"Give me that!" I grabbed the paper from his hand and squinted at the tiny type of Miss Peggy Lee's Bel Air address and phone number. Without thinking of the time, I picked up the cordless phone and dialed.

Ring. Ring. Ri—

"Hello," answered a young-sounding woman.

"Hi. May I speak to Peggy?"

"Who's calling, please?"

"Jamie."

"Okay. Hold on."

I covered the mouthpiece and looked at a slack-jawed Mr. Parker and stage-whispered, "I'm on hold. For Peggy. *Lee*."

He shot back with "This is *wild*!"

Hold. Hold. Hold.

And then "Hello?" was purred across the line in an unmistakable whisper of a voice. "This is Peggy."

Bravado trumped the surreal moment and I pushed forward. "Hi, Peggy. This is Jamie."

"Jamie?" Breath and pause. "Anderson?"

"No. It's Jamie Brickhouse. I'm a *huge* fan of yours. I met you backstage at one of your New York concerts," I lied.

"Oh. What are you doing?" Her voice was so sexy, the question could have been *What are you wearing?*

"I'm sitting here with my best friend and we've been listening to 'Is That All There Is?' I'm in New York. I missed you at Carnegie Hall last year, and I'm still sick about it. Do you have any upcoming New York dates?"

"No. Since the fall I can't even get out of bed." Her words seemed to sink into what I imagined was a cumulus, king-size cloud of a bed where she was nestled in a quilted, white satin bed jacket, a Princess phone cradled between shoulder and ear. She let her words lie there for a beat. Then with a twinkle in her voice she said, "But I've still got the voice." I could almost feel her breath in my ear.

I inhaled before speaking. "Yes, Peggy, there's no mistaking that voice." I mouthed, *Wow,* to Mr. Parker. "Peggy, it's so good talking to you. I have to tell you, I think 'Is That All There Is?' is just about the greatest song *ever.* My friend Mr. Parker and I are a little drunk. We've been listening to it tonight. Over and over. I can't tell you how many drunken nights you've gotten me through with that song."

"Well"—breath—"I guess my life was worth living."

I don't remember the rest of the conversation. After that, I didn't need to.

I guess my life was worth living. Was it a backhanded slap that if she got some lush on the other end of the phone through another drunken night, then her purpose on earth was fulfilled, or was she truly acknowledging my reverence for her and the song, meaning that if she could move people so profoundly as she had me, then her life had meaning? I suspect she meant a bit of both.

I thought about the life I had been living in the six years I'd been in New York. It was the kind of life I'd always wanted—the kind of life I imagined twitching myself into from the living-room floor in Beaumont, where I watched such movies as *Breakfast at Tiffany's,* with Audrey Hepburn as Holly Golightly in the best party scene on film, and *Humoresque,* starring Joan Crawford as a glamorously unhappy alcoholic—but never believed could happen. And here it was: the charming brownstone New York apartment, an ascending career in publishing, and a man (with some men on the side) who loved me almost as much as Mama Jean. *Well, no one could love me that much.* And a recirculating waterfall of booze and parties. Delicious booze.

The blur of our annual New Year's Eve parties, where guests with raised champagne glasses were huddled together on our freezing rooftop deck for the stroke of midnight, had become as traditional and anticipated as Mama Jean's Christmas parties. In the wee hours of the morning—after the guests were gone, after Michahaze was in bed, after those Holly Golightly parties were over—I'd stay up for just one more. One more was usually several bourbons on the rocks that disappeared as fast as I poured them. I'd survey the mess of the party and play my favorite songs: "The Ladies Who Lunch," Elaine Stritch's bitter booze ballad; *anything* by Judy Garland, whom Mama Jean once dismissed as "the worst degenerate Hollywood ever produced"; and of course, Peggy's "Is That All There Is?"

I'd sit there in the dark with the music and the bourbon, replaying the party, replaying my life. There was always such buildup to the parties: coming up with the right theme, designing a clever invitation, perfecting the music playlist, filling the apartment with a big, fun-loving crowd. Michahaze and I were always preparing down to the wire. The people showed up. The booze was broken out. A ball was had. And then it was over. And I still wanted more.

I felt like Peggy at the circus. I had the feeling that something was missing.

And I didn't know what.

FIFTEEN

Alcoholics Can't Count

The second person who called me an alcoholic was Eddie Fisher. Eddie Fisher: crooner, really bad actor, man of a thousand face-lifts, and reformed boozer and druggie. He was the first husband of Debbie Reynolds, whom he dumped for Elizabeth Taylor, who dumped him for Richard Burton. He was also the father of Princess Leia, aka Carrie Fisher. I was two sips into a perfect gin martini, sitting outside Peacock Alley in the lobby of the Waldorf-Astoria, when I looked up and saw a joker mask floating about five feet four inches off the ground. It was Eddie. I was publicizing his second memoir (second because he said he was high as a kite during the first) and waiting for him in the hotel lobby while he freshened up in his room. He sauntered up to my table looking like a Jewish gangster with his winter-white topcoat draped over his shoulders. He aimed his finger at my drink in a mock-gun gesture and said, "A martini! It's not even five o'clock. And you're drinking alone." Then in a singsong voice: "*You're*-an-*al*-co-*hol*-ic!" I laughed and didn't tell him it was my second martini.

The first person who called me an alcoholic was Mama Jean, but it took Joan Collins for her to say it.

I was riding high, four years into my second job at a major commercial publishing house. With that job I had risen to associate director of publicity, second martini to my boss, Jack, the director of publicity. Jack hired me over copious drinks in the lobby of the Royalton Hotel, a good omen since that's where Michahaze had his first audience with Mama Jean. Jack had a personality as big as a Broadway stage, called people darling and doll face, and delivered his off-color remarks such as "Titties up, girls!" with an infectious laugh trailed by a puff of smoke. I adored him. And he adored me. Jamela, he called me. In Jack I found my perfect mentor. He was gay with a capital *G,* ten or so years ahead of me in both biological years and booze years. He was a good-time drinker like me. We worked hard and we had a ball playing hard during old-school, three-martini lunches that often slid into more drinks after work.

I specialized in all the glitzy books by celebs such as Eddie, Oliver Stone, Helen Gurley Brown, Delta Burke, Aaron Spelling, and biographies of dead celebrities such as Lana Turner, Audrey Hepburn, and Jack Kerouac, who died when his booze-saturated liver exploded. In moving to New York and finding Michahaze, I had arrived. Landing at the successful publishing house where I got to hobnob with fading celebrities and drink while doing it, I had reached nirvana.

I was shooting off my mouth to Mama Jean on the phone about the publicity campaign for Joan Collins's second memoir, *Second Act. Not only do I specialize in celebrity memoirs, but I have a subspecialty in* second *memoirs by celebrities.*

"Oh!" I bragged. "There's going to be a fabulous party at Mortimer's. You know, the Upper East Side ladies-who-lunch hangout?"

"I know Mortimer's. Have you forgotten who took you to lunch there in your salad days?"

"I certainly haven't." Dad, she, and I lunched there during a New York trip after I graduated from college. We were seated in the back as we watched social X-rays air-kiss over lobster salads in the front, while a curmudgeonly old queen ruled the room with a steely gaze over his tortoiseshell readers.

"So when is the party?"

"October twenty-eighth."

"Well, I want to come, and that gives me plenty of time to book tickets for Daddy and me and line up some shows."

Before I could say that I wasn't actually inviting her to the party, she had paid the airfare, booked tickets for a couple of shows, and reserved a bed (Michahaze's and my bed). To quote Mama Jean about other headstrong women: "She had the balls of a brass monkey."

That last week of October I found myself juggling Joan Collins and Mama Jean, which was kind of funny because in the eighties Mama Jean had become known as the Joan Collins of Beaumont. Both she and Joan had their heyday in the 1980s. It's the decade when Joan reached her summit of fame and success on the night-time soap *Dynasty,* playing Alexis Carrington. That's the decade when Mama Jean made her fortune as a stockbroker and had a ball doing it. She became the second-highest-grossing broker in Beaumont and "wrote her own ticket" to build the Flamingo Road house and retire early.

Mama Jean and Joan's character, Alexis, even had the same dog, a reddish-brown Lhasa apso. I don't know about Alexis, but Mama Jean could never tame her Lhasa, Brennan. He was an incorrigible runaway. He used to air-bite at her finger as she shook it in his face, chastising him for running from the yard. It infuriated her when he did this, but it shut her up.

I spent the day of the party squiring Joan to a round of television interviews—the *Today* show, *Live with Regis and Kathie Lee*—along with her personal publicist, who had the same clipped British tongue as Joan. We had some downtime before her twelve-thirty book signing at Barnes & Noble on Fifth Avenue, and Joan wanted to "hit the shops!"

We hit the DKNY showroom on Seventh Avenue, but she was

disappointed that the Gottex swimsuit showroom next door was closed. "What a pity," she said. "I could use a new Gottex. During summers in the South of France, I absolutely *live* in my Gottex!" I imagined her drinking morning coffee on a terrace, sipping a Kir Royale poolside at lunch, hosting an evening cocktail party in an ocean-view living room, and wearing *nothing* but the same white, gold-belted, one-piece Gottex.

When we reached Saks Fifth Avenue, we had just shy of an hour to kill before her book signing at Barnes & Noble, just a couple of blocks away. But before the shopping could begin in the vast, multi-level emporium, we had to strategize. I stood back while she and her publicist leaned over a glass-topped counter and devised a fool-proof plan for us all to disperse and reconvene. With their theatrical British accents, spoken in cloak-and-dagger tones, it sounded more like they were plotting the perfect murder.

"I want to hit the shoe department *first. Then* on to better dresses," she said as if she had an imaginary clipboard.

"Yes, Joan. That sounds good," her personal publicist said as he nodded in agreement.

"And if there's time, on to the sportswear section."

"Very good, Joan. I'm going to peruse the colognes. Right. Over. *There.*" He extended his arm in a grand gesture to point to the men's cologne counter while Joan stared intently at him, her cherry-red lips puckered, cheeks sucked in, and her head nodding as if he were explaining how the stock market worked.

"Then I'm going to browse men's accessories, behind the escalators." More nodding of comprehension from Joan.

"Then I'm going to come. Right. Back. *Here.* And wait to meet you at twelve *twenty* to get into the car and go to the book signing. I'm not going to leave this floor."

"Excellent. I will see you here at twelve *twenty.*"

They looked at me and asked in unison, "And what are you going to do, Jamie?"

"I'm going to run down to Barnes and Noble to make sure

everything is in order for the book signing and then meet you two back here. At twelve-*twenty*." When I spoke "twelve-*twenty*," I involuntarily mimicked their perfect-murder accents, but they didn't notice.

At twelve-*fifteen* I found her personal publicist back in the appointed place. Twelve-twenty came and no Joan. At twelve twenty-three, he became nervous. "I don't understand it. This is not like Joan. She's *never* late."

"I'm glad you two made this plan and not I," I said, absolving myself. I checked to see if she had gone to the car that was still waiting for us on the side street. No Joan. I suggested that we have her paged. Alas, there was no paging system. To hear over a loudspeaker "Paging Joan Collins. Paging Joan Collins" would have made the aggravation worth it.

The clerk at the information desk was happy to call the obvious departments to ask where the MIA star might be. The shoe and better-dresses departments confirmed that she had been spotted. Sportswear never saw her. There must have been a black hole between better dresses and sportswear. Losing Joan Collins in Saks Fifth Avenue is like losing a float in a Macy's Thanksgiving Day Parade.

Her personal publicist was starting to perspire and I was starting to feel the pangs of LBD. I checked the side street again. The car was gone.

"I'm going on to Barnes and Noble," I told him. "You stay. Right. *Here*. In case she shows up." I dashed.

When I reached the store, where fans were lined up to get their books signed, I was relieved to see the top of her hair bobbing up and down over the stacks. I reached the back of the store to find her smiling and signing. She cut her eyes away from an adoring fan and glared at grinning me. In a stage whisper she hissed, "Where were you?" I later heard from a colleague that when she exited the Lincoln Town Car solo, she had asked the question a bit stronger: "Where the *fuck* are they?"

Apparently, intrusive fans had made shopping for her impossible. In her frustration and impatience, she forgot the meeting spot of the foolproof plan and left for the Barnes & Noble without us. Joan's brief moment of displeasure, diffused by an audience of fans, was merely a little sand in my Gottex compared to what awaited me at the office.

Glenn Bernbaum was the curmudgeonly old queen in tortoiseshell readers I remembered from the time Mama Jean had taken me to Mortimer's. *Curmudgeonly* is a compliment compared to the nasty old queen he really was. Glenn, who owned Mortimer's, was throwing the book party for Joan. The publisher was taking care of printing and sending the invitations. When I returned to the office that afternoon, Glenn chewed me out on the phone, claiming that I didn't mail the invitations to everyone on his list. As a result, he claimed I had cost him a fortune in the last-minute telegrams that he sent. *Telegrams?!* When I asked him to tell me who didn't receive their invitations, he fired a daisy chain of invectives—*mother-fucking-cuntface-cocksucker-son-of-a-bitch*—and hung up.

This was at three in the afternoon, well past what I later learned was the 10:30 A.M. point of fermentation. I ran to Jack with the tale. He accused me of exaggerating and dismissed me with a wave of smoke from his Benson & Hedges cigarette, which he was illegally smoking in his office.

Just before Jack and I reached the restaurant for the party, carrying a blowup of Joan's face, Glenn had apparently had another fit and locked the door, barring everyone from entering.

Almost everyone. There in the door's tiny speakeasy window was Mama Jean's face, her eyebrows raised. Somehow *she* had managed to get past the explosive, sodden queen while others had failed.

She let me in and rolled her eyes in Glenn's direction. "Good luck with that one."

Glenn, shriveled and peering over his signature tortoiseshell reading glasses, pointed a shaky, gnarled finger and laid into Jack and me with an automatic round of expletives so foul that they were original even to us. For once Jack was at a loss for words. We left Glenn still quivering from the shots he'd fired. After giving up trying to console the inconsolable over God only remembers what, I got myself a martini and let the party begin.

I'm sorry that I don't have a photo of Joan meeting Mama Jean. In this brief but cordial moment I don't think that Joan realized she was meeting "the Joan Collins of Beaumont." The rest of the party was a blur of more martinis mixed with the floating heads of other women of a certain age: Nan Kempner, Arlene Dahl, Blaine Trump. And Elaine Stritch.

Miss Stritch, tall and bony, whiskey-voiced, seventy-something, famous Broadway star, stood chatting in a corner with a younger woman. This was before Miss Stritch had the biggest hit of her life with her one-woman show, *At Liberty,* about her career and struggle with the bottle. But then she was most famous (and most beloved by me) for "The Ladies Who Lunch," her showstopper from Stephen Sondheim's *Company,* which was almost thirty years past. It was one of my favorite songs to drink to. It's an alcoholic rant in which she lobs acerbic barbs at the empty lives of rich society matrons who lunch—at places just like Mortimer's, come to think of it—and punctuates each zinger with an increasingly guttural "I'll drink to that."

I thought she would be thrilled that someone barely thirty not only recognized her, but was such a rabid fan. Clearly, I didn't know as much about celebrities as I thought.

I pardoned my intrusion and introduced myself. "Hello, Miss Stritch, I'm Jamie Brickhouse, Joan's book publicist. It's such a thrill to meet you. I'm a *huge* fan of yours." Nothing. Just a cigar-store-Indian stare. "I loved you in Albee's *A Delicate Balance.*" Still nothing. Not even a smile. Finally I used a variation of my Peggy Lee line on her. "Oh, Miss Stritch, I can't *tell* you how many drunken nights you've gotten me through with 'The Ladies Who Lunch.'"

She didn't thank me. She didn't tell me, "Well, I guess my life was worth living." She didn't even tell me to get lost. She broke her cigar-store-Indian stare. In a crusty voice—mouth moving like a ventriloquist's dummy's—she instantly deflated my fan balloon with "You know, it's really rude to only introduce yourself to the famous person and not to the person that the famous person is with."

I wish I had said, *Oh, is there a famous person here?* or *Jesus, have a drink,* not knowing she was sober. Instead I mumbled an apology and grabbed another drink at the bar. *I'll drink to that! And one for Bernbaum!*

Joan had a great time, despite the volatile Glenn, who, she said, "was less than charming to me." My parents had stories to tell their friends back in Beaumont. Dad fared better with Elaine, who told him that with a name like Brick-shit-house, she might even come to Beaumont for a visit. And I was happy and very . . .

"Drunk! You're *drunk,*" Mama Jean informed me at dinner after the party. Yes, I was, but I didn't need her to tell me and I didn't need her to spoil it. She looked down at the drink I had just ordered. "How many is that?"

"I don't know. Three?"

"Alcoholics can't count."

I glared at her over my martini.

"Jamie, I'm worried about you." She looked at me and heaved a sigh of disgust. "Every time I see you, you're drinking. I—" She interrupted herself with a sudden thought. "And there's nothing in your refrigerator to eat! It's all *liquor*-related." I pictured our nearly barren refrigerator: a jar of olives, lemons and limes, tonic, club soda, Absolut in the freezer. Even our cat, a Russian blue, was named Stoli. "I think you're an alcoholic." I laughed. "No, Jamie. I'm serious. I really do."

Jesus Christ! So what if I was drunk? The party had been a success. I was having a good time and wanted to *keep* having a good time for as long as possible. She shook her finger at me as she continued to tell me that I had been overserved. Involuntarily, I pulled a Brennan and began biting the air just shy of her finger. I discovered that when I did it, it had the same effect: it infuriated her, but it shut her up.

I was proud of that moment. Of having the liquor courage to force her to back down. But like everything she said to me, either praise or criticism, it left me asking, *Really?*

Not long after that night, the party started to wane for Jack. He took me to lunch to tell me that he was worried that his job was on the line. In all seriousness, and as his devoted colleague and friend, I told him that he had to stop drinking . . . *at lunch*. He agreed as we sipped our second—or was it third?—vodka tonic.

I didn't want to have that conversation, and a year later I didn't want the phone call that came one weekday morning while I lay in bed hungover, having just decided to call in sick. My rule of always showing up to work, no matter what happened the night before, had relaxed to "a sick day here and there can't hurt." Besides, I'd only taken three—or was it four?—sick days that year.

"Hello," I groggily answered the phone, sounding like Elaine Stritch.

"Jamela." Jack sounded exhausted. "I've had it. I've just checked myself into rehab."

I ran my fingers through my hair, grabbed my throbbing head, and before telling him that I'd help in any way he needed me to, I thought, *Am I next?*

SIXTEEN

Hides: Persian and Raw

I've always loved fur. Growing up, I was the coat-check boy at my parents' Christmas parties. Even though the temperature rarely dipped below forty-five degrees, all of the wives—and a couple of antiques dealers—arrived in fur. I'd place the sumptuous coats on the double bed in my room and lie on top of them, burying my face in their downy luxury. Pearly Mae, our cat, joined me in inspecting the furs: a red-fox jacket, several full-length, black minks, a silver-fox stole, a cheap calico-rabbit jacket, the occasional lynx, like the full-length one Mama Jean got after seeing Rip Taylor's on our New York trip. But the fur that fascinated me was Dorothy Loehman's three-quarter, black, Persian lamb that weighed a ton. So did Dorothy.

Dorothy was made fun of for that coat by my parents and their friends. "Can you believe she still wears that thing? Nobody but old ladies wear Persian lamb anymore. And she looks like a bulldog in it. It's not like she can't get a new coat. She has *plenty* of money."

I guess Dorothy loved that coat. I did too. It was unlike any of the others, with its strange, squiggly pattern of raised black fur that looked like a cockscomb flower but more like the surface of a brain. When brushed against the grain, it had a satiny sheen. Her coat had a brown-mink collar and oversize buttons with mother-of-pearl centers. It also reeked of mothballs, which I found repellent, but its uniqueness among a coterie of the latest-in-fashion look-alikes held my fascination long after I left Beaumont. I remember wishing that boys could wear fur. Then I moved to New York, and with each visit to the flea markets I was getting closer to a fur of my own.

I was trolling the Columbus Avenue Flea Market with Michahaze one Sunday, trying to take my mind off how much I loathed my new job at a boutique PR agency I'll call Dorothy Watts & Associates. I had left my associate director of publicity job at the publisher about a year after Jack got sober, with the illusion that I would be representing world-class luxury clients and traveling the world. The first day of the job I entered full of piss and vinegar, my temperature running high with enthusiasm. I was like a cartoon thermometer flooded to the top with red. With each discovery of the reality of the job, the red dipped, dipped, dipped, until the thermometer was bloodless.

I would not be representing exotic resorts and Michelin-rated European restaurants. I would be hawking window blinds and candles for the home-furnishings division. And the agency was run like a finishing school for girls, with Dorothy Watts as the head mistress. No one called her by name, but warily referred to her as "She" and "Her." "*She* doesn't like for us to eat at our desks. Attracts rats." "Any client meetings have to be cleared with *Her* first." "*She* can't stand it if you don't follow *Her* color-coded filing system." My new coworkers were a bevy of white girls in pearls, either perky and upbeat like Stepford Wives or beaten down with the vacant look of post-op lobotomy patients. Paula, an older schoolmarm type with a straight, greasy bob, referred to the place by its acronym, DWA, but pronounced it "Duh Wah" in the flat accent of a cyborg about to run out of battery power. I went out after that first day of work and got stinky drunk.

But Duh Wah was far away as I roamed the stalls of the flea market. I spotted the Holy Grail of vintage fur hanging solo on a chain-link fence: a Persian-lamb coat. A *man's* Persian lamb, with a brown-mink collar, it was cut like a peacoat and was two sizes too big for me. At only $150, I could swing that. God, I had to have it. I tried it on. It weighed a ton, just like Dorothy's. Sold.

I spent another $150 in alterations and mother-of-pearl replacement buttons. The first day it was ready, I wore it to work with a pair of vintage, black sunglasses. I was enveloped in so many feelings wearing it. Fur changes a person. I was impossibly chic and original. No one else was wearing Persian lamb. I was sexy like the aging divas who used to pose for the Blackglama fur ads with the headline "What Becomes a Legend Most?" And let's face it: it was delightfully queenie. *No one on the street will mistake me for a football fan.*

Then I arrived at work. Any cloak of positive thinking dissolved when I removed the fur and faced the dismal reality of the Duh Wah to-do list waiting for me:

1. Come up with three holiday ideas for Ye Olde American Candle Co. ("Sparkle, Shimmer, and *Shine* This Holiday Season!")
2. Write bathroom-window-blinds press release. ("Shade Your Bathroom in Bright Lights and Discreet Privacy with Lunetta Shades from Hailey Blinds.")
3. Slit wrists.

The only thing that got me through the day was the promise of my five-thirty drinks date with Mr. Parker at the Gramercy Park Hotel. In those days the Gramercy had a delightfully down-at-the-heels lobby bar peopled with Eurotrash, crypt keepers from the neighborhood, and dipsomaniacs such as Mr. Parker and me.

When I arrived, Mr. Parker was already seated at our corner table with a martini—less one finger of gin—in front of him. He raised his glass and exclaimed, "Whoa! Darling, that coat is fan-*taaas*-tic!"

I did a quick model turn with my hands in the coat pockets and a glance back over my left shoulder, sunglasses still on. "You like it? Good."

I nodded to Nick, the old Greek bartender, in his green livery jacket. He came over like an Oompa-Loompa in *Charlie and the Chocolate Factory,* hands behind his back. "Hello, sir. The usual?"

"Yes, please, Nick." He bowed and walked backward away from the table.

"So how's Duh Wah?" Mr. Parker asked, imitating me imitating Nancy.

"Just a little bit worse than it was the day before, but let's talk about happier times."

After that first martini—Beefeater gin, up, dry, with a twist—melted into my body, I left Duh Wah all behind. Over two or three more martinis, mixed nuts, and some chicken drumsticks, we dove into our endless banter, which ricocheted from Joan Crawford's always wearing open-toed, ankle-strap high heels, to debating the precise shade of green (chartreuse or olive?) of a wall in Michahaze's and my apartment, to the artistic perfection of Tennessee Williams's *A Streetcar Named Desire,* and of course to the exquisiteness of Persian-lamb fur and how lucky I was to have scored the dream coat.

We called for the tab, as Mr. Parker had to go home for dinner with his boyfriend, Bunny. I should have gone home to Michahaze but I was feeling too free, too sexy, too confident, with my thrilling new coat and three-martini—*or was it four?*—high not to get more out of the evening. And the Duh Wah icks were long left behind.

I decided to hit the sodomite resorts in Chelsea. First stop: Barracuda, where the dream coat got me noticed ("Fabulous coat!" "What is that, *brain* fur?" "My grandmother had a Persian-lamb fur. I *adored* it") but not laid.

Next was the View, a dismal bar that was routinely half-empty. *How does it stay open with crowds this meager? Is it a drug front?* That's why I popped in. I was looking for a wintry mix, not what the weatherman called a mix of rain and snow, but what I called a mix of booze and coke. I found it at the View and decided to take my evening down a few notches and shoot for some easy prey at the Rawhide.

The Rawhide was ostensibly a leather bar, but all were welcome. It was never just Rawhide but always *the* Rawhide, which lent it an air of foreboding. The awning boasted that the bar was established in 1979, and little seemed to have changed since opening night. To say that I was overdressed is an understatement. The clientele was almost exclusively in jeans, black T-shirts, and perhaps a flannel shirt. Not another Persian lamb in sight.

It was stripper night and the place was packed, but I lucked out and snagged the last available barstool. As I teeter-tottered a bit while removing my coat and placing it on the back of the stool, I felt disappointed that no one complimented my coat. *Wrong crowd. Know your audience.*

"Gin and tonic," I said to the bartender. Then I swung around to introduce myself to whoever was there. "Hi. How's it going?" I said to Mr. Right Next to Me.

"Not bad. You?"

"Oh, I'm having a *swell* night and enjoying life!" I said just a little too loudly.

"Seems like it. You're kinda drunk."

"So? Isn't *everybody*?" I said with a crooked smirk.

He turned away to the person on his other side. *Fine.*

Someone tapped me on the shoulder. I turned around to see a handsome coffee-colored guy holding his leather bomber jacket in the crook of two fingers. "Mind if I park this on your stool? It's crowded in here."

"Sure. Be my guest." As he placed his coat on top of mine, I remembered the dime bag of coke in my pocket. "Be right back."

I took my drink and popped into the bathroom for a snort or three. For another thirty minutes or maybe an hour, I boomeranged from the barstool to the bathroom and points in between. After the coke dried up, I decided I had had enough. Actually, I had had enough because I'd had all there was to have.

The crowd had thinned a bit. I headed back to my stool. The leather bomber jacket had been replaced by a peacoat. I lifted it to get my Persian-lamb coat. But it wasn't there.

Hey. Wha' happened?

A beefy, mustached, bald man appeared. "Excuse me, but that's my coat." He pointed to the peacoat I was holding.

"Oh, sorry. I was looking for mine. It was right here."

"I just put mine there. There was no coat there."

I panicked. Maybe it was the wrong stool. I looked left and right. The stools on either side were empty.

"Hey," I yelled at the bartender. "I had a Persian-lamb fur coat. Right *here*." I pointed to my stool.

"A what kind of coat?"

"A black, furry coat with a mink collar."

"Haven't seen anything like that in here."

I careened around the bar looking for the coat or anyone wearing it. I ran out to the street to see if I could spy the thief casually sauntering off in it. Nothing.

I went back inside and did what I knew how to do best in a moment of crisis: I ordered another drink. In the time it took to finish two gin and tonics I went through the five stages of grief:

Denial: *It can't be gone. Okay, it's got to be here somewhere. I'll find it.*

Anger: *Who in the Rawhide would want a Persian-lamb fur? Where is he going to wear it? Motherfucker!*

Bargaining: *If only I had carried it with me. If I ever find it, I'll never let it out of my sight, and I certainly won't wear it in a place like this.*

Depression: *You idiot! You didn't even get a chance to wear it to a party. You blew it all on a nothing night. You might as well have handed it wrapped in a red ribbon with a complimentary cocktail to the first guy you spoke to. You're such a fuckup!*

Acceptance: *God* damn *it! It's gone and was never meant to be. Maybe I never deserved it.*

As I left the dark cave of the bar, a gust of frigid wind hit my coatless body, a final slap in the face. *Damn, it's cold outside.* "Taxi!"

SEVENTEEN

Forgive Me, for I Have Sinned

I scanned John's plywood-and-cinder-block shelves, heavy with titles like *Sexuality and the U.S. Catholic Church*, *The Case for Clerical Celibacy*, and *The Vatican and Homosexuality*. I'd met John, last night's hookup, at the witching hour in a dark corner of a Lower East Side, poultry-themed bar, the Cock.

As John handed me the two Advil I'd requested and a mug of black coffee, I said, "Judging from your library, I'd say that you're either a lapsed Catholic or a priest."

John sat opposite me on his futon, curling his long legs under his six-foot-two, meatless frame, and took a sip of his coffee. "Actually, I *am* a praacticing Caatholic"—his *a*'s were pronounced long and flat—"but a laapsed priest."

His shrug of the shoulders and so-sue-me grin told me that he wasn't joking. Besides, his goofy, puppy-dog, fortyish face instantly conveyed that he didn't have an ironic bone in his lanky body.

"If I'd only known, I would have called you Father John last night."

"Oh, Gad," he said with a roll of the eyes. "I'm glaad you didn't.

I'm actually on leave from my church in Minnesota." *Minnesota. That explains the accent.* "I'm at Fordham getting my maaster's. My thesis is on sexuality and the Caatholic Church."

"You're doing some *excellent* fieldwork."

"Ha. I'm making up for lost time. I've been a priest for fourteen years. I wanted to be a priest my whole life. When I was a little boy, I used to pretend to be a priest and say Maass in the basement with a makeshift altar and everything."

"Wow. I grew up Catholic too, but I spent my make-believe time pretending to be Ann-Margret falling off of a Vegas stage. I don't know what's gayer." He laughed. "Were you celibate the whole time you were a priest?"

"Well, I'm *still* a priest, just on leave. Yep. I was celibate. The *entire* fourteen years." *Fourteen years? I can't imagine being celibate for fourteen hours.* "A lot of my fellow priests used to sneak over to Minneaaapolis and spend entire weekends at the baaths. But I never strayed." He took a sip of coffee from the mug he held with both hands and looked past me with a blank stare. "Celibacy fucked up my life." Then he broke the mood by scolding me. "I was pretty drunk laast night, but *you,* my son"—he shook his index finger at me—"were *very* drunk."

I hung my head in mock shame. "Forgive me, Father John, for I have sinned, and I have the hangover to prove it."

I chuckled at my mock display of contrition while I winced inside at having pulled another all-nighter. Michahaze and I had classified our marriage as "modern" years ago. We went through couple's therapy for a brief time after the Zurich trip. Neither of us could stand the therapist, an Ernie the Muppet of a man whose earnest smile hovered over praying hands while he spewed a litany of therapy jargon—"comfortability," "anger transference," "projecting"—in hushed tones. But he did get us talking to each other about what we wanted. It came out that Michahaze was no angel either, just not as sloppy in his transgressions. (My drinking never came up. At that time I didn't get the equation that too much booze equals you never know where you'll end up. I was always bad at math.)

End result: we loved each other and our life together, but wanted the excitement of other men, so, like many gay couples we knew, we decided to have an open marriage. Old salt that I was at thirty-three, I believed from experience and observation in two kinds of long-term gay-male couples: those who fuck around and are open about it, and those who fuck around and lie about it. Whenever I espouse this theory, I get three different reactions: straight women's faces fall; gay men nod in agreement; straight men are jealous.

But the deal was no love affairs, and no sleepovers—always come home. I repeatedly broke the "always come home" part of the bargain. Once I was out there and a couple of drinks became half a dozen, I couldn't stop until I found sex. I had to have it. By the time I found it, it was often so late, I'd pass out in the strange bed I was in before I could pour myself into a cab. It meant my head hung in *real* shame, profuse apologies, a couple of days of silence from Michahaze, and a slow thaw over the week. A social engagement could melt the ice into manageable cubes, when we'd put on a good face for our friends, pour some booze over those rocks, and by the end of the evening have put on good faces for each other too. *Wash. Rinse. Spin.* Until the next dirty load piled up.

After that first night with Father John, I remember slinking home soiled with guilt and shame, hoping Michahaze had already left the apartment to have his Sunday alone so I wouldn't have to face him. *Oh, shit.* I remembered that my friend Kelly and her nine-year-old son were coming over to retrieve that filthy, caged rabbit they called a pet. Michahaze and I had kept the rabbit for a week while they were on vacation. *Great. What's Michahaze going to tell Kelly?* I turned the corner onto West Eighty-second Street, and Kelly and her son were walking down the stoop of our building carrying the rabbit in its cage. They could have been a photo in a real estate brochure for the family-friendly Upper West Side. I felt naked. I ducked into the entrance of a closed restaurant and hid. *How long should I hide here? How long can I hide?*

During the rest of that autumn I helped Father John make up for those barren fourteen years. We usually met during my lunch hour, so no more all-nighters. And sex only. Some heavy affection, but no love. Then he disappeared until right after the New Year. He called me at the office with a nervous catch in his voice. "I've got the claaap. Gonorrhea." *Ah, that explains the silence. Nothing kills a beautiful thing like an STD.*

"Oh, dear. I'm so sorry to hear that."

"Have you, um, noticed anything?"

I told him that I hadn't. *Glad we always used condoms.* I promised to get checked out, but I never saw Father John again.

EIGHTEEN

Lost in Rio

"I'll make this book a bestseller if I have to suck every cock in Manhattan!" I said to my boss, Liz. She doubled over in laughter and let her auburn bob fall across her broad face. She composed herself and grinned with a twinkle in her half-moon eyes, which resembled lunette windows, and replied, "Use whatever works, I always say." I was in her office discussing the publicity campaign for a book that we had huge bestseller dreams for, the kind of book for which I had been hired as publicity director.

I had been born again two years prior when I left the dismal employ of Duh Wah. Not only had I landed back in publishing, but at the top of my field as a vice president, executive director of publicity, at a respected publisher of serious nonfiction. I was going to bring razzle-dazzle to its dusty shelves with my glossy résumé. It was a bit highbrow for my taste—the likes of Joan Collins and Eddie Fisher would never spill ink there—but I was running the show. And there was Liz. Harvard-educated, robust, former lover of black men, current lover of one woman, Karen, self-described "gay man trapped in a woman's body."

Liz. I think I fell in love with her the first time I noticed a signature look of hers. She gave this look when someone was talking to her and spewing drivel—saying outrageously stupid things, inane things, crazy theories, offensive remarks, blah, blah, blah. She would cock her head in disbelief, her already-narrowed eyes turning to slits, her eyebrows raised, staring at the oblivious person who was prattling on. The look was almost involuntary and for the benefit of the person behind the person talking, usually me.

Our conversation turned from my bestseller-making strategy to Lent.

"Are you back on Lent?" she asked.

We had been out the night before with colleagues after an author event, and Liz asked me if I wanted my usual martini. After a slight hesitation, I said, "Sure, why not? But I'll be breaking my Lenten vow to abstain from firewater."

Her infectious grin had dissolved into a look of panic as she extended her hand like a stop sign. "By all means, don't break your vow for me."

"No worries. One night won't hurt." For a few years running, I had given up alcohol during the forty days of Lent, but it was getting harder to keep the vow.

"Last night is behind me," I assured her now. "And I have the headache to prove it. But I'm back on the Lent wagon. It's always good to give up something you love."

"Good for you. My aunt Joan couldn't. She's been sober for years now and made tons of money as a stockbroker." *Just like Mama Jean,* I thought. *The money part, not the booze part.* "She's pretty fabulous. A striking, rail-thin woman with a shock of spiky, silver hair and Lucille Ball–blue eyes. Oh, but the stories she told me about her drinking days. She did crazy things, like give away fur coats to strangers." I didn't mention the much-lamented Persian lamb. "Aunt Joan always said that with her, there was a giant dial for booze that was either all the way on"—Liz pantomimed turning a dial to the right—"or all the way off." When Liz turned the dial to off, she cocked her head and made a clicking sound with her tongue. "Sad, really."

As soon as Lent was over, I turned the dial back on. I had another of those Persian-lamb-coat nights where two drinks after work turned into twelve. Whenever I told Michahaze that I was going to have a "quick drink after work," I wasn't lying. I had every intention of only having two—or three—martinis.

I started where I usually did, across the street at Mesa de España. This Spanish restaurant served mediocre paella and had murals on the dining-room walls, red vinyl booths, and a front, L-shaped bar with knotty-pine paneling and a large mirror behind it. The geriatric waiters in red dinner jackets were from the same school as those at the Gramercy Park Hotel. I had made this place my watering hole and routinely took my staff there. We'd make fun of the sad-sack regulars, many of whom drank alone, staring through their reflections in the bar mirror.

I left Mesa around eight-thirty. Somehow eight-thirty fast-forwarded to three in the morning across town, where I was deep in a wintry mix at a seedy Greenwich Village bar. I was doing coke (which I had paid for) with four young guys. When I returned from the bathroom, they were gone and so was my wallet.

I raced after them. They were a block away. I screamed and pleaded with them to take the cash but leave me my wallet so I didn't have to cancel my credit cards and get a new driver's license. *Again.* This sort of thing was happening so often that on some evenings I acted as a sober minder of my inevitable drunk self by stuffing twenty dollars of security money in my shoe and removing all but the necessary credit cards from my wallet. This was not one of those evenings.

The boys laughed at my plea and ran away. I stumbled to a pay phone and called the credit-card companies to cancel the cards. I'd become expert at this. Sometimes I'd call the credit-card companies the next morning only to be told that "someone" had already canceled them the night before. *Oops.*

The bars had just closed and the streets were crawling with lonesome men who had scattered like cockroaches when the lights came on. Here's the insane part: I had a sniff or two of coke in my pocket and five dollars, just enough to pick up someone, have some fun, and get home. *The night isn't lost!* I staggered along the streets searching for a playmate like a diviner who, instead of locating water, can find the debauched and willing. It didn't take long. We passed each other on the street and spoke. I don't remember what we said, but "Hey you" was the gist of it. He was cute. *I think.* I had the coke. He knew of a party. We hopped into a cab. I spent my last five dollars on that cab ride. We got to the party and bypassed the bawdy revelry in the filthy living room and went straight to the bathroom. He started to undress. I pulled out the dime bag of coke. Almost nothing was left.

His look of maniacal anticipation morphed into merely maniacal. "That's it?! That's it?! Man, you *lied* to me!" *Lied to him?* We had jumped into a cab one minute after meeting each other. *This relationship is based on lust, not trust.*

I was scared, but I tried to calm him by grabbing at his crotch to remind him of the other reason we were in the bathroom. Too late. His pants were already going back up. "We can still have some fun, right?" I said weakly—no—pathetically.

"Fun?! Man, I'm straight!" *Great. I have picked up a genuine coke whore.* "Get out!"

I did.

Back on the street, dawn was breaking. The birds were chirping against an anemic morning sky—an in-between blue as if it were backlit by a fluorescent tube. Nothing is worse than a Disney sound track of birds tweeting to remind you that another day is starting and you haven't gotten over the wreck you've made of the last one. You can't hold back the dawn.

I wandered the streets for a while, not wanting to arrive home and face Michahaze before he left for work. Finally, around seven A.M., merely twelve hours since my night began, I decided to head home on the subway. I had no money, so I jumped the subway turn-stile, feeling like trash—or as Mama Jean would say, "Not even trash. *Garbage!*"

As soon as I got to the empty apartment, I made myself a screw-driver. I stared into the drink and started to cry. I thought of the only sober person I knew, or, rather, the only person who was like me and now sober: my former boss Jack. I picked up the phone and called him at his office. I blubbered and blabbered into the phone. "Jack, I can't do this anymore."

"Jamela, you don't have to." He left work and came to my apart-ment. He sat with me as I drank my second screwdriver and smoked.

I looked at the drink. "I'm sorry."

"It's okay, precious angel. You need it." I told him how bad it had gotten—the constant all-nighters, Father John and the clap (well, his, not mine), getting rolled repeatedly. Perched on the edge of the sofa, he drew deeply on his Benson & Hedges cigarette, and when I got to the part about the coke whore telling me he was straight, Jack exhaled a dragon's puff of smoke and laughed hysterically as he fanned the smoke away. "I'm sorry, darling." He put his hand on my shoulder and rubbed my back. He stopped laughing and curled his lips over his teeth. "But you have to admit it's funny. We have to laugh at this stuff, ya know."

"I know." I simultaneously laughed and groaned with my head in my hands.

"Can you not drink tomorrow, honey?" he asked. "Today is a wash."

"Yes," I said without hesitation. *Where did that come from?*

I didn't drink. And I didn't drink the next day, when Jack took me to my first sober meeting. I loved it. Well, I was freaked out by everyone standing in a circle and holding hands for a closing prayer. When that happened, I looked at Jack with eyebrows raised. He whispered, "I know, honey, but you get used to it."

I loved the stories I heard other sober drunks share, many of which were worse than mine—getting fired, suicide attempts, detoxes, rehabs, jails, prison. *Jesus Christ! Maybe I'm not so bad after all.* At the gay meetings every other story seemed to involve debauched tragedy and humiliating loss at the Rawhide. *Nothing good ever came out of the Rawhide.*

Thirty days went by and I didn't drink and I came home to Michahaze every night. He told me he still loved me and I told him I loved him. But I didn't tell him what I was learning at those meetings. I didn't tell him that the one thing I was supposed to do perfectly was not drink.

I asked Jack if he would be my sober mentor, and through an exhale of smoke and emphatic left-right nods of his head, he said, "Oh, God no! Darling, you need to find someone who's not a friend. If I were your mentor, we'd both end up back in the gutter." So I found someone in the fellowship just like Jack to mentor me.

Like the best little boy that I wanted everyone to think I was, I wanted the world to know I was sober. I started with Mama Jean, of course. I heard other sober people say that their parents reacted in disbelief, couldn't handle that their children were alcoholics. Mama Jean? Her head came through the phone when I told her. "Well, thank *God*! Oh, I'm so proud of you." I didn't go into any of the gory details, and remarkably, she didn't ask. But when I was in Beaumont for the usual Thanksgiving visit, she couldn't contain herself for long. After a day of pushing for more details, then retreating, she finally burst out, "You didn't end up drunk in Harlem, did you?"

Well, no, but I did pick up a straight coke whore on the street, I almost said. Instead I answered, "Oh, no, of course not. I just decided I'd had enough."

"Well, okay," she said, clearly not satisfied. She didn't push, but she gave me the same look as when I told her how Michahaze and I first met in Central Park.

I also told Liz. She listened patiently with a beatific smile on her face. When I finished, she put her hand over mine, winked, and wished me all of her love and support. I would learn that it's not a good idea to share news like that unless you're sure that you're done with drinking, or rather, that drinking is done with you.

I had about fifty sober days under my belt when Michahaze and I took a vacation in the Caribbean. I'd been told that it isn't a good idea in early sobriety to take trips, go to parties, hang out in bars, basically do all the things you used to do when you drank. But I didn't listen. I'd be fine. I could handle it on my own. Two days into the vacation I ordered a beer. I don't even like beer.

"You know what? We're on vacation. I don't have that many days sober anyway," I told Michahaze and myself. "I can always get sober after vacation." *What's one day off from Lent?*

Michahaze looked skeptically at me with his head cocked and his lips pursed. After a silence he said, "Are you sure about that?"

When we returned, I went right back to meetings and started a new day count, but it was hard not to drink. And I couldn't let go of my persona as a drinker. I felt that it was the one thing I did exceptionally well. People were used to seeing me with a martini in one hand and a cigarette in the other. It made them happy. It made me happy. Of course, they rarely saw how the rest of the evenings played out.

I'd read that if you're going to be in boozy situations (such as a work function), to bookend the booze event with a sober meeting before and after. I inverted this advice. I drank before *and* after the meetings. *At least I am still going to meetings.*

I did one of those bookends at a pre–sales conference party. I drank at home, went to a meeting, and drank at the party that night. I had a ball. The next morning I was still giddy from the night before, so I decided to keep the buzz going. I had a pop with my morning juice before heading to the sales conference, at which I was presenting on the dais. I wasn't prepared, but I wasn't worried. I was always quick on my feet and superb at winging it. I started with a "Titties up, girls!"—a line stolen from Jack—and threw in some off-color jokes. I didn't hear a lot of audience response over my own laughter. Still, I thought I had aced it.

After the conference I left with Liz. We stood on a corner in the black and brisk winter night under a streetlight whose harsh rays shone down like a policeman's flashlight. As I told her that I was off to one of my sober meetings, I could swear she was giving me that signature look of hers: head cocked in disbelief, eyes narrowed, eyebrows raised. "Really?"

"Yes." I really was. *Maybe I didn't ace the presentation.*

On the way to the meeting I had a quick pop. The love I had for the strangers in those meetings had begun to sour. Through the fog of booze I saw them as whiners who used the meetings to find friends and talk about their problems. I had plenty of friends. I knew what my problems were. Besides, I wasn't as bad as they were. I was functioning. So I zigzagged on that path—dial on/dial off—but kept going to meetings.

Then Michahaze and I went to Rio de Janeiro. Unlike the last trip, this time I made the premeditated decision to drink. I even told Michahaze that I was going to do so. "How can anyone go to Rio and *not* drink? It would be a sin not to have *caipirinhas* in their native land." He said okay but looked at me with grave concern. I wiped the concern from his face with "This will be my last hurrah. After Rio I'll roll up my sleeves and figure out this sober business when we return." I didn't have this conversation with Mama Jean.

A couple of days into the trip I woke up naked and alone in the bedroom of a strange apartment. I got out of bed and walked down the hallway. Snapshot of the day before:

Visiting the towering Christ the Redeemer that stands watch over Rio and having my picture taken by Michahaze.

A crowded gay bar with Michahaze.

A crazy carousel of gorgeous Brazilian men.

Meeting a tall one. Well, many, actually, but one in particular.

Withdrawing cash from an ATM for coke.
I don't remember doing coke.
Then black.

As I reached the end of the hall, I could see the flicker of television light competing with morning sun rays. I could barely hear the TV, but the broad, repetitive sounds of *beep!* and *bonk!* told me cartoons were playing. The hall opened into a living room. There was the TV. *Yes, cartoons.* There was the watcher. A nine-year-old boy. He looked up. There was me, standing as naked as Christ the Redeemer's Father made me, still not remembering how I got there. I retreated back toward the bedroom, and the gorgeous Brazilian from the bar met me in the hallway.

He explained that I was really drunk the previous night. *Oh, really?* I was on a quest for coke and left the bar to pull money from an ATM. He intervened and brought me to his place. *Oh, Christ the Redeemer! What about Michahaze?*

"You're an angel . . ." I struggled for his name. I always forgot the names.

"Fernando."

"Truly an angel."

And the little boy? He was the son of Gladys, Fernando's roommate.

I called Michahaze and barreled over the worry in his voice, already turning the event into a wait-until-we-tell-the-folks-back-home-about-the-time-I-entered-starkers-while-a-little-boy-was-watching-cartoons funny story. After profuse apologies, I smoothed it over by pointing out the positive side: we now had some Rio insiders to show us around.

My indiscretion was packed away with all the other indiscretions in a closet fit for a hoarder. The rest of the trip was like a travel ad for Rio: a montage of drinking, dancing, drinking, dining, fucking, drinking. Not only were the Brazilians the most beautiful race of people I'd ever encountered, but they were as free and casual with their sexuality as bonobo monkeys.

On one cokie, "inside Rio" night with Fernando and Gladys, I found myself in lip-lock with Gladys as Michahaze and Fernando danced across the room. I almost took her up on her offer to have sex.

"Oh, please," she pleaded. "Besides, you have red hair like me?"

Not exactly. You have dyed-red hair like Mamou, Mama Jean's mother, who is also named Gladys, which is starting to creep me out.

She gave me sad puppy-dog eyes. "It would be fun. *Please . . . ?*"

Why not? I'm in Rio! Why not have sex with a woman! Then I remembered that on coke I couldn't penetrate quicksand, much less a woman. "No, it would never work," I told her apologetically, and it was the literal truth. "But let's dance!" I whisked her onto the dance floor into the oblivion of night.

Rio was liberating. I realized I would never be able to have that much fun and adventure without booze, so I decided to leave Aunt Joan's dial in the on position and forget sobriety. This wasn't a casual decision. I based it on a few hard facts at the time: *I have red hair. I'm a sodomite. I like to drink. Okay, I love to drink. That's who I am: a redheaded, gay, functioning alcoholic. As long as the word* functioning *is in front of* alcoholic, *I'm okay.* I saw this as a healthy form of self-acceptance.

NINETEEN

Where Have You Been, Lord Randall, My Son?

Do you smoke?"

"Yes." I pulled out a pack of Lucky Strike Lights.

"No. I mean this." The stranger with no name held up a smoke-stained glass pipe with a white pebble in it as he stood close to me in the dark of the plywood buddy booth at Les Hommes.

"Oh."

Crack wasn't on the agenda that night. It was never on the agenda the handful of times I'd done it, but when someone offered, I was never in a condition to refuse. After a few rounds of postwork Beefeater martinis, I'd popped into Les Hommes merely looking to get my rocks off, not to smoke rock.

I answered, "Sure. Why not?" as some specific why nots came to mind.

Because we might get caught.

Because we might get thrown out.

Because we might get caught, get thrown out, and get arrested.

Because coke is merely recreational, but crack is ghetto.

But the courage from the gin inside me and the sick thrill of watching my new blond friend take a drag off the pipe—his googly eyes lit by the flame of the lighter and the blue flicker of the booth's porn video screen—made me accept his offer.

With his jittery left hand he held the pipe to my mouth and tried to light its tail with the flick, flick of the cheap lighter, the kind they sometimes give you free with a pack of cigarettes. "Damn! This thing's a piece of shit." *It's free for a reason.* "What are we going to do?"

"Shhh," I said, paranoia setting in before the first hit.

He played with the flame adjuster and flicked the lighter again. The flame shot an inch high and wrapped around the pipe, dancing close to my nose. I reared back. *Wasn't this what Richard Pryor was doing when his face caught on fire?*

"Quick, man. Breathe deep."

I did as I was told, taking in the gray genie smoke in three quick gasps. The warm ahhh of euphoria was immediate, and the desire to copulate was feral. We gave each other a few sloppy kisses and his hands buzzed all over my body like hummingbirds too excited to land.

"Hey, wanna get out of here and go to my place?" he asked. "I live just around the corner."

"Yeah. Let's go." *I'm just a girl who cain't say no. I'm in a terrible fix.*

We opened our buddy booth to the harsh glare of fluorescent lights. *What a buzzkill.* But the lights weren't to blame. I had forgotten that the buzz of crack is killed over and over, almost as fast as it's ignited.

We exited Les Hommes into the orange glow of dusk. Crackie halted me with his hand as he stood on the sidewalk and looked both ways as if we were being trailed. Confident that the coast was clear, he motioned me to follow. "Okay. Let's go."

In the last flicker of the fading sun I could see that his jeans were a little grimy. His T-shirt frayed. As awake as he was, Crackie was exhausted. I was following a madman. *You're easily led,* I could hear Mama Jean saying.

Crackie really did live around the corner, a right and then another right. However, we had to zigzag across the street a couple of times. "Just in case we're being followed," he said. As he was unlocking the door to his third-floor, walk-up apartment, he froze and looked at me gravely. "Hey, I should warn you." *Isn't it a little late for warnings?* "My apartment's kind of messy. I've been really busy lately. No time to clean."

"No worries."

"I also don't have that much rock left."

My experience with tricks who apologize for the atypical messiness of their apartment is that the mess is not only typical but often downright filthy. He opened the door into a one-room apartment and fumbled for something in the fluorescent light of the hall. Click. The apartment was illuminated by a big-screen TV, silently playing porn. It was as if we'd never left Les Hommes.

He shut the door. When my eyes adjusted to the gloom, I saw that his place wasn't an apartment but a satellite office of the city dump. There were piles of dirty clothes, piles of cartons of half-eaten Chinese food, piles of unopened mail, piles of magazines, piles of newspapers, piles of CDs, piles of piles. *It's enough to uncurl your public hair.* The only piece of furniture I could see was the bed. We shed our clothes and climbed on the bed, becoming two more useless piles. We smoked what was left of the rock and stared at porn on his large-screen TV. *There's nothing more disgusting than a large-screen TV in a small studio, except for a large-screen TV over a fireplace.* The burning desire to copulate had melted away, the high of the crack having trumped the low of my baser instincts.

"Should I get some more?" He looked at me with a lunatic's eyes. "I can get some more. I'll get some more. Want me to get some more?"

No. "Okay."

I wanted to leave, but I couldn't. *Maybe just one more hit and then I'll leave.* It felt like one of those dreams in which you want to run but are powerless to move. Besides, I didn't want to hurt his feelings.

As Crackie pulled on his clothes while peeking beyond the drawn window shade—*just in case*—the phone rang. And rang. Next to the TV I could see the maniacally blinking red message light of his answering machine. *That's a lot of piled-up messages in that machine.*

"Go away!" he screamed at the phone until the machine picked up.

After his greeting answered—which didn't say, *I'm smoking crack for the next month, so don't bother to leave a message*—the caller spoke desperately into the machine. "Hey, girl. Did you get my messages? Why don't you call me back? If you're there, pick up. Come on! Now your mother's calling *me*. What am I supposed to tell her? She's really worried. I'm worried too. What's going on?"

We stopped and stared at the disembodied voice coming from the machine.

"Shut up! Shut the *fuck* up!" Crackie screamed at the speaker.

The caller paused and asked one last question before hanging up. "Where have you been, man? Where have you been?"

I could hear Mama Jean. I didn't hear her saying, *Where the* hell *have you been?*, as she was fond of saying into my answering machine or into my ear when I did pick up. I heard her say, *Where have you been, Lord Randall, my son?*, as she did when I was a little boy, whenever I had been out of her orbit for a time. The sound of her voice in my head was the sound of what was left of my conscience.

As Crackie left his apartment to get more drugs, he said, "I won't be long, man. I'll be back soon." In the scant hour we had known each other, he'd apparently deemed me trustworthy enough to guard his filth.

After he was gone, I sat among the ruins of his life, staring at that blinking red light. *How did two drinks after work turn into five and slide into smoking crack at dusk?* Michahaze was waiting for me at home. I had work tomorrow. It was still light outside. It wasn't too late to return to safety.

I finally stopped staring at the red light and said out loud, "I have to leave." I pulled on my clothes and got the hell out of there.

I never asked Mama Jean why she called me Lord Randall. I had since learned it's the name of an ancient Anglo-Scottish ballad. As I hurried home to Michahaze, the ballad echoed in my gin-cracked head.

> "O where have you been, Lord Randall, my son?
> And where have you been, my handsome young man?"
> "I have been at the greenwood; mother, make my bed soon,
> For I'm wearied with hunting, and fain would lie down." . . .
> "O I fear you are poisoned, Lord Randall, my son!
> I fear you are poisoned, my handsome young man!"
> "O yes, I am poisoned; mother, make my bed soon,
> For I'm sick at the heart, and fain would lie down."

TWENTY

Account Past Due

C an I get my bath now?" Mama Jean asked as she stood impa-
tiently in the bedroom doorway of the new apartment
Michahaze and I'd just bought in Chelsea.

"Yes." I sailed past her toward the kitchen to get more coffee.
"Bathroom is all yours." She always took a bath, never a shower,
because a shower would threaten her once-a-week hairdo, which
she had had done to travelproof perfection the day before she left
Beaumont.

"Good. Because I have to hurry. Jeffrey's picking me up at nine."

"Me too. I have to be out the door in twenty minutes for an early
meeting."

Mama Jean's solo visit was for three reasons: to see our new
Chelsea apartment, which she had helped us get, to see my brother
Jeffrey's house in the Berkshires, and to see her current heart-
throb, Hugh Jackman, in the Broadway musical *The Boy from
Oz*. Actually, four reasons, the fourth being to see Jackman a
second time in *The Boy from Oz*.

Michahaze and I were not quite ready for her visit. We had barely
been two weeks in the place, a fabulous, sunny, tenth-floor loft

apartment with windows as tall as the twelve-foot ceilings and views of the Hudson River and the Empire State Building. We hadn't worked out its kinks, such as the air-conditioning. She was here during an unseasonably hot June week. Our bedroom was the only room that had AC, and luckily, that's where Mama Jean was staying, sleeping in the ornate Victorian bed that had been in her family for years. When she gave it to us, she said, "Generations of my family on Mother's side were born in this bed. I guess this is the end of the line."

Mama Jean could barely wait to visit. She wanted to see where her money had gone. She had taken a second-mortgage loan on her house to help us with the down payment, a loan I was to pay the monthly interest on until the day I could pay her back. I didn't want to ask her for the loan. I didn't want to be in the red with her. Even when she lovingly lavished on me the trips to Europe in high school, the cars, the expensive college education, to my mind she was always waving a bill that showed past-due amounts that added up to a grand total of "prove you love me as much as I love you." I felt that I could never thank her enough, never level the playing field, never pay off the grand total.

The night before, we had seen *The Boy from Oz,* the musical about singer/songwriter Peter Allen, who had been Judy Garland's lover, married Judy's daughter Liza, but was gay and died of AIDS. *And Mama Jean thinks my life is sordid?* When I was a kid, I was watching old footage of Judy on TV as Mama Jean cut a diagonal swath across the den in a hurry for work. "Look, Mom! It's Judy Garland." Without stopping, she dismissed Judy with "*Uh!* Worst degenerate Hollywood *ever* produced!" She'd since revised her opinion, classifying Judy an alcoholic victim of both Hollywood and her stage mother.

"I'm telling you, Hugh Jackman is going to be a *huge* star! Listen to me. I can pick 'em." The second time she saw the show, Mr. Jackman called her name from the stage during a riff with the audience. She sounded like a schoolgirl when she retold the story. "You should have heard him! He called my *name*! He said, 'Jean!'"

I wasn't as hopped up as she was to see the show. I'd heard it was schmaltzy and maudlin, so I wasn't expecting to flood tears as Peter Allen lay dying of AIDS while his devoted mother sat by his side. I hid my tears from Mama Jean.

At intermission I left her in her seat to go to the bathroom but sneaked in a quick pop. I always—almost—controlled my drinking around her, but especially after the aborted attempt to get sober. When I told her that I was drinking again, she said, "But you told me that 'one's too many and eleven is never enough.'" She was throwing back in my face some of the bumper-sticker wisdom I'd picked up at meetings. "Well, those meetings taught me how to keep it under control." *Let's not think about that night in Rio.*

Shaking her head, she said, "If you say so," making it clear that *she* didn't say so.

So on that hot morning as we were rushing to get ready, the combination of the heat in the apartment and the heat in my body from last night's bourbon nightcaps left me cranky and wet with sweat. By the time I reached the kitchen to pour my second cup of coffee, I thought of how I had Mama Jean–proofed the apartment: hidden the blue movies, hidden my old books on alcoholism, and hidden anything in the nightstand drawers I didn't want her to see. I wished she had waited until later to visit, after we had worked out all the kinks in the apartment— *Oh, shit!*

"Don't turn on the"—I heard the bathtub faucet go on, which meant that she was leaning over the tub and beneath the showerhead—"shower!" One of the kinks we hadn't worked out was the shower valve, which was stuck in the on position, so that when the water was turned on, it automatically sprayed from the showerhead. I had forgotten to switch the valve to the faucet position.

"My hair! My hair!" I heard her shriek like the Wicked Witch of the West after Dorothy douses her with a bucket of water. I ran to the bathroom. She was standing at the door clutching a towel to cover her naked body. She pointed with her thumb at her hair. "My hair is *ruined*!" I didn't know what she was talking about. The proscenium arch of hair around her face looked as perfect as it had only seconds before.

"It looks okay to me." She turned her head to show me the back. It resembled the side of a mountain after a mudslide. She jabbed her thumb at the air in front of it. "Does *this* look okay to you?!" She didn't wait for an answer. "What am I going to do? This hair was supposed to last me a week!" Jeffrey was picking her up at nine to drive her to his house in the Berkshires.

"I . . . I don't know." I turned to Michahaze, who had emerged from the den, where he and I had been sleeping on the pullout sofa, and shot him a desperate look of help. "But I have to get to work."

Michahaze, always the calm voice in any storm, said, "Jean, it'll be okay. I'm sure that once you get to the Berkshires, you can find a hairdresser."

She shot back, "They don't know how to do hair like this up there!" As always, she was right.

During that trip, a tumor of dread was growing inside me like cancer. It was the fear of giving her bad news, news that couldn't have had worse timing, given that we had just moved into the apartment that she had helped us buy. I didn't tell her on that trip. I waited until I absolutely had to, later that summer. It was the fear of telling Mama Jean that Michahaze and I were not coming home for Thanksgiving. Every year, for thirteen years straight, Michahaze and I had made that trip to Beaumont for Thanksgiving to decorate the tree. And I returned not quite four weeks later for her big party, Christmas, and to de-decorate the tree.

That we weren't coming home for Thanksgiving was a big deal.

Logically, I knew it shouldn't be, but with her this was a breach of contract. We were going to Mr. Parker's brother's wedding in Mexico. I knew the conversation wouldn't be pretty. Usually dreaded conversations don't go as badly as one expects. This one went worse.

Before the conversation, on a Sunday morning, I fortified myself with my usual weekend *day* drinks—Bloody Marys and Greyhounds (grapefruit and vodka)—to gather the courage to tell her. That's not quite true. As usual when I told her something she didn't want to hear—such as coming out to her on the phone—it was because she asked. I was on my third drink when she called to ask when Michahaze and I were going to book our tickets for Thanksgiving. LBD hit. I felt as if I were ten years old on top of the high dive at the Beaumont Country Club swimming pool, terrified to take the plunge. I took a supersize gulp of my Greyhound and jumped into the deep end.

"Did I tell you that Mr. Parker's brother Doug is getting married?"

"No."

"Well, you know, Michael and I got to know Doug well when he was living in DC, and of course their mother, Suzanne, has become a good friend since she's been living in DC and visits New York all the time."

"Uh-huh." It felt like the lead-up to the "two kinds of sex" talk.

"Well, they've invited us to the wedding. And Doug has asked me to be a reader at the wedding." I lied about the reader bit to add gravitas to my being there.

"Mmm . . ."

"Anyway, they're going all out for the wedding. It's going to be on the beach about forty miles from Cancún."

"He's going all that way to get married? Who's he marrying?"

"A girl named Esther. She's actually Mexican, but grew up in California. The thing is, the wedding is Thanksgiving weekend.

And Suzanne really wants Michael and me there. She considers us family."

"Just what exactly are you telling me?"

"I'm telling you that we're going to Doug's wedding in Mexico this Thanksgiving."

"And you're not coming home?"

"No."

"But you come home *every* Thanksgiving. I count on that. You know how important the holidays are to me."

"Well, I'll be there at Christmas, like I am *every* year."

"We're not talking about Christmas. We're talking about Thanksgiving."

"I know, and we've been there every Thanksgiving for the last thirteen years. We really want to go to the wedding, and I've been asked to be in it. And it's important to Suzanne. She considers us family." *Wrong thing to say.*

"Suzanne?! What about *me*? *She's* like family to you? She's *not* family! *I'm* your family!"

"That's *not* what I said. I said that she *considers* us family." Another gulp of the Greyhound.

"That's what you meant. I can't believe you're doing this to me, and after all I've done for you."

"I didn't say that I'm never coming home again, and I'll be there at Christmas."

"And who's going to decorate the tree?"

"That's what it's about!" I exploded. "That damn tree! Fine. I'll *hire* someone to come decorate the tree. It'll be my present to you."

"Oh, stop it. It's not about the tree. It's about having you here where you belong."

Neither of us spoke for what seemed like a month of Thanksgivings.

"So you're not going to be here?" she asked, giving me a last chance to cave and redeem myself.

"No."

More silence.

"Well, you have really shit in the nest this time. I have nothing more to say to you."

And she didn't for about three weeks, which left me tortured and guilt ridden. I called Dad to at least get his blessing and absolve myself of some guilt. "She'll get over it," he said with resignation. "Go on and live your life."

Once again I was in the red, and the grand total of "prove you love me as much as I love you" of that imaginary bill was in the negative digits, but I had finally broken the pattern. I had finally stood up for myself. It just took a few drinks to say what I needed to say, that's all.

TWENTY-ONE

Lost in Paterson

Just as there's a photo of me somewhere in Kansas, there's a photo of me somewhere in Paterson. I've never seen it, but the details of that snapshot are as cloudy to me as every other detail of the day it was taken. I'm standing on an icicle-covered bridge and oozing an anemic smile; my eyes are as dull and dingy as the frozen snow surrounding me. Besides that wan smile, I'm wearing a charcoal-gray topcoat over yesterday's outfit. My face is puffy, and if the photograph weren't in black and white, you could see that my skin is splotchy red, almost the color of my fading copper hair. Instead of an Acapulco beach, raging waterfalls are behind me and I'm facing the photographer, but I'm not looking at him. I'm standing with my gloved hands in my pockets, shoulders hunched, and looking in the direction of Manhattan, wondering how I ended up in Paterson. *New Jersey*.

When I woke up—came to, really—on the morning that photo was taken, I wondered why Michahaze had put the alarm-clock radio on a Spanish talk station. An animated, but one-sided, conversation in Spanish was emanating from a corner of the bedroom. I pried open my sleep-encrusted eyes, but I wasn't staring at the deep-red ceiling of our bedroom. Instead, I faced a drop ceiling, the kind with rectangular panels of alternating Styrofoam-esque material and fluorescent lights, like in an office building. I wasn't next to Michahaze in the Victorian bed that Mama Jean had given us. I was alone in a twin bed. *Where am I?* "Uhhh," I groaned. *It is going to be an orange-alert hangover.*

Across the bedroom in the opposite corner was the source of the talk radio: last night's amigo sitting next to a brown, dorm-room fridge and talking on the phone in Spanish. I wasn't in a bedroom, but a studio apartment. Well, not even that. It was just a narrow room, about the size of a middle manager's office. On top of the fridge was a collection of black-and-white photographs in drugstore frames.

Fragments of last night started to descend like snowflakes: each one was different, just hard to make out. The last venue of what must have been a multi-venue night was a scant half block from our Chelsea apartment. *Oh, I was so close to ending up in my own bed, and now I'm . . . Where am I?* The evening's preamble before that penultimate stop was a wash. *Where is Michahaze in the tally of the evening's events? Had we started out together and I kept going? Or had I been flying solo the whole evening?*

Just one more must have been what I was thinking. *Just one more.*

Here's what I could piece together:

Stumbling up Seventh Avenue to my street, but turning west away from the safety of my apartment because it occurred to me that in the basement of the Chelsea Hotel was a new gay hot spot.

Descending into a murky sea of faceless heads floating in a dark nightclub.

Three Latino guys—a tall drink of rum and two pocket-size ones— giggling like geishas.

The raising of glasses. "Salud!" The locking of lips—mine and those of Mr. Glass of Rum.

"You come home with us? Ees not far. I would bery much like you to be my guest tonight. Sí?"

"Sure. Why not?"

Sailing in a van with my new amigos while in deep lip-lock with Mr. Glass of Rum. Did I get his name?

Visions through the winter-crudded window of a cluster of Manhattanites bundled up under a red DON'T WALK *sign, then the beady, white eyes of vehicular fish swimming toward us in the black abyss of a highway.*

Me asking, "Hey? Where are we going?" The geishas answering with giggles, "We already told you!"

The van dropping me and Mr. Glass of Rum—Juan? Julio? Carlos?—in a deserted back alley of what looked like a cheap office building.

Then black.

As I lay there staring at the drop ceiling—about the only thing I remembered from the previous night's sex—I remembered why the building looked like a cheap office building. Because it *was* a cheap office building. Mr. Rum told me it had been converted into "studio" apartments.

While cradling the crescent-moon phone receiver between his ear and shoulder, my host turned and smiled beatifically at me from across the narrow room. He was older than I remembered him to be from seven hours ago, like ten to twelve years older. *Thank God he isn't coyote ugly.* Actually, he was a hot daddy with salt-and-pepper, close-cropped hair—always a sexy look to me.

"Sí, Mamacita."

Oh my God, he was talking to his mother.

"Él tiene pelo rojo, Mamacita. Sí, es natural!"

I didn't speak Spanish, but I'd traveled over enough South American sheets to pick up that he was telling her I had genuine red hair. *Did he tell her that he could prove it?*

"Su nombre es Jaime."

Correct. My name is "Hi-may." But what, pray tell, is yours?

After he hung up, he walked across the room and sat on the edge of the bed and smiled down at me. "That was my mother in Colombia. I talk to her e'ery Sunday. I was telling her about chu. I tell her *e'erything*."

"I'm close to my mother too." *But not that close.*

Mr. Glass of Rum caressed my earlobe. "Are you hungry, my dear Hi-may?"

"Oh, I really should be getting back to town." I sat up in bed and ran my fingers through my hair to the back of my neck, which I grabbed to keep my throbbing head from exploding. I looked out the window through yellowing white plastic miniblinds to discern where I was. All I saw were telephone lines and rooftops of gray asphalt shingles set against a dirty-white sky. "Uh, where exactly are we?"

He chuckled. "Aw, baby. You don't remember, do you?" I sheepishly shrugged my shoulders no. "We are in my town. Paterson."

"New Jersey?"

"*Sí.*"

Oh, God. I did it again. I'd broken my no-outer-borough rule for hookups: Manhattan only. I'd ended up in various Brooklyn neighborhoods, Queens, even the Bronx—but Paterson? New Jersey? *This deserves a special Wanderlust Travel Award (emphasis on* lust*).*

"Oh. Well, fancy that. But, really, I'd better be getting back to the city."

"Why you have to go so soon? You should eat first. Have you ever been to Paterson?"

"I don't think I have."

"Ah. Then I will show you *my* Paterson! Then I will drive you home."

Before I could say, *"Buenos días, Mamacita,"* we were in his truck. A large, professional Nikon camera sat between us on the bench seat. The truck crept along the quiet Sunday Main Street, which was lonelier than a Hopper painting. A border of snow-caked cars of a decade ago was in front of crumbling beaux arts–style buildings mixed in with aluminum-sided storefronts promising weaves, wigs, and Checks Cashed.

My ambassador to Paterson told me his life story: besides his beloved *mamacita* back in Colombia, he had a teenage son from a onetime romp with a woman (*All it takes is one time,* I could hear Mamacita Jean saying) when he was a teenager himself; a move to the States for a better life, where he worked as a graphic artist and indulged his passion for photography on the side.

He took me to an empty Colombian restaurant where the staff outnumbered the patrons ten to two. They all knew him, but to my frustration never said his name. After a screwdriver and some Colombian empanadas, I started to feel human again.

I slipped away to the bathroom and called Michahaze on my cell phone, hoping that the answering machine would pick up.

He answered with a terse and suspicious "Hello?"

"Hi, Michael. It's me."

Then a formal "Hello, James. How are you?"

"Oh, I'm okay. Last night lasted longer than I anticipated"— weak chuckle—"but I'm headed home soon." As always during those morning-after calls, I decided to keep the details to a minimum.

As always, he kept his responses curt. "Very well, James. I'm headed out to start my day and run some errands. Maybe I'll see you later." That meant he wouldn't be there when I got home, so we could both have some time to recover.

"Well, señor," I said when I returned to the table, as if *señor* were my sexy moniker for him, "this was *delicioso.* Shall we head back to the city?" I just wanted to get home, pour a tall Greyhound, and crawl into bed for a few hours.

"*Sí.* But first I must show you the most beautiful part of Paterson."

No! Please just take me home, I wanted to whimper. "Oh, I really should get back to town. I have a lot to do today."

"Okay, but you cannot leave Paterson without seeing the Great Falls."

Can't I just go home? "Oh, that's very sweet but I really should get back."

"Do you know the Niagara Falls?"

"Yes. I've been there."

"Well, the Great Falls are like these Niagara Falls. Like a—how you say?—*bebé* version."

I give up. "Sure. Why not?" I said, not remembering that those words had landed me in places—figurative and literal—like Paterson all the time.

His truck snaked up hilly streets until we reached the parking lot of the Paterson Great Falls National Historical Park. He grabbed that giant camera and we got out of the truck. Just as we were the only customers at the restaurant, we were the lone spectators at the waterfall.

"Someday I would like to live where you do, over there." He pointed west to Manhattan. We could actually see the northern tip of Manhattan from where we stood. "But the Great Falls make me very proud to live here. It makes me happy to show them to you for the first time." *And to think that all these years I was just a van's ride from the Great Falls.*

We crunched our way across the snow-covered, icy ground toward the Great Falls. I heard them before I saw them. Their cacophonous roar sounded the way my head felt. We crested a hill and there they were, frantically flowing into the Passaic River hundreds of feet below. Their hyper three-dimensionality almost seemed fake, set as they were against that still photograph of frozen tundra. They looked like a giant reproduction of a reproduction of a waterfall, the kind you used to see on a lighted Coors-beer clock. My tour guide was behind me, repeatedly firing his Nikon camera. The only two things alive at that moment were the Tour Guide of Paterson and the Great Falls. I felt as dead as the landscape surrounding us.

"Beautiful. *Sí?*" he shouted above the crash of the falls.

"Yes. Beautiful." *And terrifying.*

"Please. Stand on the bridge." He pointed with the long lens of the camera to an icicle-covered pedestrian bridge. "I want to take your photo so I can remember this day."

I really don't *want to remember this day.* "Oh, no. I don't want my picture taken. Not today." It was so cold. I was shivering and the reprieve I felt from the screwdriver and food was dissipating.

"*Para mi,* Hi-may. *Para mi.*"

I sighed. "Okay."

I walked onto the bridge and faced the Great Falls. They were falling, falling, falling into the swirling river, just a quick jump below. I thought of that van ride and how I was sucked up into the current of the night. I fantasized riding the falls down to the river and being swept away, never to see days like this again.

"*Hi-may!*" he shouted.

I turned around to see Latin Avedon pointing the camera at me. I was facing him but looking westerly, toward Manhattan. I tried to keep from shivering. I stuck my hands in my pockets and hunched my shoulders forward in a futile attempt to warm my body.

"*Say chis!*" he yelled.

I just want to go home. I cobbled together all the energy I could to birth a smile. "Cheese," I murmured, certain that he couldn't hear me.

The number one tourist attraction checked off on my tour of Paterson, we finally, *finally,* headed back to Manhattan. I explained to him that I had a longtime boyfriend, a husband, really, but we were open.

When Mr. Glass of Rum dropped me off in front of my apartment building, he held up the camera that contained the frozen image of me in front of the Great Falls of the Passaic River. With his other hand he gave me a slip of paper. I looked at it. *(973) 321-4568— Manuel Antonio.* Manuel Antonio!

"*Gracias,* Manuel Antonio." I enunciated every syllable of his name.

"Call me sometime, *mi amigo,* and I will send you the photo."

"I will do that," I said, but I knew I wouldn't because I never wanted to lay eyes on that photo.

I could see him back in Paterson boasting to his visiting *mamacita* about the copper-headed lush he'd picked up at a trendy club in Manhattan. When he tells that story, he points to the top of that dorm-room refrigerator, lousy with a collection of black-and-white photos in drugstore frames. In the center is a picture not of a bright-eyed, ripe teen, but of a puffy-faced man, wanly smiling in the gray of day as he stands in front of the Great Falls of the Passaic River—forever forlorn, forever hungover.

TWENTY-TWO

The Bare Truth

"What's barebacking?" Mama Jean asked as I cringed. She and Dad were visiting Michahaze and me, and I'd taken the day off work to spend it with them. She and I were watching the tale end of an episode of *Oprah* devoted to crystal meth addicts. Oprah was interviewing a gay man whose fabulous, successful life was destroyed when he became addicted to crystal and lost everything. As he explained it, he started barebacking and became HIV-positive.

I explained the phrase to Mama Jean. "It's when you have unprotected sex. Sex without a condom."

She screwed up her face in disgust. "Oh, God."

An hour later she, Dad, and I were having a drink in the living room when Michahaze came home from work. He said a brief hello and went directly through the open archway into the adjacent den to deal with a work issue.

Mama Jean leaned forward with a mischievous grin and whispered, "Bare-skinned? Bare-assed?"

"What?" I asked.

"What's it called? That thing that boy was talking about on *Oprah*? Bare-skinning?"

"Oh. Barebacking. Why?"

"Never mind." She held up her finger to silence me and leaned back into the sofa with a just-you-wait smirk on her face. Then: "Michael?"

"Yes, Jean?"

"Have you been barebacking lately?"

Dead silence.

Dad was shaking his head in resigned exasperation, his eyebrows raised.

Mama Jean was silently tee-heeing. She cocked her perfectly coiffed head with her ear in Michahaze's direction. "Michael? Did you hear me?"

Michahaze appeared in the archway with his expert poker face, which made him unflappable in any situation. "I heard you, Jean. But I'm not sure that I understood you."

"You don't know what barebacking is?"

"Riding sidesaddle?"

"Oh, come on. If you don't know what barebacking is, I'm worried about you."

I broke the charade and explained that she was just showing off the new term she had learned. We laughed uneasily over Mama Jean's little gotcha. The story became an instant classic before it was even dry, an award-winning entry in my repertoire of Mama Jean dinner-party stories—right up there with "two kinds of sex: oral and anal." But every time I laughed at the reaction it got, I cringed inside because of the secret I had been carrying around since the fling with Father John had ended, when we were still living on West Eighty-second Street.

Back when Father John called to tell me that he had the clap, I got checked out as I promised him I would. A few days after the exam, my doctor called me at my office at four-thirty.

"Hi, Jamie, it's Dr. Connolly."

"Oh, hey." I held a press release in my hand that I was proofreading.

"I have good news and bad news."

I laid the press release down. "Okay?" I said with a nervous rise in my voice.

"The good news: you don't have gonorrhea."

"That's a relief." But I wasn't relieved.

"The bad news: you're HIV-positive."

I closed my eyes and held the phone in silence. My mouth went dry. When I opened my eyes, they were still fixed on the press release, but I couldn't read a word. My vision was blurred.

I shouldn't have been surprised, but I was. All the negatives of tests past had lulled me into a false sense of being one of the lucky ones. When I went in for the clap check, Dr. Connolly asked if I wanted an HIV test, since it had been over a year since my last one. "Might as well," I said with nonchalance to hide from him— but more from myself—my fear that I had reason to worry.

"Are you sure?" I asked. Had he been joking, it would have been a cruel joke, but a cruel joke would have been better than the truth.

"Yes, I'm sure. But these days, it's a *manageable* condition." His voice was suddenly upbeat, as if I had just won the lottery, only it was the lottery in that famous Shirley Jackson story where the winner is stoned to death. "You may not even need to go on medication right now. Make an appointment and come into the office next week and we'll talk about it."

"Okay. I'll make an appointment." I hung up.

Is he supposed to tell me this on the phone? What if I opened my twenty-third-story window and jumped out? I shut my office door and sat at my desk like a zombie waiting for the workday to end. Why I didn't leave immediately, I don't know. At five on the dot I robotically rose from my desk and left the office as if I worked in accounting. If ever I *needed* a drink, it was then.

How many years do I have left? Five? Will I have to take those pills that give you sunken-face syndrome? How long have I been positive? Was there ever a more negative term than positive? *Did I get it from that guy in the bathhouse that time I did crystal meth with him? I know I didn't get it from Michahaze because we always have safe sex. Who knows where I got it, there were so many morning afters when I suddenly remembered that a condom hadn't been part of my night before. How stupid am I? I came of age when the AIDS epidemic was full-blown and safe sex was standard protocol. I'm not supposed to get this.* Mama Jean's warning echoed in my ear: "Remember, a moment's pleasure isn't worth a lifetime of regret." I couldn't tell her she was right and face her I-told-you-so wrath, but mostly I couldn't tell her because it would kill her. God, I needed Michahaze. But more than anything else, I needed a drink.

I sat on the crowded subway white-knuckling the ride until I could gulp a martini. Someone seemed to be staring at me. I looked up, and floating in the sea of strangers was the pale, wan face of a man who was a dead ringer for the actor who played the sad, middle-aged uncle with AIDS on the gay soap opera *Queer as Folk.* Maybe he actually was that actor. Once when I was watching the show while visiting Mama Jean and Dad in Beaumont, Mama Jean walked into the room. "What's on TV?"

"*Queer as Folk.* Ever seen it?"

"Uh, yes!" she said in disgust. "If your life's that sordid, I feel sorry for you." *My life is that sordid and I love it,* I wanted to say as she walked out of the room.

The hangdog, pallid face of the man stared at me. *Is he cruising me?* I moved to the end of the car to get away from his gaze. I couldn't. No matter where I went, his eyes followed me, like the Uncle Sam I WANT YOU poster, only it was Uncle AIDS who wanted me. As if I were the only one in the subway car who could see Uncle AIDS, I was convinced he was an apparition.

When I got out of the subway, I headed straight for the Works, aka the Last Chance Saloon, glancing behind me to make sure my fate wasn't following me. I parked myself on a stool and ordered my drink, Beefeater martini, dry, up, with a twist, and drained it. "Another, please." It was barely five-thirty, so only a handful of people were in the bar. I felt a man standing behind me, watching. I turned around and was relieved not to see Uncle AIDS, but instead a new stranger with a concerned face. He asked me what was wrong. The dam broke and in a flood of tears I told this nameless stranger that I was positive. That my life was over. That no one would want to have sex with me again. He said that it wasn't true. To prove it, he took me to Les Hommes and had sex with me. Only then did I truly understand what Blanche DuBois meant about always depending upon the kindness of strangers.

By six-thirty I was home drinking a fresh gin and tonic and robotically blowing cigarette smoke into the air when Michahaze came home. He kissed me as he always kissed me when he came home from work. He looked at my red, puffy face. "Is something wrong?" He sat on the sofa across from me with his unflappable poker face.

I put out the cigarette and I nodded my head yes. My lips curled inside my mouth as the tears started to break again.

"What is it?"

"I had an HIV test. I'm positive." The tears broke.

"Oh, no." His face cracked—a hairline fracture—but it cracked.

I abandoned my chair and crawled onto the sofa and lay my head in his lap and guttural cried as he held me and caressed my head.

TWENTY-THREE

Gown Days

S top making me laugh," Liz's reflection in the nightclub mirror said to mine as I sipped my usual martini. "It hurts when I laugh." She turned away from my reflection in the mirror to my actual face. She was dolled up for the company Christmas party in black velvet pants and a winter-white angora cardigan with rhinestone buttons. Trash disco played to an empty dance floor while the rest of our colleagues ate and drank on the sidelines.

I was imitating the Brits, which always made her laugh, and telling her one of my blue tales from the time I lived in London my junior year of college. "Well, you lived over there," I said to her. "You know how disgusting and *wrong* the food is in England. So I was having a *very* playful time with a new boyfriend. 'I have an idear,'" I said, mimicking his Cockney accent. "So he ran naked to the kitchen and returned with some creamy, white stuff spread on his dick. When I swooped down to inhale every sweet drop of what I assumed was whipped cream, I gagged. It wasn't sweet at all. It tasted like paste. 'Puh! Puh!' I said, and spit it out. 'What *is* that?' He looked at me, hurt. 'Plain yogurt.'"

At "plain yogurt" she spit out the cabernet she had just started to swallow. Laughing with closed eyes, she waved her left hand at me to halt while holding her abdomen with her right. "I told you. Stop making me laugh. It hurts too much."

"What's so funny, dearies?" Jo Ann asked as she joined us. Jo Ann was the editorial director and Liz's second-in-command. A veteran editor who specialized in psychology books, Jo Ann was one of those native New Yorkers of a certain age who mixed a dry wit with maternal concern. Anne Bancroft would have played her in the movie.

"Him," Liz said, holding her abdomen with both hands. "A blue tale involving yogurt."

"*Plain* yogurt," I said.

Jo Ann cut both of us a look over her glasses. Then, in a falsetto singsong: "I can only imagine." She pointed to Liz's abdomen. "So, do we know more about what's going on there?"

"No!" Liz said, annoyed. She'd been having abdominal pain for several weeks. "And it's starting to interfere with my sex life. That's not good. Because I like sex *a lot*." She looked at me with a twinkle in her eye, a mischievous smile as if it were meant only for me, and kiss-ready lips—the Look of Liz, I called it—and said, "Oh, I long for the day when we don't work together and we can *really* get to know each other. I have so much more to tell you."

"Me too, but come on. Let's at least dance tonight!" I dragged her to the dance floor.

"Wait for me, dearies!" Jo Ann was as in love with Liz as I.

The three of us punished the parquet, twirling and laughing to my favorite disco hits: "Don't Leave Me This Way," "I Will Survive," "Love Hang Over." Our joy was contagious. Soon our colleagues danced around us. My martini buzz was perfect, so I was feeling no pain. I pushed aside the anxiety over the recent Caine Mutiny of my staff, which had been causing me enormous worry and pain. If Liz was worried about the mysterious pain in her abdomen, she ignored it for that brief, euphoric moment.

Early in the 2006 New Year, a few weeks after the disco music had faded from the office Christmas party, Liz took me out to a come-to-Jesus lunch to discuss the near collapse of my small department. A series of petty rivalries had broken out among my staff over my favoritism of Jason, the comely, gay one. He was like a young me (only much more handsome), and I was replaying the dynamic between Jack and me, with me starring in the Jack role. The resentments exploded when I promoted Jason, eventually causing two staff members to resign. My management answer throughout all of this was to throw alcohol on the rising fire and treat everyone to drinks at Mesa de España after work. *But I'm a fun boss. Why don't they like me?* Not thinking to ask, *Why don't they respect me?* Eventually, they all stopped accepting my Mesa de España invitations. *Have I become Michael Scott, the boss from The Office?*

The New Year lunch with Liz didn't come after the shit hit the fan, but after it hit the corner office. Before Lea, one of the resigning staff members, left, she had an exit interview with the CEO of the company. Lea sold me down the river. What Lea told the CEO I don't know, but everything was probably prefaced with the adverb *too*: *too* much attention to Jason, *too* many drinks at lunch, *too* many drinks after work, *too* many sick days. The CEO shared with Liz the conversation he'd had with Lea, which is why Liz took me to lunch. Liz didn't tell me what Lea unloaded in the corner office, other than to say, "She was one angry bitch."

When the waiter took our drink order, I made a big show of ordering Perrier, and Liz winked at me. Then she got serious. She was wearing the same Christmas-party sweater of winter-white angora with the rhinestone buttons that sparkled like the bubbles in the Perrier I was drinking.

"My heart is so heavy over all these problems with your staff." Her heart either sang or it was heavy. She acknowledged that I had had a bad mix of people working for me that had caused the stars to align against me. She gave me a pep talk about needing to hire good people—and fast—to get the department back on solid ground.

With her elbows resting on the table and her hands pointing at me in a prayer gesture, she said, "I know you've battled your demons with alcohol, so if you need help, honey, find it." I shook my head yes. "But trust me, you *don't* want the CEO to get involved." She didn't mention my disastrous spin on the dais at that sales conference nearly three years ago. She didn't mention the time I showed up late to an author meeting, my body a Niagara Falls of sweaty booze. What a mistake to have ever told her I was getting sober during that "dial on/dial off" time of not drinking. *How long ago was that trip to Rio?*

Later that January, not long after five P.M. one day, everyone but me heard Jo Ann let loose a shriek straight out of a Hitchcock movie. Karen, Liz's partner, had phoned to say that Liz had been diagnosed with ovarian cancer. Stage four. I didn't hear the scream because I had already left the office for Mesa de España to have my usual martinis before my commute home. My commute was a mere ten-minute walk, but come quitting time I needed that drink and couldn't wait until I got home.

I sat alone on the red vinyl seat of the barstool along with the other solo regulars, bitterly drinking over work, drinking over my department, who'd done me wrong, and drinking over yesterday's drinking. *So what if I drink a lot after work. So what if I have a few at lunch. I still come back to work and do my job. So what if I have a few sick days. So what?!*

The warring voices in my head shut up long enough for me to focus on one of the regulars. He always sat in the middle of the long end of the bar drinking a martini and reading the newspaper, occasionally staring at his reflection, which floated above the bottles in the mirror behind the bar. He looked kind of like me, but ten years older. We never spoke or even acknowledged each other as I sat at the short end of the bar, drinking my martini and reading the paper. Watching him was like staring into a looking glass:

The martini is placed before the man. He looks down at it, almost salivating. He reaches out his right hand to pick it up, but sees that the hand shakes like a palsy victim's. Then he reaches out the left hand to help the right hand pick up the filled-to-the-brim glass that he knows from experience will spill with the least tremor. The left hand is equally shaky. So he waits until no one is looking, and like a trained seal playing a horn, he dives into the drink to suck up two robust sips. The hit of booze is the medicine he needs, and it calms his shaking hands enough to allow him to pick up the glass with both hands like a toddler holding a sippy cup.

When I heard the news about Liz the next day, my first thought was *Jesus Christ. This is curtains for Liz.* My second thought: *This is curtains for me.*

This job was no longer any fun and I didn't want to be there without Liz, but I was going to hold it together while she was out sick. "Titties up, girl! Titties up," I said to myself. I was going to whip my department into shape. I was going to make bestsellers out of all of our books. I wasn't going to be out "sick" anymore. I was going to be early to work. I was going to cut back on the drinking and not drink at lunch. I was going to do it for Liz.

Liz had not returned to the office after the diagnosis. Sometime in early February, after we had received intermittent reports of her progress funneled through Jo Ann, Liz surprised me with a call on my cell phone as I was returning to the office from lunch. I read the caller ID, "Liz Cell," and couldn't flip open my tiny phone fast enough.

"Hello, Liz?"

She answered a staccato "Hi," her voice almost ethereal.

"Oh, Liz! Hello. *Hello.*" She was probably having nothing but "gown days"—Mama Jean's name for days when she didn't get out of her nightgown or put on her face. However, I didn't imagine Liz in a nightgown when I spoke to her. I saw her in that winter-white angora sweater with rhinestone buttons. She asked how *I* was, then asked if I would attend a dinner for a Catholic conservative author of hers in her place. "Tell him that I can't attend"— she said her next lines in mock horror—"because I have *ovarian* cancer! That's a good excuse, right?" We both laughed. "I may be sick, but I'm still funny." It made me think of Peggy Lee: *Can't even get out of bed. But I've still got the voice.* When the call ended, I stood on the corner holding the phone as if it were Liz herself.

After that her prognosis grew more dismal every day. Jo Ann classified the reports she received from Karen as "not good." I tried to cobble together my department. I tried to be on top of my game. I tried to do it for Liz, but my titties began to sag. If the road to hell was paved with good intentions, the road to the bar was paved with broken promises.

In mid-February I lost it on Mr. Parker's bed in the middle of his studio apartment, which was packed ass cheek to jowl with party guests. I was in hot-pink corduroy pants and a faux-mink jacket (a sad substitute for the Persian lamb), so I wasn't exactly inconspicuous. Here's what I remember:

Arriving with Michahaze at four in the afternoon in good spirits.

Three hours later crying hysterically in a puddle on Mr. Parker's bed about the dying Liz.

Sliding repeatedly into the snow like a Pink Panther rag doll while Michahaze tried frantically to hail a cab.

What I don't remember: *biting Jason on the neck on my way out of the party.*

Then black.

The hangover the next day was award winning, even though I slept until two in the afternoon. I thought I was going to die. No, really. I thought I was going to die. Michahaze and I were shopping at Home Depot. My head was the weight of a bowling ball, my legs were wobbly, and the right side of my abdomen throbbed. I didn't tell Michahaze how sick I felt. I pressed on the spot on my abdomen where it hurt. *Isn't that where the liver is? Oh, God. My liver is going to explode just like Jack Kerouac's. Right here in the Home Depot in front of the $19.99 orchids.*

Every day wasn't a question of *would* I be hungover, but to what debilitating degree? If the degree was major, I'd call in sick and have a gown day.

After one of those gown days I was sitting at my desk, paralyzed by an overwhelming to-do list that had piled up. I was praying that a guillotine would relieve me of my head and its throbbing pain when Jo Ann walked into my office. I sat up and tried to perkify myself. "Hey! What's up?"

Jo Ann didn't smile and didn't sit down. She stood at the edge of my desk and peered down at me over the reading glasses she had chained around her neck. "Jamie, I'm not your boss—"

"Sorry I missed yesterday. How was the meeting?"

"Listen to me. I'm not your boss and I can't tell you what to do—"

"What are you talking about? I was out sick. I mean, I'm sorry but—"

"Let me finish. I hope you're feeling better, but you've been out a lot lately, and now that Liz is"—Jo Ann closed her eyes, searching for the word—"out, the CEO has started to notice. When I showed up to yesterday's meeting without you, he asked where you were. 'Out sick,' I said. *'Again?'* 'Apparently.'" She gave me what must have been the same *Who knows?* shrug of her shoulders she had given the CEO. She paused and glared at me over her glasses before adding, "'Not good,' he said. 'Not good.'"

Not good is almost British in its understatement because it always means more than "bad." It means "disastrous," "calamitous," "critical condition." I tried to rationalize the phrase as "not great," "slightly marginal," "could be better." I was deluded.

"Uh-huh. Well, thanks so much for telling me. I appreciate that. I promise I won't miss another meeting."

She sat down. "Jamie, dearie," she said with a nervous chuckle to try to lighten the moment. "I used to have a colleague who drank so much every night that he had to drink at lunch to steady his nerves the next day, the hangovers were so bad."

"Uh-huh."

"He didn't always make it to lunch because he didn't always make it to work."

"Uh-huh."

"I'm just saying that you'd better be on the lookout."

"Thanks, Jo Ann. Thanks for that."

When I had gown days, they were usually precipitated by a dressing drink. A dressing drink used to be the cocktail or two I drank while getting ready to go out for the evening. It had morphed into the drink or two I had while I got ready for work in the morning after Michahaze had left for work. I didn't drink every morning, but I needed to. When I lost the battle, it meant drinking a couple of vodka screwdrivers. By the time I left for work, the crispy, crunchy feeling and penetrating self-loathing had temporarily lifted and I walked with a spring in my step.

But I liked the mornings when I lost the battle completely. If after two dressing drinks the self-loathing hadn't evaporated and the routine barfing hadn't relieved my physical malaise, I'd tell myself that tomorrow is another day, wave the white flag in complete surrender, and call in sick.

It was a tremendous relief.

Then I'd pour a tall vodka on the rocks in an iced-tea glass, abandoning the pretense of fruit juice. I'd place the untouched drink on the nightstand, not even taking a sip until everything was in place. I'd close the louvers on the tall window shutters and block out the day. I'd undress. I'd unmake the bed. Then I'd slip between the sheets, my head slightly propped up on the pillows. I'd pick up the drink with both shaking hands and hold it up like a chalice. I'd take a long, deep gulp and allow myself to luxuriate in the sensation of the booze sliding down my throat, making me warm, pulling me down into oblivion. At last I could enjoy the drink without worry or fear that someone might see me. I was at one with the drink. The annoying sounds of the city ten floors below, coming more alive as the day blossomed, faded with each sip until I started to feel myself slipping, slipping . . . *Ahh.*

I never saw Liz again, and the "I'm still funny" cell-phone conversation was the last time I spoke to her. She died in early April 2006. I was able to pull it together for her one last time, long enough to write her obituary with Jo Ann. "She could make an ordinary editorial meeting into a stand-up comedy act" was Jo Ann's quote for the obit.

At the funeral I was a wreck, shaking and hyperventilating with sobs in a rear pew at St. Ignatius Loyola Catholic Church on Park Avenue. Michahaze was by my side, holding my hand. Jo Ann was behind me clinching my shoulder. Liz was in front of the altar in a casket.

At the post-funeral reception I made a point of waving around my can of club soda in front of my colleagues. After two of those, I gave up and switched to a Bloody Mary. As I moved in a fog through the mourners, I spotted a striking, spindly older woman with spiky silver hair and Lucille Ball–blue eyes. Aunt Joan. I took a sip of my Bloody Mary and walked past her without introducing myself. She was drinking a ginger ale and wearing a beautiful fur coat.

Two weeks after Liz's death I returned to the office after one of my solo lunches. I had started to frequent the Irish pubs that lined Third Avenue. With their day laborers clutching the sports section of the *New York Post,* eyes glued to the wall-mounted TV stuck on ESPN, and drinking beer with a shot of whiskey—*boilermakers!*—I was certain that no one would ever think of finding me there. *My version of a witness protection program.* I sat in the back with a lunch of three or four vodka tonics and a shepherd's pie on the side. After I had amassed a pile of red swizzle drink straws, I surreptitiously pushed them off the table onto the floor on the off chance that anyone I knew did arrive.

When I returned from lunch, there was a message waiting for me. The CEO wanted to see me in his office to discuss a press release. *Not good. Not good.*

With a heavy heart and sudden LBD, I walked into his office. It was four-thirty, the witching hour of Dr. Connolly's call. Even though I knew what was coming, I sat there stunned. I only caught fragments of what he said:

"We appreciate the service you've given to this company . . .

"But there have been mounting complaints . . .

"I know that Liz spoke to you before she got sick . . .

". . . mounting complaints . . .

"It's best if you leave the company . . .

". . . mounting complaints . . .

"The announcement will be made tomorrow . . ."

By five o'clock I was sitting on a barstool at Mesa de España alone. The regulars hadn't arrived yet. I was the opening act.

But out of the corner of my eye I saw the reflection of my doppelgänger. His bloated, red face hovered above the backlit bottles in the mirror that lined the rear of the bar. I turned away, and the bartender silently slid a cocktail napkin across the bar. With shaky hands hidden at my side, my head poised for the trained-seal act, I said the only thing I knew how to say at that moment: "Beefeater martini, *dry,* up, with a twist. Please." Then I realized that the reflection in the mirror was mine.

TWENTY-FOUR

Dangerous When Wet

J oan Crawford made suicide glamorous. In *Humoresque* she plays an alcoholic socialite in love with John Garfield, a concert violinist whose star rises as she sinks. She's listening to him play Franz Waxman's "Tristan Fantasy," broadcast live on the radio. She's dressed for the evening in a black, sequined gown by Adrian, but she's not going anywhere. She pours glass after giant crystal glass of Scotch and replays every moment of her dissolute past, convincing herself that she's no good. Each thought drives her away from Garfield's haunting music and toward the ocean outside, just beyond her terrace. She sees her reflected image in the glass door of the terrace, floating over the racing sea as she throws back another drink. The sea is calling. She stumbles toward the ocean, and under a moonlit sky the sparkles of her gown become one with the glistening whitecaps as the sea claims her.

Even though I knew the end, I always hoped that she would change her mind, realize that she was good.

I spent every day of those last few months of drinking obsessed with suicide—it was the last thought when I passed out at night and the first thought when I came to in the morning—but

I didn't have the guts to do it. I kept hoping for divine defenestration, some magical force to pull me from bed and throw me out of the tenth-floor window, or maybe I'd walk in front of a bus and make it look like an accident. Then I'd think of Mama Jean, and Michahaze and Dad. I couldn't do that to them. Myself, yes, but not to them.

When I found myself watching Joan's suicide waltz over and over and pouring myself tumbler after tumbler of booze on the rocks along with her, I thought, *I think I get it. I understand how she feels. Just like Genevieve.*

Genevieve. That friend of Mama Jean's who shot herself. I could hear Mama Jean saying, "She was an alcoholic. A *bad* alcoholic." I barely remember Genevieve, but what she did haunted the rest of my childhood. Every time I passed her house, I imagined her last day on this earth. I saw her in her bedroom upstairs in the dark of day, the only light from a bedside chinoiserie lamp and the morning sun bleeding through the corners of the closed shutters. She sits on the bed in a quilted, powder-blue robe, crying and downing a gin on the rocks, as a Smith & Wesson waits on the nightstand. After draining that heavy crystal glass with both hands, she sits erect, pulls herself together, and takes a deep breath. Then she swallows the Smith & Wesson.

I didn't understand how Mama Jean must have felt about Genevieve until I got my own Genevieve in Paul Rosenfield. Paul was an author with whom I had worked early in my career. I adored Paul. He wrote a book about his adventures with the old guard of Hollywood. Though a good book, it didn't light any fires, and he was always a little sad that he didn't have a boyfriend. He disappeared for a while. When he resurfaced, he told me over a lunch of salad and copious Bloody Marys what had happened to him. He'd taken an overdose of pills. He felt that he was all used up.

"I'd hit the Peggy Lee 'Is That All There Is?' wall," he said. "Unlike her, I *was* ready for that 'final disappointment.'" I looked at him, uncomprehending. He explained further. "I felt that I was...I don't know...*done*." *Done* dropped onto the table like a dead pigeon from a ledge.

He was about forty-two and I was twenty-six when he told me that. I couldn't understand how anyone as talented and beloved as he was could sink to that point. But all that was behind him, he told me. He said that he was much better after a few weeks in the nuthouse.

"Thank God," I told him as I raised a glass. "Stick around. I know we'll be friends for life."

The next day I sent him a book as a gift with a note that said:

Dear Paul: We'll meet again. Don't know where. Don't know when. But I know we'll meet again some sunny day.

Kiss, kiss, Jamie

I didn't hear from him again until he mailed my note back to me barely a year later. He had written in the margin:

Jamie, You couldn't have known how prescient your words were. Love, Paul

By the time I received the note, he was dead. The second overdose took.

In those last months of my nearly intravenous drinking, I came to understand how Joan, Genevieve, and Paul felt. I no longer needed to watch that scene from *Humoresque*. I was living it. I spent each day replaying every scene of my dissolute life—sans gown by Adrian and John Garfield playing "Tristan Fantasy." I had been fired from a job that represented the pinnacle of my career. I was a laughingstock among those former colleagues and in the industry. Even though I had landed a new job immediately after being fired, I couldn't enjoy the satisfaction of saving face, so deep in the depression of booze was I. I had been destined for great things and reached marginal at best. And the good things got all drunk up. I was nothing but a lush—a "positively" diseased one at that. My looks—what looks I'd had—were gone.

"You disgust me" was my daily affirmation to the red, bloated face in the medicine-chest mirror. "No. *Really*. You disgust me." Every day that I couldn't get out of bed—and there were more of those days than not, near the end—I lay there with the shutters closed and the covers pulled, until I passed out from a few tumblers of vodka. I didn't have the ocean beckoning to me from a terrace, but it called to me in a recurring dream I had on those dark mornings.

I'm on a ship. It's night, and I awake from a drunken slumber. I'm still intoxicated and feel as if the room were spinning. I put one foot on the floor. Then the other. I immediately lose my bearings and fall and slide across the room into a corner. My head is spinning. I slump in the corner of the room. I'm dizzy. The room seems lopsided. It is *lopsided. I stare across the room, blinking my half-shut eyes. I place my hands on the walls and slowly pull myself up. My crotch is wet. Did I piss myself? I stand. My feet are wet. I look down and see that I'm standing in a small puddle of water. When my blurred vision comes into one-eyed focus, I see a stream flowing toward me. My eye follows the oncoming stream across the room to the opposite corner, where there is a shut door, a door I somehow know I can't open and walk out of. I see water bubbling under the door. I am powerless to move. The water begins to flow toward me, but in slow motion, and I awake in a panic.*

I always woke before drowning.

The morning I decided to take the plunge wasn't so different from any of those other mornings. It wasn't premeditated. It was a sunny, clear, crisp late-September day—as deceptively beautiful as a 9/11 morning—with a nip of fall in the air. It was a workday and I came to after Michahaze was long gone. The night before had been the usual routine: a few martinis after work, a couple of gin and tonics at home, wine with dinner, a bourbon on the rocks, plus several more, a couple of Ambien. *Nighty night.*

I had started taking Ambien for three reasons: to stop drinking as much by bringing on sleep sooner, to lessen the crush of the hangovers, and to insure an uninterrupted night of sleep. Once I started taking the pills (over time the one pill became one and a half, then two, then two and a half), three things started happening: I'd pound more drinks faster before I fell asleep, the hangovers become worse because a residual Ambien wooze was on top of the liquor every morning, and I never wanted the sleep to end. What I loved most about Ambien was the awareness of being put to sleep. It was like the moment before a movie begins in a theater. You're aware that the lights are swiftly dimming as the room goes to black. Then the screen lights up and the movie plays. Only with Ambien the movie never plays.

On that morning I had overslept as usual, but I was slowly moving through the miasma of my daily hangover to get ready. *Will I or won't I?* (Throw up, that is.) *I will.* I did. I lay on the bed to recover as the city ten floors below continued to come to life with honks and bus farts and the sounds of another day starting without me.

Don't drink.

But a drink would stop me feeling so sick from feeling so sick. The cycle was vicious.

I drank.

When I came out of the shower, the half-drunk screwdriver was waiting for me on the toilet. I finished it and made myself another. The second "dressing drink" would either put a spring in my step, like Fresca on a jockstrap (to paraphrase a classic Joan Rivers joke), or it would make my bed beg me to return. I was half-dressed when I finished the second drink. The bed was begging.

My only intention was to sleep another hour. I shot Debbie, my boss, an e-mail with the bogus excuse that I would be late after an author breakfast, then removed my half an outfit, poured a tall vodka on the rocks, unmade the bed, closed the shutters, and jumped in. I couldn't call in sick again, since in four months on the job I had already racked up enough sick days for a cancer patient.

When I came to, it was after lunch. *Shit!* I looked at the time on the clock in disbelief. Then I checked my watch. Same time, which was the wrong time. I threw open the shutters. I looked at my e-mail.

Debbie had responded to my author-breakfast excuse with *"Again???"* Apparently, I had had breakfast with that author a scant three weeks prior.

Busted! I thought. Not just caught, but smashed, broken, unfixable. Busted.

I poured another vodka on the rocks. I dashed around the apartment in circles, picking up and throwing down my shirt, rereading Debbie's e-mail, rechecking the clock—frantic, rudderless.

"I can't keep doing this. I just . . . I can't," I said out loud, my hands nearly crushing my head like an egg.

I looked at the mirror and stared hard into the eyes of a ghost, or was it the picture of Dorian Gray (the one he keeps in the attic)? I wanted to join Joan in the ocean. Genevieve was waiting for me in the bedroom. And I finally understood Paul.

"I'm done," I said, nose-to-nose with myself in the mirror. "Done."

The ocean wasn't a terrace away. I didn't own a gun. I'd have to take Paul's way out. I didn't let myself think about Mama Jean or Michael or Dad. I didn't let myself think. I was operating on vodka and a mountain of self-loathing.

Then I got hold of myself. I poured another vodka on the rocks. I brought it into the bedroom and set it on the nightstand. I closed the shutters again. I stood next to my bed in the dark of day like Genevieve. I emptied what was left in the Ambien bottle into one hand. I stared down at the blue pills as if they were the deep end of a pool, like the times when I was a kid too terrified to jump off the high dive into the water below. I did what I did in those days. I forced myself by not thinking about anything but what I *had* to do. *Just jump. All you have to do is jump.* I closed my eyes, cupped my hand over my mouth, tilted my head back, let the pills slide down my throat, took a big gulp of vodka, and "jumped."

I sank into bed and pulled the covers up as the sounds of traffic and life ten floors below drifted away.

Part III

Palm Springs Follies (2006)

Starting here, starting now, honey, everything's
coming up roses!

—Mama Rose from *Gypsy* (lyrics by Stephen Sondheim)

A few times in my life I've had moments of absolute
clarity. When for a few brief seconds the silence drowns
out the noise and I can feel rather than think, and things
seem so sharp and the world seems so fresh. It's as though
it had all just come into existence.

—Christopher Isherwood, *A Single Man*

TWENTY-FIVE

Ready or Not, Here Comes Jamie!

W hat's happened to your hair?! It's not red anymore!" That was the first thing Mama Jean said to me when Michahaze returned me to her after my week in detox. She was in our apartment, where she'd been waiting ever since she slapped on her face in Beaumont and flew to my rescue. It was just before noon and she was having a gown day. She wore the black satin nightgown with oversize red roses that she'd picked out for me to give her one Christmas as she held on to the art deco bar she'd reluctantly given to Michahaze and me years ago. Gathering dust in the bottom cabinet of the bar was a laptop computer, also a gift from her, but given with the vain hope that I'd start writing. It was the first time I'd seen her since I came to on that emergency-room gurney following my melodramatic suicide attempt.

As obsessed with hair as Mama Jean was, it was no surprise that she immediately pounced on the fading of my copper-red "crowning glory." It was cataclysmic that my hair had gotten as out of her control as my drinking. My hair was still red, but it was no longer the shiny-penny hue of my youth. It had merely dulled with age, but it seemed to match the dullness in my eyes, which had deadened with drink.

I had been wrong when I was on that emergency-room gurney and lay in fear of her reaction. She didn't jump on me with "God . . . *damn* it!" She didn't give me a red-fingernailed I-told-you-so point. She didn't glare and bare her teeth to declare, "You don't know what love is." Standing there in her nightgown without her face on, holding on to the bar as if it were a crutch, she wasn't in charge. She almost looked lost.

After she scrutinized my fading follicles, she hugged me long and hard, as if I were a doll that someone had threatened to take away from her. She held my face in her hands, a pose that Dad had captured in so many photos of us. Then she pulled back and penetrated my gaze with her eyes. "Oh, I'm so glad to finally see you. I knew you had to be in that place, but it was killing me being this close and not being able to lay eyes on you. God, I love you so much."

I had spoken to her from a hallway pay phone during the week I was locked on the sixth floor of the drunk tank, shuffling down linoleum floors in paper slippers. It was the detox ward of the hospital a few blocks from our apartment, where Michahaze had taken me after he'd discovered me in our bed. The ward was under lock and key and no visitors were allowed, which must have been torture for Mama Jean. Everyone there had been pulled from the central-casting department of *One Flew Over the Cuckoo's Nest*.

The first night the bed next to mine was empty, but when I awoke the next morning, I saw a ghost of white sheets rising from that bed with a gray face the color of a new bruise.

The ghost spoke in slow motion. "So how'd you end up here?"

"Booze and pills. I took an overdose of Ambien." That was the first time I'd said it out loud, but I'm not sure if I believed it. "What about you?"

"The usual. Heroin," he said matter-of-factly, as if delivering the weather report. "I'll have a nice rest here for a week like I've done a lot of times before. Once I'm back on the street, I'll pick up again. It's too late for me." Behind him, the window to the city was as gray as his face and streaked with rain.

Most of my fellow detoxers were like the Junkie Ghost: repeat offenders in for a week to dry out, rest, eat some regular meals, and then return to their old lives on the streets. The place had a post-apocalyptic feel, as if a nuclear bomb had hit and the only saved people were unshaven zombies in buttless hospital gowns and pill-dispensing nurses in pastel smocks.

As dead as I felt, I decided I no longer wanted to die. But my fantasy of life after detox couldn't stretch further than being put away in a nice sanitarium with an attractive gentleman orderly in crisp, white scrubs who'd push me down a gently sloping, verdant lawn in a cane-back wheelchair to receive the occasional visitor in the late-afternoon sun.

But I'd made it out of detox, and there I was standing before a relieved Mama Jean. "At least I got to talk to you while you were in that place. Every day we spoke, I could hear a little bit more life in your voice." Then she started to regain her dexterity. "I *knew*"—said with a red-fingernailed point—"every time I talked to you these past few months. . . . I said, 'Earl, something's not right. I'm *telling* you. There's *something* wrong.'" She hugged me again. Dad had stayed in Beaumont, probably because of the expense of the last-minute flight. Besides, this was a job for Mama Jean.

"Well, I'm better now!" I said with the phony cheer of an Olive Garden waiter.

"Not quite. You're alive." She quickly glanced over my shoulder at Michahaze.

"Uh, Jeffrey is coming over in a minute. So are Smith and Jennifer and Janine."

"Now?"

Mama Jean had told me on the phone in detox that she and Jeffrey and Michahaze had been talking to my college girlfriends

Smith, Jennifer, and Janine. Jeffrey remembered that Smith was visiting from San Francisco and called her for help.

Smith was one of the few friends of mine that Mama Jean not only liked, but unconditionally adored. "Oh, she's just precious! I would have killed to have had a little girl like that." Cupid-size with sometimes-blond hair in a pixie cut à la Mia Farrow in *Rosemary's Baby*, she was a blue-eyed sprite. On my dresser is a photo of her and Mama Jean from the night they first met after years of hearing stories about each other and periodically talking on the phone. It was the night that Mama Jean earned her name. I wasn't there. She and Dad were in San Francisco and brought Smith to Teatro ZinZanni, a blend of circus and cabaret in which the audience is encouraged to dress up and be a part of the show, never an arm-twister for either Smith or Mama Jean. Their heads are pressed together in close-up: Mama Jean is ecstatic; Smith's angelic face stares at the camera, her eyes popped in surprise. Their instant bond that night was sealed by a red feather boa draped around their necks. The day after that night Smith called to tell me, "Jame! [Smith's nickname for me] I finally met your mother. Wow! You weren't kidding. And she's one mama who loves her baby. All I can say is Mama Jean!"

Smith called Jennifer and Janine since they were psychologists. As Smith told me later, they had all met while I was detoxing, and Janine, who specializes in addiction treatment, clinically and gingerly begins to explain to Mama Jean, Michahaze, and Jeffrey the five stages of alcoholism: early/adaptive (it's all fun and an ability to drink bottomlessly—*Swingin', baby! Swingin'!*), middle (craving, physical dependence, loss of control, blackouts—*Verboten in Zurich, Dressing Drinks, Biting Jason, Lost in Rio*), late stage (severe physical effects—*that distended liver in the orchid aisle of Home Depot*—loss of family and or job—*"mounting complaints . . . it's best if you leave the company"*).

Janine made eye contact with Mama Jean as she said, "Jamie

is in the third or late stage, and at this stage, it is wise and probably necessary—"

"Cut to the chase, Janine. Are we going to have to lock him up?"

Yes. Because the fourth stage of alcoholism is treatment.

Soon the apartment was filled with Jeffrey, Smith, Janine, and Jennifer. I had agreed over the pay phone in detox to go to rehab. The way I understood it, detox was merely a place to rid the body of alcohol and drug toxins under medical supervision. It was a kind of purgatory before either returning to the hell of a life of booze and dope or going on to a multiweek rehab with the promise of sober salvation. Everyone was showing up for a reinforcement intervention to make sure I didn't change my mind.

"To what do I owe the honor of your smiling faces?" I said to all of them as if they were there for a surprise birthday party for me. Jennifer was having none of my faux jolly. With a look of worry and verge-of-tears agony that could make a Jewish mother feel guilty, she said, *"Jamie.* You tried to *kill* yourself." *Do you have to remind me?* I wanted to say.

Janine, with her cascade of jet-black hair and assured air of professional confidence, quickly got to work and fanned on the coffee table a selection of handouts and rehab brochures. She opened the dialogue by saying, "I always knew this moment would come." We whittled it down to three: Hazelden in Minneapolis (*A classic, but Minneapolis in October? Minneapolis anytime?*), Silver Hill in Connecticut (*Learning to play bridge with rich housewives addicted to chardonnay and prescription pills would be very* Valley of the Dolls), and Michael's House in Palm Springs, an all-male facility (*If I'm going to rehab, I might as well get laid*). I picked Michael's House.

"I might have known you'd choose that one," Mama Jean said as she pulled out her proverbial checkbook. She, rather than insurance, was paying the $16,000 because in detox I made the mistake of not lying when asked if I was still suicidal. Had the answer been yes, my insurance would have paid. *Mental note: Next time I'm in detox and I'm asked how I'm feeling, the answer is always "Suicidal. Suicidal."*

After the decision was made, a bed was reserved at Michael's House for the next day. *Why does one reserve a bed and not a room? It sounds so Bowery.* When I imagined my entrance into rehab (I had had nightmares about it as a part of my future ever since that call from Jack), I always imagined guzzling a fifth—okay, a magnum—of gin right out of the bottle, timing the last drop to my arrival. I'd toss the empty bottle out of the taxi window, wipe my mouth on my sleeve, and roll out of the car. Like Susan Hayward in the booze movie *I'll Cry Tomorrow,* I'd flip my hair, do a tit thrust, hold my head high, and stumble through the wrought-iron gates of the alcohol-treatment sanitarium on a broken heel. As the gates closed behind me, I'd slur with conviction, "Okay. *Now* I'm ready to get sober."

But no. I was told by Janine that I couldn't show up drunk to Michael's House. They'd refuse me. That if I did, I'd have to re-detox. *Really?* I didn't believe that. "Your drinking days are *over,*" Mama Jean said. She was back in command with a fully charged battery.

To insure that I didn't drink, Smith rerouted her flight back to San Francisco so she could accompany me on the plane to Palm Springs. She couldn't afford the expense of changing her flight. Since Michahaze and I were cash-strapped and Mama Jean said she had to draw the financial line somewhere, Janine and Jennifer split the cost for Smith to travel with me.

As decisions were quickly made for me, Jennifer, Smith, Michael, and Jeffrey whirled past with an endless exodus parade of liquor bottles. *Wait! Not the banana liqueur!* I wanted to say. *What if I want to make bananas Foster?* Instead, I stood in silence, holding back the tears as magnums of Beefeater gin, Absolut vodka, Jack Daniel's, and sundry other libations were removed from my life. *What if someone wants an after-dinner drink?*

Michahaze and Jeffrey carted the booze train out the door, and Smith and Janine and Jennifer followed. Mama Jean went into Michahaze's and my bedroom for a nap. I was left alone to start pulling it together before I disappeared for sixty days. I had to call my boss, Debbie. Her last e-mail to me, *"Again???"*—the one I read before swallowing the Ambien—rang in my head like an alarm-clock buzzer that couldn't be silenced. *Have I drunk myself out of another job? I can't handle the humiliation.* Michahaze had already spoken to Debbie. I called to tell her that I'd be going away for sixty days. "Take as much time as you need. Just go and get better. Your job is waiting for you when you get back." Pause. "If you still want it."

Did I?

Oh, God. Liz.

I had been in the middle of planning with Karen and Jo Ann the publishing-industry memorial for Liz that was to happen in October. Now I couldn't finish it, much less attend it. I had gotten as far as pulling together a suggested playlist of her music. I sent Karen and Jo Ann an e-mail saying that I was sick and going away: "Be sure to include Dusty Springfield's version of 'The Look of Love'—it's what I personally associate with Liz. It's the song I played over and over the night of her funeral. I remember her sitting in my apartment, looking ecstatic while listening to the song and saying, 'Oh! It's almost as good as sex.' My speech was going to be called 'The Look of Liz.'"

I remembered riding home in a cab with Karen after the initial planning dinner for Liz's memorial. I asked her what Liz had thought of me. "Oh, she loved you." Then Karen hesitated before finishing with "She always said, 'Jamie has such . . . potential.'"

Potential. That stung.

Keep moving, I told myself.

What to pack for Palm Springs? Should I pack a tennis outfit? I don't have a tennis outfit. I don't even play tennis. What awaits me in Palm Springs? All I thought I knew of rehab was Liz Taylor in a caftan scrubbing her own toilet bowl. *Will I be locked up? Humiliated into sobriety?* I panicked. My heart was racing and my hands were shaking. *God, I want a drink. Just one—maybe two—to calm my nerves.* I looked at Mama Jean napping on my bed. *How long will it take Michahaze to deposit the booze?* I thought seriously of running to the bar across the street for a pop. I stood still and didn't do anything. Then I saw a biography of Ava Gardner that I had promised to loan to Mr. Parker. The book was juicy, with endless stories of her ravening appetite for booze and sex followed by weeks of drying out in Arizona. I dashed off a note to him and stuck it in the book: *Dear Mr. Parker: They're putting me away, like they put away Ava. L, J.* I later realized that writing that note instead of running across the street was a little miracle.

By bedtime, my bags were packed, minus a tennis outfit, and Mama Jean was asleep in our bedroom. On the sofa bed in the den, Michahaze and I lay next to each other, stiff as cadavers. From the silence of the room and the absence of breathing sounds, I knew he was still awake.

"Michael?"

"Jamie?"

"Can you sleep?"

"Uh-uh."

"I'm scared."

"So am I." He grabbed my hand under the covers. "But you'll go away and you'll get better. And while you're away, I'll be here waiting for you so we can resume our life together."

"Michael, I love you."

"I know. You're the love of my life."

I didn't think I'd ever fall asleep, but I did. I awoke to Mama Jean whispering my name. I looked up and she was standing in the bedroom doorway backlit by the dim glow of the bedside lamp inside. She motioned to me. "Come here. I want to talk to you before I leave."

I did as I was told. She went into the room and lay down on her back on the Victorian bed she'd given us. She was on the left side—her side of the bed—dressed and fully made-up, not a hair out of place at four-thirty in the morning. She had a six A.M. flight and was waiting for a car to pick her up. *At that time, who would care what she looked like?* I knew the answer. *She would.*

I lay on my stomach, half on the bed, my feet still on the floor. I thought the tableau could have been in her bedroom in Beaumont until I looked at the nightstand on my side of the bed. The last time I had looked, a drained glass of vodka and an empty bottle of Ambien had been on it. It was also where I kept the Atripla, my HIV medication, which had been hidden before Mama Jean arrived. When I was still on the gurney and Jeffrey told me she was in flight, I had been so worried about her discovering my medication. She could never know about my HIV status. Michahaze remained negative; he had been tested after I told him, just to be sure.

Mama Jean stared at the ceiling. "Thank God for those girls. I don't know what I would have done without them. You're lucky to have friends like that."

"I know."

She reached out for me to take her hand. I did. It had been a long time since I'd held her hand. It was as soft as I remembered it. "I walked around this apartment for a week in a daze—oh, your little hand is so warm. I didn't know what I was going to do."

"It's going to be okay now." I felt ashamed of the dread that had filled me when Jeffrey told me that she was coming. In the way that she had been a nagging voice in my head during so many dark moments of my drinking—the only thing left of my conscience—my fear of facing her was wrapped up in the fear of facing what had brought me to that gurney. It wasn't her I didn't want to face. It was me. I hadn't even spent twenty-four hours with her, but I felt as if she had saved me, fixed the situation like a deus ex machina in a Greek play descending from the heavens and waving a checkbook.

"You can't know how I scared I was."

"I'm sorry. So sorry." I really was.

She abruptly let go of my hand and raised hers in warning to me. She looked me in the eye. "Let me tell you something. You can never drink again. *Never.*"

"I know."

"Do you understand me?"

"Yes."

Silence. She folded her arms across her chest and stared back at the ceiling, her mouth slightly open and lips curled tightly over her teeth.

After a beat she spoke, still staring at the ceiling, not looking at me. "You know, suicide is a mortal sin. It's a good thing you didn't succeed. If you had, you couldn't spend eternity in heaven with me."

TWENTY-SIX

If They Could See Me Now

Look, Coach, I'll run three laps around the baseball diamond instead. Just don't make me play baseball. I hate competitive sports. I hate *sports*." I was pleading with a sixty-something, potbellied, snow-topped, bulbous-nosed, *sober* man in polyester shorts and a baseball cap who insisted on being called Coach.

"Everybody plays the game, Brickhouse," Coach said.

"But Coach, the point of this is physical fitness. I want to be fit and lose this liquor fat. Believe me. But I'm telling you, playing baseball is *not* going to help my sobriety. In fact, it *threatens* my sobriety."

He was silent, his reaction unreadable. Where his eyes should have been, two palm trees stared back at me in the mirrored lenses of his aviator sunglasses. I felt as if I were back in junior high PE class: scheming, bartering—anything to get out of playing the game. It was one thing to be in rehab, but to be forced to throw and catch a ball with my fellow alkie, druggie inmates was a sick joke. And to think I had been worried about being forced to scrub a toilet bowl with a toothbrush. I thought of that song from *Sweet*

Charity: "If my friends could see me now ... they'd never believe it!"

"Come on, Coach, there are seventeen of us. The teams will be uneven."

"All right, Brickhouse. Run the laps. But run four."

"You got it, Coach!"

After I ran two in the afternoon desert sun, I noticed that Coach was engrossed in refereeing the game, blowing his whistle and calling fouls or strikes, touchdowns or home runs ... whatever. I parked under the shade of an oak tree far in the outfield—my favorite location on any baseball diamond—and pulled out my copy of *The Best of Everything* by Rona Jaffe. *The movie starring Joan Crawford is better.*

The negotiation with Coach was in week three of my eight weeks in rehab, but back in those first twenty-four hours, I was convinced I had made a terrible mistake in choosing Michael's House. Oh, the setup was nice. Anonymously nestled between two tony hotels, and a block off Palm Canyon Drive, the main drag, this former condo complex of Spanish haciendas was in an L around a kidney-shaped pool and Jacuzzi. A volleyball court was in back, where a rowdy game always seemed to be in play.

Intake—registration in rehab lingo—felt more like being booked into prison: confiscation of valuables, mug shot taken, and a litany of rules presented. I nodded and blinked in a haze, as if I were still drunk. I couldn't let the last rule—"You are expected to not participate in sexual behavior of any kind"—go without comment. *Seriously?* "Does that include masturbation?" I asked the tech (administrative staff member) in good faith.

"As long as you keep it to yourself." Sage "pressing" advice I already knew.

Turned out that the no-sex rule wasn't going to be an issue—I was the token faggot out of about twenty men. Most of them were in their twenties, a mix of heroin junkies, pill poppers (OxyContin snorters, mostly), cokeheads, and only a couple of alkies. *Dipsomania is* so *twentieth century*. Their maturity level was barely above pubescence. When they weren't playing volleyball, they were sitting around the patio smoking table and trying to light their farts.

After a starchy dinner of public-school cafeteria food that dashed any fantasy of California-spa fare of poached chicken breasts and alfalfa sprouts, we were driven to an off-site 12-step meeting in a short bus like special-needs kids on a field trip, which is what we were. Classic rock blared from the speakers, and everyone howled with delight when a Journey song came on. *I knew then that I was in Sartre's hell.*

Despite the dismal picture I saw before me, I was ready to dive into the deep end of getting sober—recovery, they called it—the next day at my first group-therapy session. I sat with the boys and the case manager (aka therapist) in a circle of chairs. Posted on the wall was a list of emotions (happy, sad, angry, depressed, fearful, excited, melancholy, euphoric, anxious, etc.). As we went around the room, everyone declared the emotion or emotions he felt: "Today I'm feeling _____"—fill in the blank. I scanned the list but couldn't find the one that fit me: numb. So I went with "Today I'm feeling anxious."

Since I was the new kid in town, I was invited to share my story. I threw the facts out onto the cutting board like raw meat: gay since birth; drinking since fifteen; everyday drinker by mid-twenties; healthy—and unhealthy—doses of drugs along the way; became suicidal; *tried* suicide. *Voilà! Here's Jamie!*

The shares followed. (Shares as in sharing what's on your mind, what you're feeling, where you're at, man.) No one was as witty as Bob Newhart's group-therapy patients. Someone commended me on how courageous I was to reveal that I'm gay. *Courageous?* It was a simple, obvious fact, like the red hair on my head. Coming clean on my full story, complete with suicide attempt, *that* was courageous. Then Hank from Indiana, one of the few older guys, piped in with "Jamie, I'm struggling with something and maybe you can help me understand it." I knew where he was headed. Basically, he wanted me to help him understand gay people—*he never will*—and get over his "uncomfortableness"—*did he really just say that?*—when seeing "them." *And I thought I was going to get laid? Flayed was more likely.*

I scrapped "anxious" and did an emotion do-over. "Hank, today I am feeling *angry*. It is a waste of my time for me to explain myself or homosexuality to you. I'm not here to deal with my sexuality, but to get sober." My face must have been as red as it was before detox.

Dave, the case manager, jumped in and started explaining the nature of sexuality and how any man is *capable* of having sex with another man. (Dave was gay.)

As he said this, Copper, an overpumped G.I. Joe police officer with an Ambien addiction, was writhing and twitching with every syllable of Dave's words. I thought he was going to put his fist through the wall. "I am *absolutely* . . . *incapable* . . . of having . . . *sex*"—then he spit out rapid-fire—"with-another-man." He let his words lie on the floor where he'd spewed them, then added, "But if my three-year-old son turned out gay, I'd still love him." *Big of him.*

When the session ended, anger was the only feeling I could see on the emotion cheat sheet. "Hey, man, come play volleyball!" one of the guys suggested, as if the Homo 101 lesson hadn't just happened. I gave a terse no.

If one other person asked me to play volleyball or looked at me as if I had three balls when I explained that I played no sports nor had even a passing interest in sports, I thought I'd get on my knees and ask if they'd like a free blow job—my sport of choice. I was certain then that I'd made a terrible mistake. I should have gone to Silver Hill with the pill-popping, chardonnay-swilling, rich housewives. *It would have been a hell of a lot better than being the only girl on the dorm-room floor.*

But thank God for my case manager, Dave. Every client (rehab inmates are not patients but clients) is assigned a case manager, who evaluates your drunk file from the forms you fill out, has one-on-one sessions with you three times a week, and makes written comments of encouragement, wisdom, or blunt-force honesty in the daily journal you are required to keep. A former New Yorker and recovering garbage head (an addict who ingests any readily available substance), Dave was a tall, olive-complected Italian American and a fifty-two-ish sixty. To me, he was the homosexual with the heart of gold—sage, pragmatic, insightful, and manicured—the kind of homo Stanley Tucci played in such films as *The Devil Wears Prada* and *Burlesque.* When he dubbed me Miss Lawson, as in Helen Lawson, the Susan Hayward diva from the film *Valley of the Dolls,* I knew I was in good hands.

My first journal entry was a rant about that initial group-therapy session. Dave wrote in red ballpoint pen, "I believe there is a reason you are at MH. It will be a challenge in some respects, but hard-won sobriety is the best kind (and most lasting). You'll get what you came here for—don't let the world get in your way. I'm glad you're here." I could see him staring down at me over his reading glasses with a hand on my shoulder.

He was right. The fog started to lift. Hank apologized. Copper thanked me for enlightening him about homos, and I found my first real friend in Keith. He consoled me after that inaugural group-therapy session at the smoking table by the pool while the boys hit the volleyball court.

"I'm not gay, but they all think I am." Keith gestured in the direction of the volleyball game with a lit cigarette that twitched like a hummingbird between his shaky fingers. "So I might as well be." He could have been one of my left-field friends from childhood. Twenty-something Keith was as thin as the cigarettes he fiendishly chain-smoked. (We all smoked like fiends.) With his dilated eyes and steady tremor, he looked like one of Robert Crumb's fried cartoon characters.

"How long have you been here?" I asked.

"Almost a month."

A month?! I thought he was still high. I guess my face didn't mask my surprise.

He cut his dilated eyes toward his jittering hands. "It's the benzos. They're still in my system, and it's been over two months."

"Oh. I mean . . . What are benzos?"

"Pills. Psychoactive drugs. I'm a pill popper. Klonopin, Xanax, Librium."

"I took a Xanax a couple of times."

"Only a couple? You *are* an alkie. Benzos take forever to get out of your system. You alkies are lucky. One week in detox and you're done."

"I suppose it's all relative."

"I was at Sober Choices in Arizona for a month before coming here. Michael's House is my third rehab. I'll probably go to a sober house after this." *My God, he's a rehab careerist.*

After a week's moratorium on contact with the outside world, I was talking to Mama Jean and Dad for the first time. It felt as if I were calling them from college—*How's the food? Who's your roommate? What's the syllabus?*—except I was in my bathing suit talking on one of the two pay phones by the pool. The only way to communicate with the outside world was via those pay phones and good old-fashioned mail. Cell phones and e-mail were *verboten*.

"Every time I see an ad for Ambien, it strikes terror to my heart," Mama Jean said.

I didn't tell her about Copper the homophobe and Ambien

addict. I did tell her about the endless volleyball games and dressing down my brethren addicts in group therapy.

"You'll teach those sons of bitches a thing or two," Mama Jean said.

"And who's your roommate?" Dad asked.

"Oh, yeah. Chris. He's a really nice guy with a family. He drank nothing but Coors Light. *Cases* of it. Every day."

"My God, is he fat?" Dad asked.

"No. Go figure. Weirder than the Coors Light is his thing for Katie Couric."

"What?" they asked in unison.

"He has photos of her cut out from magazines and tacked all over his bulletin board."

"Katie Couric?!" Dad said. "I could see Diane Sawyer, maybe, but Katie Couric?"

"I blame it on the Coors Light. *That's* the infatuation he can't get over. Like a lot of guys here, he's been through multiple rehabs."

"Bless his heart," Mama Jean said. "That's just pitiful. You're smarter than those other guys. You know what will get you through this? Your intelligence."

I lied and told her that she was right, but I didn't have the heart to tell her that intelligence was as effective as an umbrella in a hurricane when it came to alcoholism. *Why else would I, Little Miss Straight-A Student, have a couple of pops at nine in the morning, then show up unprepared for a sales-conference presentation and hope for the best?*

Like a good pupil, I fell right into the routine of the place. Up at six-thirty. Smoke a cigarette. Breakfast. Smoke. Morning meditation. Puff. Group-therapy sessions. Puff. Puff. *Puff.* Free time for volleyball, swimming, TV, reading, or back-to-back cigarettes. Lunch. Afternoons were spent at either a workshop (journaling, art collage, educational video), the dreaded baseball field with Coach, or an off-site gym with a perfect view of Bob Hope's spaceship of a house. The drive was the best part. The special-needs van would glide along Bob Hope Drive, Ginger Rogers Road, Frank Sinatra Drive, and Dinah Shore Drive. It made me feel safe knowing that Dinah and Ginger were right under my ass. Back to the dude ranch for more volleyball and fags—*the carcinogenic kind*. Dinner. Off-site 12-step meeting. Round-robin of daily affirmations: "Great game, Hank." "Love ya, man." "Today, I'm grateful to be sober and I thank my HP [higher power] for Marlboro Lights." Hot tub and one last butt. Lights out at midnight.

Once I asked Hank what day it was. He replied, "How the fuck do I know? Every day is like *Groundhog Day* around here."

There was also the privilege of "town time" three days a week. We were allowed to leave campus unsupervised in buddy groups of two or more. Since we were a scant block from the main drag of town, we could cover a lot of ground in the two or three hours we were given. If anyone thought of sneaking a drink or scoring some dope—and we all thought about it—there was the threat of random urine testing back at the ranch. A stroll down Palm Canyon Drive in the warmth of the arid desert air was heaven. I was no longer dying for—or from—a drink, but as I passed all of the alfresco restaurants, I could name every drink caught in my peripheral vision: martini with a twist, salted margarita on the rocks, cosmopolitan, perfect Manhattan, whiskey sour, Bass ale.

A stronger distraction was the sidewalk, a knockoff of Hollywood's Walk of Fame called the Palm Springs Walk of Stars. The marginal and forgotten names kept my head staring *down* at the stars: Rona Barrett, a 1970s gossip columnist; Cheetah the chimp from the Tarzan movies; Mr. Blackwell, the queenie arbiter of best- and worst-dressed celebrities; Mamie Van Doren, a cheap Jayne Mansfield, who was a cheap Marilyn Monroe—*that's pretty cheap*.

Lining the Walk of Stars were shops and art galleries of every caliber. My favorite was the gallery of Thomas Kinkade, aka the Painter of Light. Keith and I would pretend to be serious buyers of the vomitus, mass-produced paintings of saccharine, bucolic scenes with candles *glowing* and stars *twinkling*. The paintings appeared to have pin lights in them, but, no, it was the magic of the master's technique that made the light shine. The saleslady positively radiated like a lit fire in one of the pictures as she told us that she was a graduate of the Thomas Kinkade University of Art. "You mean that you can actually *teach* people to paint that way?" was our response.

Most of my town time was soaked up by some of the seriously chic antiques and design stores. We weren't allowed to carry credit cards, and our petty cash of forty dollars maximum wouldn't buy a crystal ashtray in these shops. I had my eye on a Czechoslovakian glass bowl from the 1930s. The glass was lacquer-shiny—the outside Halloween-cat black, the inside an orange the color of a taxicab when a taxicab isn't yellow. I had to have it. It was only $150, but it might as well have been $150,000 when all you're carrying is piddling change left over from the Jamba Juice smoothie and Starbucks scone you just had.

"You simply don't come across glass with a sheen this pure," the effete shop owner raved rhapsodically.

"It would be perfect in my art deco apartment in New York."

"New York? Do you have a place here too, or are you just visiting?"

"Actually, I'm here on extended vacation." I glanced at my watch. *Yikes.* "You know what, I have to dash or I'll be late for an appointment. Can you place it on hold and I'll get back to you in a couple of days?"

"Certainly." He handed me his engraved business card with his well-manicured hands, the nails of which had a sheen almost as pure as that glass bowl.

"Really, I must dash or I'll turn into a pumpkin." I had less than ten minutes to make curfew back at Mission Rehab.

I made it back just in time for the afternoon mail delivery, always an endorphin rush.

"Brickhouse, get over here!" Hank shouted from the patio smoking table where the mail lay in stacks. "You have a package and it looks like food. Open 'er up. I'm hungry."

"In a minute." I bypassed the table where heads bobbed amid a cloud of smoke over the mail. I went straight to the pay phone.

"Michael Hayes," Michahaze said in his clipped, professional, office voice.

"Hey, it's me."

"Howdy. How are you today?"

"Good. Just got back from a *lovely* town-time afternoon."

"Oh, yeah? What did you do?"

"The usual. Grabbed some treats from Jamba Juice and window-shopped. You know, they have some exquisite antique shops here."

"That's what I hear. I can't wait to check them out."

You'd think I was on a solo vacation, but that was Michahaze's way of coping—keep things upbeat and normal. We hadn't had a heart-to-heart since that moment in the dark on the pullout sofa before I left.

"Well, there's a tiny shop off the main drag that specializes in vintage glass and ceramic vases. . . ." I described the bowl.

"Sounds fabulous. It would be perfect for the dining-room table. You should get it."

"Actually, *you* should get it." I reminded him how strapped for cash I was. "I have it on hold. Why don't you call the store and have them ship it?"

"Ha! Did you tell them where you're staying? In Palm Springs, they're probably used to that." I pulled the salesman's card out of my pocket and gave him the number, before heading to the mail party.

I had quickly become the most popular gal in rehab since I received more mail than anyone else. Part of the reason was my advanced age. Since most of MH's clientele was under thirty, none of them nor their friends had ever written a letter. On one town-time afternoon I had to walk some of them through how to address and stamp a letter at the post office. "Didn't they teach you kids *anything* at school?" I asked them in my best Texas mawmaw voice.

The letter from my brother Jeffrey—who had been my third parent and mentor growing up and held vigil next to me in the emergency room after Michahaze went home to make sure my HIV medication was hidden before Mama Jean arrived—filled me with hope: *I am looking forward to having my brother back. The brother whom I adore. The brother whom I will always, always be there for.*

The most entertaining letters came from Mr. Parker. He didn't need a best girlfriend in rehab as an excuse to write letters. He'd never abandoned them and was valiantly fighting to keep the art of letter writing alive. His missives were a work of art, not just in content but in presentation. They were written in royal-blue fountain-pen ink in an affected, exquisite script—flowing, upright letters, sans slant, like the cursive font of Neiman Marcus.

Dear Jamie—

So I checked out Michael's House on the internet, as you advised. The place looks nice ... comfortable I suppose; like a dude ranch. I guess you can think of it as a Reno, Nevada, divorce ranch not unlike the one such prosperous New York matrons as Mrs. Lorna Hansen Forbes, the Countess De Lave and Mrs. Stephen Haines were obliged to spend six months (!) because of a world that didn't understand. I suppose your time in the desert is your Reno-vation from the bottle. ... Maybe it will be the answer. (Well, not the answer, exactly, but a way to get at it.) The only danger I see are the quilted bedspreads I saw on the website. Fiberglass, insulation-filled, poly-cotton bed "linens" cannot be considered therapeutic. It really is the only thing in the Michael's House environment that might drive one to drink. ... I want only the best for you, no matter how much your life does or does not change and I love you wet, dry, or otherwise.

Much love to you, darling,

Michael Parker

I heard from friends whom I hadn't seen or spoken to since college. Rehab really does bring out the best in people. Keith would chain-smoke with nothing in front of him but a pack of cigarettes as I sifted through my mail or read choice bits of Mr. Parker's letters to him.

After I'd plowed through one particularly robust stack of letters, he offered me one of his cigarettes. I accepted.

"You know," he said, exhaling smoke, "after the second or third rehab the phone stops ringing and the mail dries up."

Rehab wasn't what I expected, but it was better than I expected. First I had to wrap my booze-soaked head around the idea that I was in rehab, which wasn't an idea, but a dry, hot fact. Once I got to know my inmates and learned how to negotiate with Coach, the novelty of being sober became a thrill. Just not being hungover every day of my waking life was worth the price of admission. It was better than any vacation I ever took. For the first time in my adult life I could completely let go of work and family and spend time *thinking* about me and not *running* from me. Being free of the outside world became sexy superfast. *Okay, this is all I need. Three meals at the same time every day, a little therapy, a dose of recreation, some free time in town, and back to the safety of MH's white stucco, dry walls.*

I was making progress with a cast of characters—some unexpected—to help light the way. If Mama Jean was my benefactress, Dave my guardian angel on earth, Keith my kindred spirit, then Liz was my patron saint. Liz's ghost arrived during the middle of my "extended Palm Springs vacation." I was still in mourning and marinating in my favorite emotion, guilt, over not being able to be a part of her memorial. But the core of my guilt about Liz was that I'd tried to throw away what she would have given anything to have. Every time I thought of my feeble suicide attempt in the harsh glare of her death—"But I have so much more to do," she had said when she was told she was dying—shame scalded my every nerve.

When the program for her memorial, along with *The Many Moods of Liz* CD, arrived in the mail with her beatific face on the cover of both, I wept all over again for her death and for my sins. I tacked the program to the wall above my bed so she could watch over me. Then I grabbed some headphones and a CD player, went outside under a canopy of desert stars, and let her talk to me through her "many moods." Some of the songs I had suggested for her CD were on there: Judy Garland singing "The Man That Got Away," Dusty Springfield's version of "The Look of Love," and Madeleine Peyroux's "Dance with Me." I thought of that marvelous, euphoric moment of disco dancing with her at the company Christmas party. It was our last happy moment together, the last time booze made me happy, joyous, and free. Four months later Liz was in a casket at the front of St. Ignatius Loyola Catholic Church. That was the last time I had been to Mass.

When I left for college, I stopped going to Mass. After eighteen years of going every Sunday, I didn't have to anymore. Besides, why was I going to sit for an hour under the roof of a church that didn't want my sinning sodomite self? During one of my visits home, Mama Jean, who was no longer attending Mass regularly herself (much to the consternation of Dad), spoke for both Dad and herself about their disappointment that I wasn't attending church anymore.

"Come here. I want to talk to you." She pulled me into the Miss Havisham living room, which was always as quiet and somber as a sanctuary. She sat in a wingback chair while I stood before her. "Your father is really upset that you've stopped going to church.

He won't say anything to you about it, but I will. Listen to me. I may not go to Mass every Sunday—and believe me, there is no church for me *but* the Catholic Church—but I was born a Catholic and I'll die a Catholic. You'll never see me under a Baptist roof—or even Episcopalian. No, ma'am! But I've *never* lost my faith. Not even during 1963."

That was the black year. The year that her first husband, Len, died in the plane crash and her father, Big Daddy, died, three months later. Two thousand and six was my 1963.

"After the plane went down, I waited a week for them to find his body. A *week*. You can't imagine what that was like." She was right. I couldn't. "And when they found him, I didn't know how I was going to go on. But I had to. I had two little boys to take care of. Do you know what got me through it?"

"The Church?"

"No. My *faith*. My faith carried me. I cried and I prayed and I cried and I prayed some more. And when I didn't think I could cry any more, Big Daddy died. Well, I thought they might as well bury me. But as hard as that time was, I learned that I'm a survivor and there's a God more powerful than me." *Really? There is something more powerful than Mama Jean?*

"Your father disagrees, but I don't need to go to Mass every Sunday to prove my faith. I'm secure in it, but you're too young to understand faith. That's why I think it's a big mistake for you to stop going to church until you find it."

I promised her that I'd think about it, but I never went back to the Church, except for Christmas and Easter with Dad and her. And faith? I poured my faith into all those beautiful liquor bottles that came in gem shades of green, amber, and blue like the stained-glass windows of St. Anne's.

After listening to *The Many Moods of Liz* that night, I wasn't ready to surrender completely to the notion of a God, and I hadn't prayed in years, but I assumed my former altar-boy position at the foot of my bed and got down on my knees. I prayed to Liz as her twinkling lunette eyes stared back at me. I prayed for forgiveness. I prayed to her for help. I prayed for my life. Dave's words bled into the page of my journal entry on November 1 about that moment: "As an old Catholic girl you must know that today is the Feast of All Saints. Perhaps you've found a saint to help take care of you."

The next afternoon, when I returned from my successful negotiation with Coach on the baseball diamond, Liz's photo over my bed had been framed with a rosary. My bottle of Wet, my personal lubricant of choice, had gone missing. Dave eventually confessed to hanging the rosary. The Katie Couric lover said he would swear on a case of Coors Light that he didn't take my lube. Some things can't be explained. I choose to believe that Liz took my Wet away.

The "wet" was gone, but the guilt and shame were like oil stains that continued to spread. Mama Jean couldn't get over that I had tried to kill myself, and I hadn't fully accepted that I actually did that. I wrote in my journal, "I know I did it, but I keep rationalizing it. I only did it because I was drunk." With bloodred ink, Dave had underlined the last sentence and written in the margin, "I would rethink this."

I took Dave's advice and thought about Paul Rosenfield. And Genevieve. And then I thought about myself. I was glad to be alive, but my feelings vacillated from waking up filled with joy and enthusiasm—*I'm an alcoholic, and I'm sober!*—to being hopeless and fatalistic by nightfall—*I've squandered my passion, ambition, and thirst for life.*

"Where is Susan Hayward from *I Want to Live!* when you need her?" I wrote in my journal. To which Dave shot back in red, "You'd better start channeling her."

TWENTY-SEVEN

Feelin' Good

The Fabulous Palm Springs Follies was something to live for. Located on the Walk of Stars strip, the show boasted "the world record for the oldest chorus line!" *Who's tracking these figures?* "1940s Music, 1940s Cast!" It was made up of showgirls and boys old enough to have seen Ginger and Fred, Gene Kelly, Ann Miller, and Cyd Charisse. Heaven.

Keith and I were strolling along the Walk of Stars slurping our Jamba Juice pomegranate smoothies one Saturday afternoon of town time when I stopped dead in my tracks on Liberace's star to read the marquis announcing GOGI GRANT: OUR FABULOUS GUEST STAR, OCT 31 TO DEC 31, 2006.

"No!" I said to Keith, and pointed. "Gogi Grant. She can't still be performing."

"Huh?"

"You don't know who Gogi Grant is?!" I said, sounding like Mama Jean and Dad.

"Jamie, I barely know who Debbie Reynolds is." Keith pointed to her star beneath his feet.

"I have to investigate." I walked up to the box-office window and left Keith behind, shaking his head as he stood on Debbie.

The lady behind the window was preserved in frost: frosted-blond helmet, frosted-pink lipstick, frosted-silver nails, frosted, snow-white dentures.

"Excuse me, but next month's guest star: Is that *the* Gogi Grant? As in 'The Wayward Wind'? Was the singing voice for tons of Hollywood stars? Dubbed Ann Blyth in *The Helen Morgan Story*? *That* Gogi Grant?"

She let out a Virginia Slims bronchial chuckle. "Only Gogi Grant I know of, hon."

Back at the dude ranch I was on the pay phone to Michahaze. "I know what we're doing when you come to visit. We're seeing *The Fabulous Palm Springs Follies,* and Gogi Grant is the guest star!"

"Sounds wonderful," Michahaze said with true enthusiasm. Then a beat. "Remind me. Who is Gogi Grant?"

I had accepted that Michahaze was coming for a conjoint. *Conjoint* is a bear of a rehab term. This term I looked up. It has multiple definitions. In recovery it means: "a type of therapy in which a therapist sees the two spouses, or parent and child, or 'other partners,' together in joint sessions."

From the beginning Dave had been pushing for a conjoint with Michahaze. I agreed and he was on board, but I wasn't completely. I subtly tried to deflect him from coming. "Don't worry if you can't get the time off or if airfares are too expensive. I'll be back in New York soon enough." Even though we spoke daily, I hadn't shared many of the details of my therapy sessions, of my "recovery." Kind of like I hid just how excessive my drinking was. I ruminated in my journal that I was unsure about how much I wanted to let him in on what I was going through. Dave's red ink: "Translation—how much I need him."

One of my care packages was a box of books from my boss, Debbie. I grabbed one of them as if it were a forgotten diary, *Exiles in*

America, by Christopher Bram, about a gay couple in a long-term, sexless—and open—marriage. I put all of the recovery self-help books Dave had given me on the bottom shelf and dove into that book, hoping to find the answer about whether Michahaze and I should be together. It only brought up the same questions, and a few more, that I had already been asking: *Is companionship, deep friendship, a good home, and a little on the side enough?* Dave's red ink posed one more question: "There is no answer because it is not an intellectual issue. The real question is 'Is Michael my emotional home?'"

Michahaze showed up. After we hugged, he pulled back and looked at me. His blue-green eyes, with that beautiful circle of gold around his pupils that I'd noticed the night we first met, looked different. The look of fear and worry of the last few years had been replaced by relief. He looked at my no-longer-bloodshot eyes and said, "Do you know that in our sixteen years, this is the longest we've ever been apart?"

Sixteen years. Forget straight people. We've been together longer than most lesbians. "I hadn't realized that. Wow." I hugged him again. Long and hard. "I'm so happy to see you."

"I got the tickets to *The Palm Springs Follies,* and the Czechoslovakian bowl arrived last week. It's beautiful. You're right. It's perfect in the apartment. It's sitting on the dining-room table . . . waiting for you."

The next day we saw the Sunday matinee of the follies. The poster for the show barked, "Every performer 53- to 83-years young!" When Michahaze and I stepped into the theater, I took a look at the audience with canes, walkers, scooters, and wheelchairs and said, "And the audience is *slightly* older." I looked at the show's poster and saw a one-word ringing endorsement of it from Katie Couric: "Wow!" *Wow, indeed.* I thought of Coors Light and turned to Michahaze. "I'm so glad that Gogi Grant *and* Katie Couric have been a part of my recovery."

That night Michahaze got to go to a 12-step meeting with me. I gave him a primer of what to expect. "Now, if you don't want to introduce yourself when they ask if there are any newcomers or visitors, you don't have to. There will be a speaker who will tell his story about what a booze bag he was and how he got sober and how his life now is all singing birds and sweet-smelling farts. Then they open it up to shares from the room—"

"I understand."

"This particular meeting is a round-robin, where they go around the table in order and everyone shares. You don't have to share if you don't want to, you can just pass. And you can share whatever you want to share—if you want to share—but I understand if you don't want to—"

"*Okay*. I get it."

He chose to share.

I cringed and held my breath as he told the roomful of strangers about coming home from work to find me passed out in our bed with an empty pill bottle and a glass with three fingers of melted ice on the nightstand. It was my first time hearing this and was typical of how we communicated. We left the big things unsaid until asked by an outsider, and then we'd share with the outsider in front of each other.

"I had a bad feeling all day," he said to the room of strangers. "We speak several times a day, and all of the voice-mail messages I left were never returned. When I opened the door, I knew it wasn't going to be good." *Not good*, I thought. "And it wasn't. I found my partner of sixteen years passed out in bed. I was able to wake him, and through slurred speech, he told me that he'd taken some pills. 'How many?' I asked. 'How *many*?' He couldn't tell me. I called our friend Bunny, who is a nurse practitioner and lives nearby. He came over. By that time Jamie was in the kitchen pouring shots of gin. Bunny and I took him to the hospital as he begged us to stop at a bar along the way. It was the scariest day of my life." Michahaze looked away from the table of anonymous faces looking at him tell his story. He turned back to them. "But now he's here and I'm thankful that he's going to be okay."

He didn't have to share that *honestly.*

The conjoint with Dave started to scrape away the layers of dirt that had hardened over the years and till the fertile soil that still lay beneath. We sat next to each other in Dave's sun-drenched office, Michahaze in his white linen shirt and seersucker, striped trousers (the ones I had picked out for him). We stared intensely at Dave as if we were telling a doctor the symptoms of our illness and waiting for his remedy, which is exactly what we were doing. Michahaze made it abundantly clear that he loved me and would stand by me through everything. Then he expressed his concern over the hold Mama Jean continued to have on my life.

"From a thousand miles away Jean still has a vise grip on Jamie. Emotionally." As he said this, I could feel him blocking from his peripheral vision any possible looks from me. "She continues to have this idealized view of Jamie, and I think he nearly kills himself to live up to that. Jean simply can't accept any behavior that deviates from her norm." Then he added with his trademark giggle, "She told me that she blames me for him becoming a Democrat."

We all laughed.

In her eyes, my unacceptable behavior was always someone else's fault. Some might say that she turned me into a drunk. The truth: no one turned me into a hydrophobic, liquor-swilling, sometime-cocaine-snorting, homosexual *Democrat* but me.

After the session, Michahaze and I sat by the pool and talked about what the future would look like.

"What are you concerned about most?" Michahaze asked.

Before I answered, I looked at the wavy double helixes of sunlight in the pool. I thought of a David Hockney pool painting in which a man is forever submerged at the deep end in midswim. He never has to emerge from the cocoon of that chlorinated womb. I turned back to Michahaze's gold-rimmed pupils. "I'm afraid of leaving the safety of this place and not being able to handle it out there. Of picking up again."

"You can do it. You can do anything." He hugged me and I believed that he believed in me and loved me almost as much as Mama Jean did. And now I had to love him back just as much.

Of all the *conjoint* definitions I found, the first one listed is the simplest: "joined together; combined." I shared this with Dave in my journal. Dave gave me the validation I needed: "Michael is a gem. So are you. Create a setting worthy of you both."

"You know, I still can't get over the fact that I tried to commit . . . that I tried to kill myself," I told Dave at our next therapy session. "Hearing Michael tell that room about finding me . . . made it real."

"It's called shame, kiddo." Dave stared at me over his reading glasses. "But you first have to accept that you did it before you can get over the shame and move on."

"I see what you mean. But more than that, I can't get over the fact that *Jean* can't get over the fact that I . . . did that."

"Maybe Jean can finally take you off of that gilded pedestal she erected and placed you on."

"Funny. That's what Mr. Parker said to me while I was in detox. I thought I had made a dent in gaining my independence when I shit in the nest last Thanksgiving, but I've thrown myself back in the crib. I'll never be free of her obsessive love."

"Do you feel that her obsession with you actually robbed you of being a child?"

"You think? I don't know. Maybe. I spent so much energy being the adorable, happy, cheerful boy she needed me to be that there was no room for my feelings." I shared with Dave a passage from a highbrow self-help book that I'd been reading, *The Drama of the Gifted Child*. The book's premise—that the intelligent, sensitive, "gifted" child is essentially denied a self of its own, as the needs of the parent are always paramount—was pure catnip:

> Children who are intelligent, alert, attentive, sensitive and completely attuned to their mother's well-being are entirely at her disposal. Transparent, clear and reliable, they are easy to manipulate as long as their true self (their emotional world) remains in the cellar of the glass house in which they have to live—sometimes until puberty or until they come to therapy.

I pursed my lips and cocked my head as I let the words fill the room.

Dave broke the silence. "Time to smash the glass house. You need a daddy."

"A daddy?!"

"Not *that* kind of daddy, Miss Lawson. A father."

"Okay . . . ?" I said, still not understanding.

"What about asking your father to visit and have a conjoint?"

"And not her? She'd never go for that—"

"She doesn't have to—"

"Oh, *yes,* she does. She's the one paying. There's no way in hell she's going to pay for Dad and not her to come see me." My head went from left to right as I said with finality, "Will never happen. No, ma'am."

After the session I went back to my room and reread a letter that Dad had written to me on the eve of my graduation from high school. While I was on the ER gurney and Mama Jean was on the plane to New York, he had pulled his copy of the letter and faxed it to Michahaze so it was waiting for me—along with Mama Jean—when I returned from the week in detox.

. . . You can be anything you want to be. No matter what you choose to do in your life . . . discipline, dedication and, most important, patience will get you there. Sometimes we have set-backs and detours in life, but God is directing us on a different path, one that will eventually lead to a happy and fulfilled future. . . . Your sense of the ridiculous will always keep you young at heart. . . . But, please know your Mother and I will unconditionally support you. But, most importantly you have our undying love.

It was signed "All Our Love, Mom and Dad," but the words were all his.

I never asked him to visit.

The last ritual of Michael's House was "Good-Bye Group." The client leaving sits in the center of the room, and the case managers share what they have observed about how you've sobered and matured. A black-and-white photocopy of your hideous mug shot from your first day at intake is posted on the wall. In my photo my eyes are puffy from five hours of crying on the plane. The left side of my bottom lip droops down. In fact, the whole left side of my face sags like a stroke victim's. My expression is blank, numb. *I imagine the photo of me from the Great Falls of Paterson, New Jersey, looks about the same.*

My fellow inmates handed me slips of paper on which they had written "one wish," "one hope," "one concern," and "one gift" (received from the person leaving). The general messages of the well-wishes I received were:

One wish: That you start taking care of you and stop trying to tend to everyone else, one being your mother.

One hope: That a whole new rich and colorful life unfolds for you and that you never look back to the old drinking life.

One concern: That the flashing lights of Fire Island discos, shiny

green of Tanqueray bottles, and sparkly white mountains of co-
caine don't make you forget how painful a life of using can be.

One gift: Your incredible sense of humor and always seeing the
funny side of the dark.

I looked at the wall. There hung the recovery steps and inspi-
rations that I had studied for the past sixty days. I was still con-
founded by "This is a program for those with a desire to stop
drinking." Shouldn't it be "This is a program for those who need
to stop drinking"? I knew I needed to stop drinking, but didn't
know if I had actually acquired a *desire* to stop drinking.

Dave's last comment in my journal: "Looks like your reality
holds joy and promise. Now you have to begin the process of
self-forgiveness. Yuck indeed!"

The day I left, one of those sublime cinematic moments in life
occurred when the perfect song hits at the right time. I had one
day on my own in Palm Springs before returning to New York. I
was going to spend it shopping with my newly regained credit
cards. On that first day of freedom, when I put the rental car in
motion, the song "Feelin' Good" (most famously sung by Nina
Simone, but I had the Paul Anka version) filled the automobile. I
euphorically sang along with Mr. Anka about it being a new
dawn, and a new day, and a new life for me, and I *was* feelin' good. I
sailed down Palm Canyon Drive. The car seemed to be propelled by
my elation rather than gas.

Did Janine tell Mama Jean that the fifth stage of alcoholism is
relapse?

Part IV

The Hair Is the Last to Go (2008–11)

I think that the most important thing a woman can have—next to talent, of course—is her hairdresser.

—Joan Crawford

All changes, even the most longed for, have their melancholy; for what we leave behind us is a part of ourselves; we must die to one life before we can enter into another.

—Anatole France

TWENTY-EIGHT

The Seven-Month Itch

W hat's wrong with her hair?" I asked Dad. "It looks like she did it herself."

With a look of weary exasperation he said, "That's because she did. She fired her last beauty operator. She said the gal kept getting her appointments wrong. Your *mother* was the one who screwed up the appointments." He shot me his signature eyebrows-raised, eyes-bugged look.

Mama Jean and Dad were staying with Michahaze and me for a few days before they went on a cruise. It was her first visit since the rehab rescue just two years prior. Instead of the perfect raven helmet to which I was accustomed, her hair looked like a home perm left out to dry.

Screwed up her hair appointments? That was not like Mama Jean. One time, years before, Dad almost missed a colonoscopy because of her hair. Right before the procedure, the nurse couldn't locate Mama Jean. "Mr. Brickhouse, we can't start the colonoscopy until your wife comes back and we know that someone is here to take you home. Where did she go?"

"To get her hair done," he said in a where-else-do-you-think-she-went? tone.

"Well, we have to get her back here. What's the name of the beauty parlor? We'll call."

"Good Lord, I don't know. She keeps changing beauty operators. It's next to a Mexican restaurant on College Street." The nurse called the Mexican restaurant, which called the beauty parlor. And Mama Jean came back. *After her hair was done, I presume.*

For her to show up in New York at the beginning of a two-week trip with her hair not done to perfection was cataclysmic. I should have known then that something was seriously wrong with her. I was relieved that she couldn't tell that things weren't completely right with me either.

I wanted to do something special for that first postrehab visit. I still felt guilty that she'd had to pay the nearly sixteen grand for the program. I gave her five thousand dollars and she said that was good enough. I reminded her that Michael's House was actually a bargain, almost half the price of the other places we considered. "I'd have paid double the amount if that's what it took" was her swift reply.

I threw a brunch in their honor on a sunny Sunday afternoon in October. We were people who entertained. That's how we rolled in our family. The apartment was filled with Michahaze and my friends coming to pay their homage to Mama Jean and Dad. I was chatting with guests and sipping a Dinah Shore (my renamed version of an Arnold Palmer—half iced tea, half lemonade—but with a dash of bitters), while across the room Mama Jean sat on the club chair where she had written the check to Michael's House.

As the guests came to her, she sat like a queen receiving her subjects. My friend Stella stood at Mama Jean's throne nodding her head as Mama Jean regaled her with a story. Stella, who was from Oxford, Mississippi, could be mistaken for a blond former sorority girl, which she was. But like Mama Jean, also a former sorority girl, Stella had an edge. When she was rejected as a buyer for an apartment by a snooty co-op board at 41 Fifth Avenue, she said, in her slow-as-Mississippi-mud accent, "You know whuuut? When 41 Fifth Avenue wouldn't take my money, I went up the street to *Saaaks* Fifth Avenue and bought five pairs of shoes. They took my money. No questions asked." She and I had been dear friends ever since we met at a publishing party years ago and bonded over our mothers' hair. Her mother and my mother were both Chi Omegas, but more than that, they had the same once-a-week dos. When Stella told her mother the story of Mama Jean's shower hair catastrophe, the color drained from Stella's mother's face. "Stella, that story isn't funny at all. What did she *do*?"

Stella looked slightly aghast as Mama Jean, with her right hand on her chest, dramatically recounted a story. I was too far away to hear the conversation, but I was sure that I knew the story well. It was the same story she told me over and over.

She didn't need an obvious trigger to launch into it with me. We'd be on the phone talking about Hugh Jackman's latest movie and the next second: "Oh, you don't *know* the terror that struck my heart when I received that call from Michael. . . . I still can't believe that you would try to kill yourself. I just can't get *over* that." I'd interrupt her and say that my drinking and dark days were behind us, that she didn't need to worry about it anymore. But there was no stopping her. She had to hit every lousy note of the story until she reached her final destination: "You can never go back to that dark place again. *Never*."

It was bad enough that I had to relive the nightmare almost every time I talked to her, but to my mortification I discovered that she was telling the story to her friends in Beaumont, to *my* friends in Beaumont, to anyone who would listen.

I had told Stella, as I had told all my close friends, about my "nervous breakdown." Stella referred to the sixty days at Michael's House as my "extended Palm Springs vacation." But Mama Jean didn't know that Stella knew. While I looked at Mama Jean shaking her head in disbelief as an uncomfortable Stella futilely tried to steer the one-sided conversation in another direction, I winced and thought, *Stop telling that story! It's* my *story. God* damn *it!*

Every time she told it, I was struck with the worst symptoms of alcoholism from which I continued to suffer: guilt and shame. But then I was still suffering from the number one symptom of alcoholism: alcohol.

I honestly thought I was done after Palm Springs; not cured, but done. I knew that after rehab I had to immerse myself in a solid "program," as the recovery set calls it. When I returned from Palm Springs, I went to an outpatient program twice a week (group therapy and one-on-one therapy) for three months. When that ended, I started private therapy sessions. My *analyst,* the old-school term I preferred over *therapist,* was Dr. Demma. He was Italian American and Catholic like Dave. Our weekly sessions were in the living room of his pristine apartment, decorated with Asian art and matching red velvet sofas. I'd always find him on one of the sofas serenely waiting for me as a candle burned on the table before him, like a priest ready to take confession.

We were on a first-name basis. I called him Anthony. He called me Blanche. As in Blanche Hudson, the Joan Crawford role from *What Ever Happened to Baby Jane?* In one of our early sessions I complained that I shouldn't care what others think of me, and he shot back, "But ya do, Blanche! Ya do care what others think!" That was a riff on the famous Bette Davis line from the movie: "But ya are, Blanche! Ya are in that chair!" The name stuck. Anthony was also gay.

Besides the weekly sessions with Anthony, I went to my sober meetings almost every day. Despite all that, I kept getting blindsided every seven months.

Mr. Parker, who everyone thought was going to reject my sobriety and tempt me to drink again, had remained my most supportive best girlfriend, his love and friendship unconditional. When he announced he was moving to Mexico City, I was devastated, even though I had encouraged and supported the move. It was like losing not just my best friend, but my vestigial twin.

I threw him a party and he showed up drunk and barely thanked me. His thoughtlessness was probably due to his own shock over leaving New York after ten years and moving not just to another city, but another country. Two days later I had worked myself into an inconsolable lather. I went to a sober meeting and told myself that if the first person who shared didn't say something significant to my situation, I'd leave and drink. No one spoke to change my mind. I left before the meeting was over. The bar was a short walk across the street. *New York makes it so easy for alcoholics: there's a bar on every corner and a meeting on the opposite one. Dealer's choice! I am greedy. I keep choosing both.*

My walk across the street from the aborted meeting to the bar was as deliberate as a Nazi storm trooper's. I sat down at the bar to drink away my hurt and anger. It worked. Within an hour I was drunk. The anger was gone, and I was right back where I had left off on that September morning: thinking of killing myself. Drinking in anger at someone is like wishing him dead and then drinking the poison that would kill him. A friend ran into me at the bar and called Michahaze. She got me home.

Guilty and ashamed, I jumped back on the wagon the next day and announced I had one day back.

Seven months later I was overwhelmed at work with a big project that I feared I couldn't handle. I wanted to drink to escape it. I could barely wait for five o'clock to come so I could run to a meeting. It felt like the old days of waiting for quitting time so I could dash to Mesa de España across the street. I thought, *How pathetic! I have to escape to a meeting like I used to escape to a bar.* I failed to realize that that was the fundamental point of the meeting. *What an idiot!*

Unlike the night of the first relapse, I did all the things that I had been told to do when I wanted to drink. I went to a meeting.

I shared and said I wanted to drink, rather than keeping it to myself. I told myself that if no one from the meeting reached out to me afterward about my I-want-to-drink share, I'd go drink. Someone reached out to me. *Damn!* Out on the street he asked me if I was okay, out of danger. "Yes," I lied.

Actually, I didn't do all the right things. I didn't call my sober mentor, who would have said, "It's okay if you want to drink, but why don't you put it off until tomorrow? You can always drink tomorrow." But I didn't want to make that call because after sixty days in rehab and a year and a half in a sober program, I shouldn't want to drink anymore. I should be cured. *But you're not, Blanche! You're not cured!*

As soon as that guy from the meeting was out of sight, I went to a bar. The desire to drink and escape from the fear that I couldn't do the job was more powerful than the need to stop drinking. I didn't shoot back down to suicidal, but I shot to slurry. I was hoping to hide that slip from myself and everybody else, keep it my little secret and not lose my new seven months of sober time. But when I got home, Michahaze knew immediately. With a look of sick despair, he said, "Again? What happened?"

"I drank. That's what happened," I said, ashamed, and lay facedown across the bed. A freaked-out Michahaze called my sober mentor, who basically said what I said, which infuriated Michahaze. My sober mentor told him that there's nothing to be done when an alcoholic drinks. That's what they do. To stay sober, they have to want it.

When Michahaze recounted the conversation, I thought of the slogan on the wall of Michael's House: *This is a program for those with a desire to stop drinking.* I still wanted to replace *desire to* with *need to.*

Despite all that drinking had done to me, all that I had lost, from the Persian-lamb coat on down, all that I'd *nearly* lost—such as my life—did I *still* not have the desire to stop drinking? As Dorothy Parker said, "You can lead a whore to culture, but you can't make her think." A week later I was back at a meeting announcing I had day one. And things got better, as they always did when I didn't drink.

Seven months later Michahaze and I were on Fire Island for a glorious beach weekend. Everything was right that weekend. Work was going well. Michahaze and I were happy. I was in love with life.

One full-moon night, I took a solo walk along the beach. I was awestruck by the beauty and mystery of the shimmering sea and terrified by its infinite darkness. As the waves lapped toward me, the moonlight transformed the whitecaps into silver, electrified centipedes. They'd shimmer and shimmy before being swallowed by the sea. I walked along the shore and darted in and out of the fat fingers of the encroaching ocean and thought of Joan Crawford giving herself to that same Atlantic sea in an evening gown that glistened like the electrified whitecaps. "The sea is hungry and it wants you," I said out loud, and actually shivered with fright. Even though I could swim, the holy terror of the water I had had as a little boy had never completely evaporated.

I kept walking, not letting the sea touch my feet for fear that it would grab me. My alcoholism was that encroaching sea, and I had to constantly dart in and out of the surf lest it take me completely. I could jump in the ocean, but each time I swam in it, there was no guarantee I could make it back to shore. I turned my back against the Atlantic and ran to the beach house.

The next day I went to a meeting that had a second-floor view of the glistening Great South Bay. I was as in love with the beauty of the bay as I was frightened of the sea the night before. I left the meeting feeling the way I felt the day I left Michael's House. It was a new day, a new dawn, and I was feelin' good. I felt so good that like a short-circuited robot I walked straight down the boardwalk into a bar with the same view of the bay and ordered a Cape Cod. I wasn't angry or hurt. I wasn't filled with fear. I had reverted to the fundamental feeling I'd craved when I first started drinking. I drank because I wanted to make a good feeling feel even better.

Unlike the first two relapses, which were like minor colds, this one lingered for seven months, like a virus.

I'd go for days, even a few weeks, not drinking and silently counting days at sober meetings. I never stopped going to the meetings. My plan was that once I reached ninety days, I'd then admit I had relapsed. I couldn't go through the shame of publicly counting days again.

But I couldn't reach ninety days.

I was able to keep it from Michahaze. I was drinking secretly, hiding my vodka in the closet and taking sips while he was in the shower. Or I'd go out to the street on the pretense of smoking a cigarette but dash to the bar across the street and quickly suck down two vodkas on the rocks. I'd stash a bottle in the kitchen while I cooked. But I was always careful not to get drunk. When you've become the kind of drinker who drinks to get out of control, controlled drinking is no fun. And my God, the amount of work to control and hide it was exhausting. I felt like an actor playing identical twins with ten-second costume changes.

I never reached the level of drinking that had landed me in Palm Springs, but it was merely a matter of time before I did. I knew I had to stop. I was dog-paddling through the fifth stage of alcoholism: relapse.

Alcoholism has to be one of the only diseases with shame attached. People often say that if you have a disease such as cancer, you treat it. But I think that a disease such as anorexia is a better analogy. Like anorexics, alcoholics don't want to believe they have a disease. Both are diseases in which the afflicted keeps drinking the poison—literally, in the case of drunks—the very thing that will kill them. The anorexic looks in the mirror and sees a fat person. Logically, she knows that she must eat to survive. So what does she do? She starves herself and hopes it will make her better. The alcoholic, once he begins to realize that alcohol is a huge cause of his problems, drinks more, hoping that the problems will go away, hoping he can recapture the bliss that booze used to bring. But each drink deepens the problems and creates brand-new ones. Alcoholism is a madness all its own.

No one knew I had relapsed. Not Michahaze. Not my sober mentor. Not my analyst. And certainly not Mama Jean. *No, ma'am!*

It stung deeper every time I heard or saw Mama Jean telling the story of my near destruction, as she was telling it to Stella on that celebratory day. I turned my gaze away from her and Stella. Johnny, the comely bartender who always worked our parties and knew I wasn't drinking (and I wasn't drinking that day), was making a sweep of the room. He cut his eyes at the empty drink in my hand. "Another?"

"Yes, Johnny." And then, loudly, as I handed him the empty glass: "Another Dinah Shore, please."

I looked back across the room. Stella had ended Mama Jean's story by pulling in another guest to join them. *Thank God.*

When will she stop telling my story? I thought, not understanding that it was just as much her story to tell.

And what's wrong with her hair?

TWENTY-NINE

Gown Days (Reprise)

E*lderly!* Do I look elderly to you?!" Mama Jean said through the phone to me. At seventy-three she didn't look elderly, but she was starting to act elderly. She was referring to the anonymous description of her in the police blotter of the Beaumont newspaper that described her as such. Seven months before the New York brunch (about the same time as my first relapse), she had pulled up at the Bridge Studio in her brand-new, sporty, red Cadillac CTS. When she and Dad weren't on cruises or trips to Europe funded by her nest egg from her career as a stockbroker, she was playing contract bridge and racking up trophies at tournaments all over Texas and Louisiana. She honed her game at the Bridge Studio downtown, which was housed in a no-frills, cheap, corrugated-metal building. These ladies played competitive duplicate bridge, as opposed to the more social form of bridge known as playing a rubber that the country-club ladies enjoyed. No rubbers for the hard-core Bridge Studio ladies. They went "bareback."

Lucky for her other bridge partners, Mama Jean was always early, otherwise they could have met (somewhat) untimely deaths. On this particular day, when she arrived, she didn't stop in the lot. She plowed through the flimsy metal wall of the building, swiftly pushing aside eight tables of four settings each for the luncheon bridge game and creating a paper rainstorm. The aftermath seemed staged: the red Cadillac sat parked on the industrial carpet as if displayed in a motor showroom, but with the decorative touch of two playing cards and one "Tally-ho!" score sheet artfully fanned behind the red, white, and blue Texas license plate. *Ready or not, here comes Mama!*

Mama Jean was unscathed—not a hair out of place—and the car could be fixed.

"Did you scream louder when you crashed the car or when you read that report?" I asked her. It was a rhetorical question.

My mind played a collage of the classic images I have of Mama Jean: the glass curtain of a car window disappearing into the door to reveal her behind the steering wheel of a succession of ever-grander cars—a silver-blue, 1960s Chrysler; that white, 1972 Mercury Marquis; a slightly used, 1976, lime-green Lincoln Mark IV with oval opera windows; a 1978, silver Ford LTD with maroon interior; the navy-blue Pontiac Bonneville with matching landau top; and, after the money came in, a succession of Cadillacs that made her queen of the road. Her high-heeled, lead foot always knew the fastest route, the best roads to take, and how to avoid a speeding ticket (or get it fixed, if she got one). For her to lose control over anything—for her to lose control period—was unfathomable to me.

The Bridge Studio incident came in the middle of a pileup of increasingly lunatic mishaps to which any drunk could have laid claim. A year before the car crash she'd had knee surgery. For a month after the surgery she was batshit crazy, having wild hallucinations, thinking her nightmares were reality, falling out of bed repeatedly, imagining Dad was having sex in hotel lobbies with other women. "It's like we're down in *The Snake Pit* with Olivia de Havilland," Dad told me over the phone, referring to the classic horror film about life in a nuthouse.

More devastating than the Cadillac crash was the financial crash of 2008. Despite rumblings of the coming storm, despite Dad's urging her to move the money she still had tied up at her former stock-brokerage firm, she didn't. Unlike the Bridge Studio incident, in which the only thing lost was her pride, a small fortune was lost. All of her years clawing to write her own ticket were wiped away in an instant. If a traumatic event can jump-start a latent illness, then the recession of 2008 did it for her.

When I came home for Christmas that year, I felt as if our roles were reversed, that I was now in charge. Smarting from the recession, Mama Jean and Dad decided not to have their grand Christmas party, which was by then a twenty-year tradition. No ten-foot artificial tree twinkled with a thousand lights and a thirteen-year collection of BOHs (balls of honor) from Michahaze with the Scarlett O'Hara doll from Dad in the center. Only the living-room fireplace was decked. The garlands of golden fruit hung on either side of the mantel, upon which three Venetian-glass Wise Men marched in single file bearing gifts.

Since I didn't have any investments, I was untouched by the financial crash. Here was a chance not to even the score, but to at least make up for the Tobacco Leaf china Christmas. I felt as if my whole life had been a losing proposition in which I tried and failed to prove that I loved her as much as she loved me. I still dreamed of being able to give her as much as she had given me, to somehow even the score.

I got to be Santa that year. She was no longer buying expensive St. John Knits, such as the red, rhinestone-studded gown she liked to wear at her Christmas parties, but the more casual Chico's. I gave her a catalog and told her to pick out whatever outfits she wanted. To watch her open all of those Chico's boxes filled with everything she loved because she had chosen it (not one Tobacco Leaf rabbit in the bunch) was to watch on Christmas Day the kid I would never have. It may not have been the happiest Christmas, but for me it was one of the most satisfying.

And I was sober. I had about seventeen secret sober days under my belt. While I was still in Beaumont, a past playmate (the sexual kind, not the *Romper Room* kind) texted me from New York and asked if I wanted to meet for a drink at '21.' "How about Monday the 29th at six-thirty?" he wrote. I'd be back in New York by then.

I stared at the text. *Say no. Say no.* Oh, but it was '21.' Old-school glamour with its bar of wingback chairs in front of a roaring fire. Where Mama Jean and Dad had that hundred-dollar lunch. Joan Crawford's former perch. Where Mr. Parker and I once had a glorious four-hour, *three-hundred-dollar* lunch drinking Joan Crawfords (100-proof Smirnoff vodka on the rocks). And now a date over martinis and the promise of sex afterward. The invitation mixed all the ingredients of the cocktail I always craved: booze, glamour, Old Hollywood, and sex.

Go to '21' and not *drink. Then why go?* I didn't respond for a couple of days. He wrote back, *Did you get my text?*

You know, I thought, *I only have a few days sober; why not go enjoy myself and then restart my day count?*

Remember Rio? I didn't.

I wrote back, *Yes. '21' on Monday at six-thirty sounds lovely.* But I didn't send it immediately. I cradled the BlackBerry in my hand and stared at what I had written. I had that old edge-of-the-high-diving-board feeling. After a few minutes I closed my eyes and jumped. *Send.*

I wasn't going to drink until the date, but on the plane ride back to New York the flight attendant asked me if I wanted a cocktail. Without hesitation I answered in the plural: "*Two* gins and *one* tonic, please." *If I am going to drink tomorrow, why not drink today?*

That Monday at the office I was giddy with anticipation thinking of that Beefeater martini, dry, up, with a twist, that would touch my lips in a few hours. It was dead at the office, as the week between Christmas and New Year's always is. My staff was still away, so I was the skeleton crew. I remembered that a Miró exhibit was at the Museum of Modern Art (MoMA), just a block from my office.

Why not have a nice lady's lunch at the MoMA café and see the exhibit? Why not have a couple of glasses of white wine with lunch since I'm going to be drinking tonight anyway? Why not? I forgot that "Why not?" was the question that so often led to my undoing.

The entrance to MoMA was jammed with a line of puffy-parka-ed, fanny-packed Christmas tourists that extended all the way to the street. A vat of liquid Drano couldn't unclog that mess. *No, thank you.* The white wine wasn't meant to be.

I grabbed a sandwich and went back to the office. Better to arrive fresh and dry to '21.' That martini would taste so much better without the residue of white wine.

When I got back to my office, a text from my playmate said that he was sick and had to cancel. He was *so* sorry.

And I was *so* relieved.

I looked up at the office ceiling. It was an icky Styrofoam-esque drop ceiling like Manuel Antonio's in Paterson, New Jersey. I thought of the orange-and-black bowl Michahaze had bought for me in Palm Springs. To the untrained eye the bowl was merely an exquisite example of Czechoslovakian art deco glass circa 1931. To the educated it was a beautiful reminder of my rehabilitation.

I realized that I had the choice of perception. I could either shrug off the cancellation and the aborted MoMA lunch as mere detours to my date with a drink, or I could see them as roadblocks and receive them as a sign. Still looking at the ugly drop ceiling and thinking of the beautiful bowl that sat on our dining table, I said out loud, "Uncle! I give up! I'll take this as a sign." *From God? My higher power? Mama Jean? What does it matter?* What mattered was that I took it as a sign.

The next day I went to a meeting and announced that I had two days sober and started working my way back to full-time sobriety.

"Call me as soon as you get this message," my brother Jeffrey said on my voice mail. "She's had another wreck in the Cadillac." After financial difficulties of his own, Jeffrey had temporarily left New York and moved in with Mama Jean and Dad just before the Bridge Studio incident. Jeffrey had become her chauffeur to keep her from sitting in the driver's seat as much as possible. But one day she wanted to go to the beauty parlor. *Immediately.* Jeffrey wasn't ready and asked her to give him five minutes. She wouldn't. She drove herself to the beauty parlor and backed into a light post. That wasn't the worst part. She drove there sans pants. *Her priorities are still in order, but the execution is misfiring.*

After Jeffrey finished telling me the story, he said, "You have no idea. I've watched her unravel day by day." His voice cracked. "She can't even dress herself. Something's got to be done." When she started screwing up her hair appointments and thought it was okay to show up in New York having done her own hair, we should have rushed her to the hospital. Everything at which she had been expert—cars, money, and hair—she could no longer handle.

Two months after the pantless drive to the beauty parlor, she went haywire. She saw intruders in the living room. Instead of calling the police, she faced them down and told them to get out. I knew this move. Once we were on a crowded subway in New York. When the train came to the next stop, two bruisers—black men in skullcaps—started to get on. She pointed her finger at them and shouted, "Y'all can't get on here!" They didn't. I can still see their shocked faces. I looked at her with bug-eyed reproach. She defended herself: "I didn't say that because they're black. I said that because there's no room." When the intruders in her house refused to obey her, she went into the other room and called the police. There were no intruders in the house.

By the time Dad and Jeffrey got home, she was seeing babies that didn't exist, believing that her worst nightmares were true, talking to herself. Dad and Jeffrey had to hospitalize her in a geriatric-care unit in Houston so that doctors could try to figure out what the hell was going wrong.

As soon as I could, I jumped on a plane to Texas. This was my chance to come to her rescue. I flew down to visit on her Leo birthday, July 30. I didn't bring an extravagant gift: just a card, a framed beefcake photo of Hugh Jackman, and my newly brightened, copper-red hair (thanks to an expensive visit to the colorist). I also brought seven months of sobriety.

However hard I tried to prepare for the worst, I kept harboring fantasies that I would somehow master the code and bring her back. Jeffrey warned me that she might not know me. I nodded yes, but part of me didn't believe that was possible.

Dad made a great fanfare over my arrival when he brought me to her in the visiting room. She was having a gown day, as all of her days had been that month. My presence didn't have the joyous effect for which Dad had hoped. There was no hug for dear life. No "I've missed you so much." Or even "Where the *hell* have you been?" She had that lost look of which I had seen glimpses during her last visit to New York—the weekend of the celebratory brunch. Worse, she was totally out of it and hallucinating like someone tripping on acid. She wept when she saw Dad, telling him that she thought he'd been killed in a grisly car wreck.

And her hair . . . I don't even want to talk about her hair. A drink was starting to look good. Scratch that. A drink was starting to feel necessary. *Who could blame me?*

I'm not sure if Mama Jean even knew me. At one point she smiled and told me that with my pretty red hair I reminded her of . . . And then she trailed off. All that she said that day lacked the one thing she had never lacked: conviction.

Actually, not all that she said lacked conviction. As we said goodbye—a moment that will stay with me forever—her parting words chilled me with fear and warmed me with love, giving me a strength I didn't know I had.

The following September (nine months sober; I'd passed the seven-month itch) I was in the passenger seat of Mama Jean's red Cadillac. Jeffrey was in the driver's seat. In the back sat Dad holding Mama Jean's hand. We were on our way to see a neurologist in Houston whom Jeffrey had found, so we could finally get some answers.

By this time she had been moved from the geriatric-care unit to a traditional nursing home in Beaumont. The hallucinations and agitation had dissipated, but she was in partial shutdown with her eyes closed most of the time. When they were open, she'd respond to us with childlike giddiness. It wasn't that she didn't know us. She didn't even *ask* who we were. If we were strangers to her, she didn't bother to wonder why we were in her room.

But there were sparks of pure Mama Jean. While Jeffrey and I were feeding her (she now had to be fed with a bib around her neck, her meals puréed like baby food), two male staff members banged some trays outside. She had always been sensitive to loud noises, but she no longer knew how to shut out background noises. She turned away from Jeffrey and me and yelled out to the hall, "Hey, fellows! Y'all want a blow job?"

She turned back to us with a giggle and then back to the hall. "Well, you're not getting one in here!" Then back to us: "Uh-*uh*! I'm not putting that thing in my mouth. No, ma'am!"

I brought a playlist of her music that included the Burt Bacharach songs she used to play on the hi-fi when she still sewed. The music brought her back to us in flashes. As "More," her and Dad's song, played, she'd sway and hum along, pointing in the direction of the speaker and saying, "Listen to that beat. I'm telling you, that's *good* music." Puccini's *La Bohème*: "Mimi's aria has to be my favorite." "High Flying, Adored" from *Evita* rekindled memories of seeing the show on Broadway with Dad when she lived in New York while she was training to be a stockbroker. "My Best Girl" from *Mame* was just for me.

On the drive to the neurologist's appointment I played her music. You would never have known that the Cadillac had been driven through a wall. It had been expertly repaired and was as good as new. *Why can't any of us repair Mama Jean?*

She slept most of the way, but just as we were approaching the doctor's office, the song "Jean" (from the movie *The Prime of Miss Jean Brodie*) filled the car:

> Jean, Jean, you're young and alive
> Come out of your half-dreamed dream . . .

Mama Jean suddenly awoke and brightened as if a spotlight shone on her. "Jean!" She pointed to herself. "That's me!" It made me think of the time when Hugh Jackman called her name from the stage, and like a schoolgirl she told me, "He called my *name*! He said, 'Jean'!" I fought back tears.

She remained alert for the doctor's visit. When the handsome neurologist hit her knee with a rubber hammer to check her reflexes, he discovered that her reflexes worked just fine. As she blurted, "God *damn* it!" she punched him in the stomach.

He reared back, blinked, and with with a nervous chuckle said, "Wow. I've never had a patient do that before."

Dad replied with pride, "You've never met Jean Brickhouse."

Diagnosis: not good. She had Lewy body dementia, or LBD. This type of dementia causes paranoia, agitation, and wild hallucinations. *Check*. Patients also often experience repeated falls. *Check*. Problems with spatial perception. *Check*. Fluctuating cognition with great variations in attention and alertness from day to day and hour to hour. *Check*. Visual hallucinations of people or animals. *Check*.

Like alcoholism, it is progressive. Unlike alcoholism, there is no way to arrest it. A person could live with it for five to seven years, each week, each day, getting just a little bit—*or a lot*—worse.

Her decline seemed to play out like a blossoming flower filmed in time-lapse photography. But in reverse. Michahaze went back to Beaumont with me for Thanksgiving. It was our first Beaumont Thanksgiving since the time I had "shit in the nest" when we went to Mexico instead. Michahaze barely recognized her. She sat slumped over in a wheelchair in a front window of the nursing home. Her hands were balled up in arthritic fists (the physical toll of LBD at work). Dad sat next to her with his ubiquitous pile of newspapers, looking up every now and then to rub her shoulder or pat her hand and read aloud the kind of item from the paper that used to spark her interest. "How are you, honey? Can I get you anything?" No response. This had become his morning routine, his life. Jeffrey would relieve him at noon to feed her lunch. Then one or both of them would be back at dinner. My brother Ronny rarely visited. Not because he didn't care, but, as he said, "Man, I just can't look at Mama that way."

When Michahaze saw her, he looked stricken. Borrowing Dad's signature look, I glanced at him with my brows raised and eyes popped.

Dad left and we wheeled her back to her room. I played music from her playlist. "Listen, Mom. It's Hugh Jackman." He was singing "I Go to Rio" from *The Boy from Oz*. Nothing. Her eyes remained firmly closed, as if she didn't want to open them to the life she was living. Her hair had patches of gray and had been ineptly combed by Dad. Her beauty operator had offered to come to her and do her hair, but Dad refused, as he refused to let her friends visit. Echoing Ronny, he said, "I don't want anyone to see her this way."

Her food arrived. Michahaze and I looked at the puréed brown and orange sludge and screwed up our faces. Then I threw on a false expression of good cheer for her unseeing eyes. "Look, Mom! It's lunch." She refused the first few bites. (Dad and Jeffrey said that with each day it was increasingly difficult to get her to eat.) Suddenly she started taking bite after bite. I cheered her on. "Yes! You like that, don't you? Doesn't that taste good?"

Eyes still closed, she shook her head emphatically left to right, "Uh-uh. Uh-*uh!*" She'd always told me, "Never shit a shitter."

When it was time to go, a nurse came in with a giant cherry picker to lift her dead weight out of the chair. When she hit the bed, her eyes popped open like a giant doll come to life. She looked at me, then Michahaze.

"Michael?"

"Hi, Jean."

"Yes, Mom! It's Michael. He came here just to see you."

"Well, I'm impressed." That's what she'd told me after she first met Michahaze at the Royalton.

"Michael flew all the way from New York."

"Why anyone would want to come to this godforsaken place is beyond me." *Does she mean the nursing home or Beaumont?*

During that Thanksgiving visit I paid back Dad the loan she had given Michahaze and me for the down payment on the apartment, in case he needed extra money for her care. How ironic that I was back home for Thanksgiving and had settled my debt, but she was oblivious to both. As I sat in the study contemplating this, Dad walked in carrying a bottle of wine. He stopped in front of me. "In the morning I pray to St. Mary. In the afternoon I pray to St. Anthony. And in the evening"—he held up the bottle and pointed to the brand name on the label—"I pray to St. Genevieve."

I laughed, but thought of Genevieve the alcoholic. *That's not a good omen.*

He poured himself a glass and we sat in silence. After he finished it, he got up to leave the room, but stopped midway and gave me his signature look. After a beat he said, "I want my life back."

It wasn't a completely thankless Thanksgiving. As powerless as I felt to stop Mama Jean from disappearing, I didn't indulge in a glass of Genevieve—saint or sinner—to try to escape that feeling. For that, and not much else, I was thankful.

THIRTY

Driver's Seat (Reprise)

H i, Dave. It's Miss Lawson."

"Hey, kiddo. How are you doing?"

"Not good." *There's that deceptively understated term.* I was talking on my BlackBerry to Dave, my rehab counselor from Michael's House, as I walked home from one of my weekly sessions with my analyst, Anthony. I needed to talk to Dave. I'd seen him the previous month when he was in town to visit family and friends. Dave, Michahaze, and I went to see Carrie Fisher's *Wishful Drinking,* her one-woman Broadway show about growing up in Hollywood and her battles with drugs and alcohol. It was a perfect choice to see with my rehab case manager, a show by a woman in recovery who was also the daughter of the man who was the second person to call me an alcoholic, Eddie Fisher. I'd told Dave what was going on with Mama Jean, and he told me that his colon cancer had returned after being in remission for a couple of years. I confessed my relapses to him and that I was finally on my way to being sober a year. "Sounds like you're the one in remission now," he had said with a wink.

Now, on the phone, he asked, "What's wrong?" in that tell-

Mama-all-about-it tone I knew and loved so well. It was barely two weeks since I had returned from Thanksgiving in Texas, and I had just made the decision that I would return the next day.

"My mother. My dad just moved her to hospice. She's dying."

"Oh, kiddo, I'm so sorry."

Days after I left Beaumont she stopped eating, refusing even liquids. By Friday, December 10, Dad had called to tell me that they were moving her to hospice. I prayed on the plane ride home for God to take her, because if her remaining gown days were going to be spent catatonic in a wheelchair, well . . . Despite that prayer, I was blindsided by the news. We chose hospice rather than bringing her home. We decided that the image of her dying in her bedroom, where she'd spent so much of her time, would be too much of a stain on our memories.

For the next five days I debated when I should return. I talked to people I knew who'd had experience with hospice: Liz's partner, Karen; a sober friend who was a hospice worker; and various others in the hospice set. *What a fun set to be in.* When I told them that she was refusing food, they all said, "Go now." Then I heard the news that CBS was canceling her beloved soap, *As the World Turns*. That was the final sign I needed.

When I told Dad I was coming home, he said with odd perkiness, "Good! Come on, but you may be down here cooling your heels for a while." He was still in denial, or maybe he was still in hope.

When I stopped blathering to Dave on the phone, I asked, "So how are you?"

"Well, kid, *I* just started hospice at home today."

I stopped walking. "Oh, shit."

"Yeah. Shit. The cancer spread, and it's inoperable."

"I don't know what to say."

"There's nothing to say. That's why I came last month. To see my family and those whom I care about. People like you."

"Oh, Dave. You have to know that you made such a huge difference in my life and getting sober. You must know that."

"I do. The good thing about going this way is that I've had time to say good-bye and close up shop."

I wish I could have that with Mama Jean.

Twenty-four hours later I was in Beaumont standing next to her deathbed at the antiseptic hospice. Dad sat in a chair next to her bed with his arm outstretched to hold her hand as he read a magazine. A carpet of newspapers was spread at his feet. "Look, honey. It's Jamie-poo."

She lay flat on her back, a morphine drip next to the bed. She turned her head to me. Her eyes were open. "Hi, Mom. I'm here." She blinked her eyes and smiled at me in the way that a baby does, and you want to believe that the baby knows and understands you. She may not have known and understood me then, but she had for most of my life.

Four days later the call came in the middle of the night, when calls like that are supposed to come. Minutes later Dad, Jeffrey, and I piled into Mama Jean's Cadillac. I drove, but my sitting in that seat didn't feel right.

The deathbed scene was as slow and steady as the morphine drip by her bed but without any pain relief.

It's hard to say who needed Mama Jean most. Certainly Dad would be left with the biggest void. "Who's gonna tell me what to do?" he said. Jeffrey had had a tumultuous relationship with her. He and Mama Jean had come to a kind of mutual peace and respect for each other in that year of living together. When she got sick, he, alongside Dad, had done everything possible to help take care of her. But Ronny may have needed her the most. A loner all his life—he definitely "marched to a different drummer," as Mama Jean said—he talked to her about *everything,* from his roofing business to his Neil Diamond obsession to his adventures at tittie bars in Houston.

We stood around her bed speechless as her heave-sigh breaths dominated and hushed us. Hours later, we collectively held our breaths as hers came further apart. Each long pause in between fooled us into thinking that every breath was her last. We'd start to let go of our breaths, let go of our tears, let go. But then she'd breathe again. This edge-of-the-cliff breathing—hers and ours—must have gone on for an hour. "Oh, God, she's gone." Tears would start, and then another of her long exhales would fill the room. *Not yet!* "She's still with us. She's still here."

Finally, she took her last breath. The room was silent and airless. I know the exact time of the moment, because when it happened I instinctively sent Michahaze an e-mail from my BlackBerry. My friend Smith had dubbed her Mama Jean after witnessing her Auntie Mame side that night at the Teatro ZinZanni in San Francisco. But I never called her that myself. Not until I sent the e-mail to Michahaze: "1:14 PM. Mama Jean is dead."

The next afternoon, Dad and I sat across from each other at his desk as we wrote her obit. We had planned the funeral right down to what she would wear. "Your mother was so excited because we were going to have our Christmas party again this year. She was going to wear the red St. John Knits gown with the rhinestone buttons down the middle." We buried her in that dress.

The obit read: "A force of nature, Jean Brickhouse was known to all for her dynamic personality, irreverent sense of humor, generosity and deep appreciation of family and friends." We chronicled the list of achievements—Chi Omega, American Real Estate Million-Dollar Producer, top producer and Chairman's Club at her brokerage firm—all of which I knew well. Except for one: president of Jefferson County Council on Alcoholism.

I shot Dad his signature look. He mirrored the look from across the desk as he said, "Your mother liked to say I was an alcoholic, but I'm *not*."

"No, you're not. But she hit the jackpot with me."

The obit ran with a photo of her flashing her thousand-watt smile, from that night when Smith dubbed her Mama Jean. She was "decorated" for the evening. A beauty mark is affixed to her left cheek like Peggy Lee's, and a red feather boa is wrapped around her neck. *Showtime!*

When she died, I was two weeks away from finally having a year sober. Through it all, not once did I need to drink.

Not at her deathbed.

Not on the drive in her Cadillac to view her body, supine, dressed in the red St. John Knits gown, and looking as if at any second she would turn and tell me, "There are only two kinds of sex."

Not at the funeral, where her casket lay at the steps of St. Anne's altar, where she and Dad knelt to get married, where I knelt for my First Communion.

Not at the Flamingo Road open house after the funeral for "Jean's Last Christmas Party," which was decorated last-minute by me because after thirteen years of decorating that house, I knew where she wanted every last ornament placed, right down to the Venetian-glass Wise Men on the mantel.

Not during any of those times did I need to drink. But more significantly, I didn't have the desire to drink. I had her to thank for that.

Five months before she died, I had my last moment with her lucid. It was on that July 30 birthday visit in the geriatric hospital in Houston when I had shown up with a Hugh Jackman photo, my newly reddened hair, and seven months of sobriety. It was my first time seeing her after she had gone haywire, after she stopped being Mama Jean. I wasn't even sure if she knew me.

When it was time to leave, Dad said that I should kind of drift out of sight rather than say good-bye. He and Jeffrey slipped away first. I stood alone with her in the unforgiving glare of the hall's ugly fluorescent lights. I hugged her and turned away from her vacant eyes without saying good-bye.

As my mind tried to erase what I had just seen—a madwoman in my mother's body wearing a worn, pink nightgown, no makeup, and a crushed hairdo—she clamped my forearm in a vise grip.

I turned around and she stood glaring at me. The look on her face was a mix of teeth-baring anger and fear, the same look she wore the night she declared, "You don't know what love is." She was furious with me and about to let me have it. She kept one hand gripped on my arm and released the other to point her index finger at me in accusation. "You've been drinking." The nail polish was chipped.

"No, I haven't."

"Don't lie to me."

"I'm not." I wasn't. I never did reschedule that December 29 drinks date.

"You better not be."

"Remember, Mom? That's all behind us. You took care of that. I have you to thank." With seven months sober *again*, I was treading water through the critical period. *Who would blame me if I drank over Mama Jean losing her mind?*

But there was another way to look at it.

God damn *it! If you can't stay sober for yourself, do it for her.*

I looked her straight in the eye. "You don't have to worry anymore."

She stared at me warily before she accepted what I said. "Okay." She raised her finger at me in a warning halt. "But promise me. *Promise.*"

"I promise."

She froze in that position: eyes narrowed, jaw set, finger raised. Resolute.

The anemic wash of the fluorescent lights seemed to fade away. I saw her again as I always knew her. She was no longer without makeup and unmanicured hands, no longer wearing a nightgown that needed changing. And her hair wasn't a crushed bouffant. Instead, she was bathed in the glow of a warm spotlight, dressed in her Christmas-red St. John Knits gown, face on, with superbly manicured nails, hair done to perfection: camera-ready. It was the last time she was Mama Jean. The last time she was in the driver's seat.

THIRTY-ONE

Destiny (Reprise)

I t is said that the things an alcoholic loses during the throes of drinking start to come back in sobriety. We're not talking about material items like a wrecked car, a diamond ring, or a Persian-lamb coat so much as big-picture things like dignity, hope, self-respect, family life, job. At nearly three years sober, not only had those things come back to me, but they came back improved.

December 7, 2011, was the gayest day of my life—and I didn't go near a cock that wasn't my own. It was gray and drizzly outside, and everything that went on inside was beautiful. It was almost two years to the date since Mama Jean had died and three weeks shy of my third sober anniversary. I went to an auction of the estate castoffs of Joan Crawford—mostly flea-bitten—in the morning and a preview of Elizabeth Taylor's jewels at Christie's in the afternoon, with a life-changing lunch in between.

I'd perused the online catalog of the Crawford auction to consider what I wanted to bid on: her 1969 Golden Globe Award (*too expensive*), a set of silver-plate escargot dishes (*forget it, my grocer never carried snails*), a Margaret D. H. Keane painting (Keane paintings had gone from a joke to collectible kitsch) of one giant, sad eye with a single tear (*now we're talking*), and various fur coats and stoles (*bingo!*).

I'd never been to an auction before. When I signed up at the counter, I admitted to the clerk, "This *is* my first time at the rodeo." My reference to a line Faye Dunaway says as Joan Crawford in *Mommie Dearest* sailed over her head. I was registered as Bidder 134 and given a kelly-green plastic paddle with the corresponding number.

When I bid for the first time on the big-eyed Keane portrait, I displayed my gaucherie by throwing paddle number 134 high in the air like a first-grader begging his teacher to call on him. I quickly saw that the other poker-faced bidders merely flicked their wrists to raise their paddle from resting position to just under their chin. The eagle-eyed auctioneeress, who looked more like a Realtor with her bubble of blond hair and reading glasses, had no problem spotting all serious bids. But I worried that I'd have a Lucy moment and scratch my nose and mistakenly bid and win the Golden Globe Award, which went for $25,000.

When the furs came up for auction, I was ready for action. The petite fur coats and jackets would be fun to have, but I couldn't *wear* them. *I'm a practical gal.* Lot number 1157 was the one that seemed just right. It was a six-and-a-half-foot-long, chestnut-brown, ranch-mink scarf. It was finished with long tail fringes that looked like sinister, glamorous fur fingers. I could see it draped around my neck, dramatically cascading down the front of my coat, the fur fingers wiggling in the cold air. "Nothing keeps you warmer than fur," I could hear Mama Jean saying. I had to have it.

The bidding began at $300, lower than the estimated value of $600 to $800. Up went paddle number 134. Over the top of her reading glasses the auctioneeress glanced at me in subtle recognition of my bid. "I have a bid of three hundred dollars. Do I hear three hundred fifty?"

With pursed lips and a just-sucked-a-lemon expression, a gray-headed man on the end of my row nonchalantly flicked his paddle. I hated him.

"I have a bid of three hundred and fifty dollars. Do I hear four hundred?"

I raised paddle 134 again. It was a heady moment. The bidding was between me and *Him,* whom I strongly suspected of being a homosexual. The auctioneeress's eyes darted between Him and me like those of a cat watching a metronome.

"I have a bid of four hundred dollars. Do I hear four hundred fifty?"

Him flicked his paddle again.

"I have a bid of four hundred fifty dollars. Do I hear five hundred? Do I hear five hundred dollars?" Paddle 134 spoke again and she listened. "I have a bid of five hundred dollars. Do I hear five hundred fifty?"

Please don't raise your paddle, I silently willed Him. My sphincter muscle was so tight, a midget flea couldn't have entered. *God damn it, I want that fur!*

She scanned the room over her reading glasses like a schoolmarm in search of the pupil with the right answer. I held my breath. "I have a bid of five hundred dollars. Do I hear five hundred fifty? This is fair warning." No paddles moved. "Sold! For five hundred dollars." She pointed to me. Lot number 1157, or the Crawford Scarf, as I dubbed it, was mine.

I didn't have to be sober to get that fur, but if I weren't sober, I probably wouldn't still have it. I lament the loss of that Persian-lamb coat, but the Crawford Scarf trumps it.

Elizabeth Taylor had died earlier that year, and Christie's was about to auction her famous jewels. A friend of a friend had invited me to see a preview of the loot before the auction. I thought it was going to be a few well-lit galleries of her most prized jewels. Wrong. This was a blockbuster, ticketed event filled with ten-plus rooms of antiques, paintings, movie memorabilia (including her Oscars), and eye-staggering jewels, as exquisitely curated as an exhibit at the Metropolitan Museum of Art. I wasn't prepared for the exhibition and the wave of grief that hit me—not for Miss Taylor, but for Mama Jean—because I hadn't counted on the clothes.

The show opened with two rooms of Miss Taylor's wardrobe. The second room of clothing was the size of an airplane hangar. One entire wall was lined with dozens of tunic dresses in a riot of colors and patterns, full-length with long, wide sleeves. *What do you call those figure-forgiving tunic dresses? Mama Jean loved them.* The image from my childhood of Mama Jean's kelly-green knockoff of the Halston version made famous by Miss Taylor unfurled like a bolt of fabric. I was a little boy back in that vast closet of hers that could swallow me whole in sequins and marabou and suede and *ultra*suede and fur and leather as it drowned me with the scent of her Wind Song perfume. Had I met an early death in that closet, I would have perished happy.

Two years after she died, Dad was still trying to unload the warehouse of clothes in her closet. It was a Sisyphean task because the closet seemed to replenish itself like the bottomless salad at the Olive Garden. As I helped him go through the clothes, I discovered her wedding dress. It was as I remembered it from the photo albums I spent hours flipping through as a boy: chiffon, triple-pleated shawl collar, blurry green the shade of a Spanish olive submerged in a martini.

"Look what I found," I said, presenting it to Dad.

"Oh, look at that. Your mother had taste. She paid money for that dress. She got it at some fancy dress shop over in Houston. Probably Tootsies."

The label had a woman's name written in the kind of script that graced 1950s strip-shopping-center signs. "Helen Rose?" I asked Dad, pointing to the name.

"She was a famous designer at the time. She used to make clothes for Hollywood pictures before she got her own line."

A week after that conversation I was flipping through a coffee-table book on iconic dresses. There was Elizabeth Taylor dressed in the satin slip from *Cat on a Hot Tin Roof.* The designer? Helen Rose. What a shame that Christie's didn't have a satellite gallery in Beaumont to auction off Mama Jean's wardrobe.

The memory of being sucked back into her closet overwhelmed me with grief as I stood before Miss Taylor's tunic dresses. I was on the verge of crying when an elderly woman next to me nudged her friend. She pointed to the dresses and said, "She sure did like afghans."

The gallery walls were decorated with famous quotes of Miss Taylor's, but my favorite one of hers was missing: "It's not the having, it's the getting."

It could have summed up Mama Jean's life. As much as she was always in want of something and loved all that she had, she was at her best when she was in pursuit. I was just beginning to appreciate the getting, and not just the having. Although the having of the Crawford Scarf felt pretty damn good—and I knew exactly how I was going to wear it for the first time—the getting part of getting sober was an ongoing way of life, I had finally realized.

But the big "get" that was in the middle of that day? I was finally becoming a writer, something Mama Jean always wanted me to be. I had decided to tell our story. She was right all those times when she said I knew how to tell a story.

Three years sober, the creative ambition that had disappeared—not as quickly as the Persian-lamb coat but drink by drink—was starting to come back. In that first year after Mama Jean died, Mr. Parker kick-started it. He was working for a travel magazine and asked me to contribute an article to a feature about restaurants around the globe that are frozen in time. He wanted me to write about Le Veau d'Or. This Upper East Side restaurant is virtually unchanged since it opened in 1937, a combination Parisian restaurant fantasy and Old New York preserved in aspic. Including the patrons. I used to have boozy summer-Friday lunches there with Mr. Parker. Then, after he moved to Mexico City, alone.

The piece I wrote was good, and the gratification of having worked hard to produce a sharp, clever, and witty article had me hooked. It was my calling card to get into a private writing workshop. That's when the fun really began. I showed up almost every week with new work, work that I had labored on, worried about, agonized over. Some pieces that I wrote with little effort turned out decent. I used to believe that if something didn't come easily and automatically to me, I was incompetent, a failure, and I'd stop trying. I didn't have faith in myself, the blind faith that Mama Jean always seemed to have and I never trusted. *Another martini, please, waiter.*

But the pieces over which I struggled and fought to get right? The "getting" of those pieces produced a high that was way beyond the best high I ever had drunk or the most mind-blowingest orgasm. *Well, let's not get carried away.*

For me to become a writer and push aside, rather than drink away, the fear of doing something I believed in couldn't happen until I got sober. Before I got sober, if anyone had asked me what I was afraid of, I would have told them snakes, being drafted into the army, team sports, and water. Those are fears of tangible things. Everything else I labeled anxiety, anger, discomfort, hate. But they were all fear wearing different outfits. My fear of water, I've come to realize, is fear itself. Specifically fear of the unknown, which is where the bulk of fear resides. My alcoholism is the sea, always rushing toward me—sometimes with enchanting whitecaps that shimmer in the moonlight, sometimes with terrifying black waves ten stories high—but always ready to wash away whatever I've created.

Between the Crawford auction and the Taylor preview, I had lunch at Le Veau d'Or with Lisa, a former colleague turned literary agent. She had read some of my workshop pieces about Mama

Jean and wanted to represent me. In one day I had acquired the Crawford Scarf, seen Elizabeth Taylor's closet, and found a literary agent. To have actually had sex after that day would have been superfluous. What a bitter irony that Mama Jean was gone and I was finally sober and becoming what she'd always wanted me to be. And I finally *wanted* what she wanted for me.

By five o'clock I was back on the street. Night had fallen, the drizzle had stopped, and the city glowed with the usual red, yellow, and green blur of traffic and taxi lights, but with the added twinkle of Christmas cheer in every window. Even in my darkest days, I'd never fallen out of love with New York. It still had the magic of that first visit with Mama Jean and Dad at Christmastime twenty-nine years ago. My party line to friends had always been that ever since that visit, I knew I *had* to be in New York.

The truth: Mama Jean pushed me to go to New York. At the beginning of my senior year of college in San Antonio, I told her that I might stay there for a year until I figured out what I wanted to do.

"Stay in San Antonio?! Uh-uh!" She handed me a brochure for the Radcliffe Publishing Course with its promise of launching pupils into the publishing world. "New York is where you need to be . . . especially with your lifestyle." Had she truly been selfish in her love, she could easily have manipulated me with golden handcuffs to stay close to her in Texas, say eighty miles away in Houston.

I had recently asked Michahaze about the night he called Mama Jean after he found me. When he told her that I had tried to kill myself, she asked dumbfounded, "Huh?" as if she hadn't heard him, but it was because she didn't believe him. He repeated himself, and she went into action. "Earrrul! Pick up the phone!"

I asked Michahaze, "Why did you tell her then? Why didn't you wait until you got me to the hospital and knew I was okay?"

"Because. She needed to know."

Did she need to know I'm HIV-positive? I still don't know the answer. I know that she always feared it, that she suspected it. While I was in detox, she asked Jeffrey if I was positive and if that's why I tried to kill myself. (It wasn't.) He knew I was positive, but he told her I wasn't to protect her. She even asked me more than a couple of times, "You'd tell me if you were, wouldn't you?"

"Yes," I lied to protect us both.

I didn't tell her because I was afraid of her reaction. "God *damn* it! I warned you." I am lucky. I take my Atripla pill once a day and have never been sick. Dr. Connolly was right: it is a manageable disease, physically. Managing the shame and stigma of it is another story.

The excuse I gave myself for not telling her was that I thought it would kill her. That's bullshit. Mama Jean could handle anything. Besides, she already knew that I was an alcoholic sodomite *and* voted Democratic. HIV would have been the copper-red cherry on top.

After she died I found an old birthday card she'd sent me with the message "I may have tried at times to change you, but I love you just the way you are." She always told me that she admired me for always knowing who I am. I think she meant being openly gay, which from her generational and geographical perspective was a brave and bold move. No matter how old I was, she never stopped saying to me, "I wish I could shrink you back to age five. *That* was the perfect age!" I think it's because she believed that at that age she still had my unconditional love and devotion. Did she ever know that Lord Randall, her son—no matter how far from her I strayed—never stopped loving and idolizing her? Did she know that she would always be a bigger star to me than Joan Crawford or Elizabeth Taylor?

She was right all those years ago when she told me, "You don't know what love is." I didn't. Her love was complicated. It was possessive, generous, narcissistic, selfless, smothering, and liberating. To outrun her love, I was always trying to match it, to even the score. I was a fool to think that the perfect gift or the right number of days visiting her or the number of times I decorated that damn tree could put us on the same level playing field.

I never could "out–Mama Jean" Mama Jean because her love was love in its purest form, and it saved me. Now, twenty years later—after Mama Jean helped me get into publishing in New York City, after Michahaze and I spent countless family holidays with her, after I became an alcoholic and she funded my rehabilitation, after I became HIV-positive and never told her—if she declared, "You don't know what love is," I'd answer, "I didn't then, but I do now."

When Dad and I were cleaning out Mama Jean's closet, I asked him if I could have her full-length lynx fur, which I could just fit into. She'd bought it in the eighties when she was hitting her stride as a stockbroker, but hadn't worn it in years. Candice Bergen wears one just like it in the 1981 movie *Rich and Famous* after her character hits it big. Knowing Mama Jean, I wouldn't be surprised if she had been inspired to get her lynx after seeing that movie. *Or maybe after seeing Rip Taylor in his lynx at the Russian Tea Room on my first New York visit. Or both.* Dad said I could have her fur. If the Crawford Scarf trumps the Persian lamb, Mama Jean's lynx coat trumps the Crawford Scarf. And my love for Mama Jean? Hers trumps mine.

I continued to walk through the Christmas-bedazzled sidewalks until I found myself in front of '21.' The second-floor balcony of lantern-carrying horse jockeys was festooned with an evergreen garland. Through the picture window below I could see glasses being raised and drained, lit by the glow of a fire. I was still high from both the day I'd had and the thrill about the new direction my life was headed. *Wouldn't it be nice to go inside? Wouldn't it be nice to have one drink while sitting in a wingback chair in front of the fire-place? Wouldn't it be nice to get blotto?*

I saw ghosts: Joan Crawford at her table at the top of the stairs; Mama Jean and Dad blowing a hundred bucks on lunch; Mr. Parker and me sailing through a blizzard of drinks. *Wouldn't it be nice?*

I continued to stare through the window at the silhouette of so-phisticates as they laughed and clinked glasses. I watched myself as I entered the restaurant, and walked straight to the dimly lit bar to place my order. *"Beefeater-gin martini, dry, up, with a twist."* No. *It's winter. "Make that a dry Manhattan."* No. *I'm at '21.' "Make it a Joan Crawford, one-hundred-proof Smirnoff on the rocks, please."*

I could see myself in the bar mirror waiting for the drink. Then I snapped out of it. The person I saw wasn't me. It was a ghost of me, like my doppelgänger at Mesa de España. And I wasn't look-ing in a mirror. I was still on the sidewalk, looking through the win-dow. The shopping bag with the Crawford Scarf was safe in my clutches. I didn't have a need for a drink then. It wasn't even de-sire I had. It was nostalgia. There's a difference.

All those times—moments like this—when I was on a natural high and thought I needed booze to make the high higher, I didn't. It was superfluous. I was drowning the moment rather than savor-ing it. I didn't need or want that drink at '21' because I had at least two more highs left waiting for me that day.

I had a new piece to present at my writing workshop that eve-ning, but first I was going to run home, where Michahaze and the orange-and-black, Czechoslovakian glass rehab bowl were wait-ing. I'd have him take my photo next to our Christmas tree wear-ing the Crawford Scarf. And nothing else.

I turned my back on '21' and kept walking west. As I walked, I smiled. In her later years, Mama Jean would make her usual declaration—"You should be writing! *That's* what you should be doing!"—then she'd leave the room. Five seconds later she'd return with a finger pointed at me like a butter knife. "But *don't* write about me . . . until *after* I'm gone."

George Anttila

Jamie Brickhouse has been published in *The New York Times, International Herald Tribune, Salon, Out, Lambda Literary Review, POZ, Publishers Weekly, The Fix.com,* and is a guest blogger for *The Huffington Post.* He spent over two decades in the publishing industry, most recently at two major houses as head of their publicity and lecture divisions. Brickhouse is founder and CEO of redBrick Agency, a speakers bureau. He is also a spoken word performer, a two-time Moth StorySLAM champion, and has recorded voice-overs for the legendary cartoon TV show *Beavis and Butthead.* Brickhouse lives in New York City with his common-law husband Michael. Visit him at www.jamiebrickhouse.com and follow him on Facebook, Goodreads, or Twitter @jamiebrickhouse.

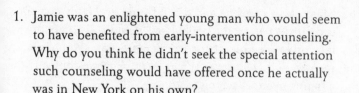

1. Jamie was an enlightened young man who would seem to have benefited from early-intervention counseling. Why do you think he didn't seek the special attention such counseling would have offered once he actually was in New York on his own?

2. Why do you think Michahaze stayed with Jamie after everything he put him through?

3. Do you think any of the blame for Jamie's drinking lies with Mama Jean? Do you think Jamie is to blame for his drinking or do you believe it is a disease?

Discussion Questions

4. Jamie makes the claim that he could not understand Mama Jean's pronouncement "You don't know what love is" or her all-consuming love until after he got sober from twenty years of "drinking a silo of booze," and that ultimately that love saved him. Do you agree? Do you think her love was more harmful or helpful to him?

5. Voice is crucial to any book—fiction or nonfiction— in the telling of its story. How did Jamie's strong voice and irrepressible humor help you get through some of the darkest parts of the book?

6. Given that *Dangerous When Wet* is a recovery memoir told through the lens of Jamie's relationship with Mama Jean, how would you compare it to other memoirs of alcoholism and addiction?

7. If you have or have had substance abuse problems, was Jamie's story one with which you could identify, even though his circumstances were different? Would you recommend *Dangerous When Wet* to people who are suffering from or affected by alcoholism and addiction?

8. Mama Jean's decline and death from Lewy body dementia is a salient part of the book. How would you compare it to other memoirs that cover dementia and would you recommend *Dangerous When Wet* to anyone coping with a family member's dementia?

9. What lessons can mothers take away from *Dangerous When Wet*? What lessons can sons take away?

10. Jamie reveals many incredibly personal secrets in *Dangerous When Wet*, including his HIV status, which he never told Mama Jean. Even though HIV is a manageable disease, do you think it is still stigmatized and should more HIV-positive people "come out" to relieve that stigma?

BURNHAM MEMORIAL LIBRARY
COLCHESTER, VT. 05446